Is the Bible *Really* the Word of God?

THE DOCTRINE OF SCRIPTURE

Andrew W. Wilson

*Biblical Christianity
Volume One*

BELIEVERS PUBLICATIONS

Is the Bible *Really* the Word of God? The Doctrine of Scripture

Copyright © 2016 Andrew W. Wilson

Believers Publications, P. O. Box 485, North Lakes, Queensland, 4509, Australia

All rights reserved. No part of this publication may be reproduced or transmitted in any form or by any means, electronic or mechanical, including photocopy, recording or otherwise, except for brief quotations in printed reviews, without the written permission of the publisher.

Scripture quotations, unless otherwise noted, are taken from the New King James Version, copyright © 1979, 1980, 1982 by Thomas Nelson, Inc. Used by permission. All rights reserved.

Scripture quotations marked (KJV) are taken from The Holy Bible, Authorized King James Version

Scripture quotations marked (ESV) are taken from The Holy Bible, English Standard Version® (ESV®), copyright © 2001 by Crossway Bibles, a publishing ministry of Good News Publishers. Used by permission. All rights reserved.

Scripture quotations marked (NIV) are taken from the Holy Bible, New International Version®, NIV®, copyright © 1973, 1978, 1984, 2011 by Biblica, Inc.™ Used by permission of Zondervan. All rights reserved worldwide. www.zondervan.com The "NIV" and "New International Version" are registered in the United States Patent and Trademark Office by Biblica, Inc.™

ISBN: 0994397712
ISBN-13: 978-0994397713

In God (I will praise His word),
In God I have put my trust
Psalm 56:4

CONTENTS

	Abbreviations	vi
	Preface	vii
1	Ten Reasons Why the Bible is the Word of God	1
2	What does it Mean that the Bible is Inspired?	18
3	The Highest Court of Appeal	34
4	Isn't the Bible Full of Mistakes and Contradictions?	48
5	The Best Way to Start a New Religion	72
6	Where is Your Scripture for That?	86
7	But the Bible is Dry, Boring and Difficult to Understand!	101
8	That's Just Your Interpretation!	114
9	Didn't a Fourth Century Council Decide which Books went into the Bible?	132
10	All we have are Translations of Translations of Copies of Copies	151
11	What Bible Version should I read?	164
12	The Parable of the Four Fishing Boats	176
	Epilogue: How to Read the Bible	198
	General Index	207

ABBREVIATIONS

BDAG	Bauer, Danker, Arndt and Gingrich, *Greek-English Lexicon of the New Testament and Other Early Christian Literature*, 3rd Ed., Chicago, IL: University of Chicago Press, 2000
BDB	Brown, Driver, Briggs, *A Hebrew and English Lexicon of the Old Testament*, Oxford: Oxford University Press, 1906
ESV	English Standard Version
KJV	King James Version
LSJ	Liddell, Scott, Jones, and McKenzie, *A Greek-English Lexicon*, Oxford: Oxford University Press, 1940
LXX	Septuagint (Greek translation of the Hebrew Scriptures)
NASB	New American Standard Bible
NEB	New English Bible (1970)
NET	New English Translation (2006)
NIV	New International Version
NKJV	New King James Version
NLT	New Living Translation
NT	New Testament
NRSV	New Revised Standard Version
OT	Old Testament
RV	Revised Version

PREFACE

In the Garden of Eden, the serpent first cast doubt upon God's Word, and then denied it outright: 'Has God indeed said, "You shall not eat of every tree of the garden?" . . . "You will not surely die"'. By contrast, when Satan tempted Christ in the wilderness, the Saviour quoted God's Word three times, refuting Satan's falsehoods and relying totally upon its trustworthiness.

Today, God's Word continues to be challenged, denied and doubted. It is not too much to say that the battle over God's Word is the constant spiritual conflict of the ages. Down through the centuries, when the world has tired of burning the Bible, other more subtle attempts have been made to undermine Scripture: adding to it, or setting other sources of authority alongside it, or arguing that it is full of errors and contradictions, or that it is impossible to interpret. In more recent times, the flashpoint has been the canon and the text of Scripture – we are told we can't be certain what books truly belong in the Bible or that its original wording has been faithfully transmitted to us. The point of attack may shift, but the target always seems to be God's Word. The aim is the same: to stop us loving and worshipping God by trusting and obeying what He has said in His Word.

As much as we would prefer there were no such attacks, one of their beneficial side-effects is to force us to think more deeply and state more clearly what we believe. As a result, this book not only defends the Bible, it also sets out the different doctrines Christians believe about Scripture. In addition, it is also historical and practical, because it is helpful to reflect on the way the truths about Scripture have been attacked and clarified in the past, and how they apply to our lives today.

A number of people deserve my special thanks for their help: Don Stormer, Phil Page and my father Raymond Wilson, whose encouragement and suggestions have improved the book in many ways, and above all, my wife, Gillian, without whose help and support this book would not have been possible.

CHAPTER 1

Ten Reasons Why the Bible is the Word of God

Rosalind Picard, Professor of Media Arts and Sciences at the Massachusetts Institute of Technology, has won multiple awards as a scientist and inventor and was named by CNN as one of seven Tech Superheroes to watch in 2015[1]. Brought up as an atheist in a loving and happy family, Picard had no need for religion and didn't think very much of people who did. Religion was something for people who were emotionally crippled, or who weren't very intelligent or who were taught some myth and never thought to question it. However, in her teens she became friends with some Christians. They invited her to church, but because she didn't want to go (or to dress up in special clothes), she made excuses. However, her friends said it didn't really matter whether she went to church or not – what matters is what we believe.

They asked her whether she had ever read the Bible. Picard says, 'I just believed the Bible was wrong without having read it, and it occurred to me that that was actually an inconsistent intellectual position – to think that I was so well educated and knew about the Bible, but actually hadn't read it'[2]. So she got herself a Bible and read it through in a year, as a result of which she became a Christian. She said, 'I started reading the Bible not because I believed in Christianity, but because it was the best-selling book of all time. To my surprise, it started to change me'[3].

In this chapter we are going to look at ten reasons why the Bible really is the Word of God. As we will see, extraordinary evidence points

---

[1] http://edition.cnn.com/2015/01/20/business/7-tech-superheroes-watch-2015/index.html, accessed 15/4/2016
[2] See the 'www.testoffaith.com' video at youtube.com/watch?v=jnS2ovwtx-g
[3] See the graphic from Veritas Forum: twitter.com/Veritas/status/679450688481406976/photo/1

to the fact that Scripture is inspired by God. While this evidence does not *prove* that the Bible is God's Word, it is exactly the sort of evidence that we would find if the Bible were the Word of God, and it provides good reasons for us to believe in the Bible's divine inspiration. Robert Morgan writes, 'If there is a God, if He has revealed Himself through Jesus Christ, and if that message is recorded in a book that He Himself has inspired, then we should find evidence for that in that book. The Bible should authenticate itself. It should be different from every other book and give evidence of supernatural origin, design and insight. It should be a book like no other'[4].

Ten Reasons the Bible is the Word of God
1. The Bible's Own Claims for Itself
2. The Permanence of the Bible
3. The Popularity of the Bible
4. The Unity of the Bible
5. The Fulfilled Prophecies of the Bible
6. The Historical Accuracy of the Bible
7. The Scientific Accuracy of the Bible
8. The Character of the Human Authors
9. The Witness of Jesus Christ
10. The Living Power of the Bible

1. The Bible Claims to be the Inspired Word of God

The fact that the Bible claims to be the inspired Word of God does not prove that it is. Sceptics rightly point out that we cannot take Scripture's own testimony as any proof of inspiration; 'the Bible is the Word of God because the Bible says so' is circular reasoning and proves little. A man going to a job interview would not impress his prospective employer if he pulled out a reference written and signed by himself.

However, what the Bible says about itself is very important. If the Bible never made any claim to be the Word of God, then we would have little confidence that Scripture was inspired. Or, if the Bible's claims for itself were few, weak, or vague, the entire case would collapse, as the lawyers say. In a court of law, a defendant is asked how he pleads – guilty or not guilty. While a defendant's 'not guilty' plea does not prove his innocence, it establishes the basis for his defence. If he pleads 'guilty', he

---

[4] R. J. Morgan, *Evidence and Truth: Foundations for Christian Truth*, Wheaton IL: Crossway, 2003, p70

makes it much harder for his lawyer to defend him. Thus, the Bible's own claim to be inspired is a necessary first argument in its defence.

So frequent are the references to the inspiration of Scripture, and so varied the ways that this claim is made, that Warfield compares this testimony to an avalanche of evidence: 'We may explain away a text or two which teach plenary inspiration, to our own closet satisfaction, dealing with them each without reference to its relation to the others: but these texts of ours, again, unfortunately do not come upon us in this artificial isolation; neither are they few in number. There are scores, hundreds, of them: and they come bursting upon us in one solid mass. Explain them away? We should have to explain away the whole New Testament. What a pity it is that we cannot see and feel the avalanche of texts beneath which we may lie hopelessly buried, as clearly as we may see and feel an avalanche of stones!'[5]

The Bible's Claims about Its Inspiration

Old Testament Claims. We read about inspiration many times in the OT. Expressions like 'Thus says the Lord' (420x) or 'the Lord spoke to' (138x) indicate that the words of Moses or the messages of the prophets came from God. Entire OT books are described as 'the word of the LORD' (see Hosea 1:1, Micah 1:1, Zephaniah 1:1). The Old Testament is quoted in the New over 280 times, introduced by phrases like 'Scripture says', or 'it is written', indicating that for the NT writers, Scripture was the supreme standard of authority and truth, God's written record.

Specific instances of inspiration include David in 2 Samuel 23:2, 'the Spirit of the Lord spoke by me, his word was on my tongue'. In 1 Chronicles 28:12, David's 'plans for all that he had by the Spirit' (that is, the plans for the temple) . . . 'all this, said David, the Lord made me understand in writing, by His hand upon me, all the works of these plans' (verse 19). Thus, David was inspired by God, not simply in his spoken words, but also in writing. In Jeremiah 1:9, God says 'Behold, I have put My words in your mouth', and Jeremiah was further told to write down all these words (Jer. 36:2, 28). Moses was told by God to 'Write these words, for according to the tenor of these words I have made a covenant with you and with Israel' (Exodus 34:27).

---

[5] B. B. Warfield, *The Inspiration and Authority of the Bible*, Philadelphia: Presbyterian and Reformed, 1948, p120

New Testament Claims. There are so many verses that attest to the inspiration of Scripture, either directly or indirectly, that it will suffice to take a few examples from three New Testament books.

Matthew's Gospel quotes many fulfilled prophecies from the Old Testament, claiming that these were God's words. In Matthew 1:22, we read, 'So all this was done that it might be fulfilled which was *spoken by the Lord* through the prophet, saying . . .' (and see also Matthew 2:15 for a similar construction). Other fulfilled prophecies emphasise the written words of the prophets, as in Matthew 2:5 ('for thus it is *written* by the prophet'), or in Matthew 26:56 ('that the Scriptures (i.e. writings) of the prophets might be fulfilled'). Other fulfilled prophecies mention the human authors, like Jeremiah (Matt. 2:17) or Isaiah (Matt. 3:3, 4:14, 8:17, 12:17). Thus, Matthew's fulfilled prophecies were divinely-inspired, through human prophets, who wrote them in Scripture.

The book of Acts frequently bears witness to the divine inspiration of Scripture. In Acts 1:16, Peter says 'this Scripture had to be fulfilled which *the Holy Spirit spoke* by . . . David'. Similarly, in Acts 28:25, Paul says, 'the Holy Spirit spoke rightly through Isaiah the prophet'. Elsewhere, we read that 'God, who by the mouth of Your servant David . . . said' (Acts 4:25). These references to God or the Holy Spirit inspiring Scripture through human writers like David or Isaiah, show the dual divine-human nature of inspiration.

The letter to the Hebrews quotes many OT Scriptures, sometimes using the words 'He (*God*) says' followed by a quote (Heb. 1:5-13, 5:5, 6; 7:21, 8:8), sometimes prefacing the quote with the words 'He (*Christ*) says' (Heb. 2:12-13, 10:5), and once with 'As *the Holy Spirit* says' (Heb. 3:7). In addition, the human authors of Scripture are acknowledged in the words 'one testified in a certain place' in Hebrews 2:6. Hebrews thus equates Scripture as God's words, Christ's words, and the Holy Spirit's words as well as the words of men. Notice also the form in which the book of Hebrews quotes the Scriptures, saying that God or the Holy Spirit or Christ '*says*' (in the present tense). It is not simply that God 'said' something in the past, but that what God said in the Scriptures still speaks today. The Bible is the living word of God, through which God is still speaking to us.

The Titles of Scripture. The terms Scripture uses to describe itself attest to its inspiration. It is called 'the oracles of God' (Romans 3:2, 'oracles', meaning the 'utterances, sayings, messages, prophecies'), 'the Law of the Lord' (Psalm 19:7), the 'book of the Lord' (Isa. 34:16), the 'Scriptures of truth' (Dan. 10:21), and the 'holy Scriptures' (Rom. 1:2, 2 Tim. 3:15). In Psalm 119, the Scriptures are called 'Your (i.e. God's) Word' 35 times (see, for example, verses 9, 11, and 105). In the NT, the Lord Jesus Christ spoke of Scripture in prayer to God as 'Your Word', John 17:17.

Scripture is Equated with God. A number of times in the NT, God and the Scriptures are treated synonymously, that is, as if they were the same. In Matthew 19:4-5, Jesus said 'Have you not read that He who made them at the beginning made them male and female and said "For this reason a man shall leave his father and mother and be joined to his wife"'. Jesus here said that God had spoken the quoted words, however the words quoted from Genesis 2:24 were not part of a speech by God in Genesis, but rather were part of the narrative. Christ thus attributes to God the narration of Scripture. See also Galatians 3:8 where Paul attributes the ability to foresee the future to Scripture, a personal quality that is normally reserved for God. Again, Hebrews 4:12 says 'For the word of God is living and powerful . . . and is a discerner of the thoughts and intents of the heart'. Here, Scripture is said to possess omniscience, an attribute of God. Notice in the words in the next verse the subject changes to God: 'And there is no creature hidden from His sight, but all things are naked and open to the eyes of Him to whom we must give account' (v13). God and Scripture are used interchangeably.

Conclusion. The Bible does not present us with a few, scattered places which hesitatingly point to the possibility that the Bible is of divine origin. Instead, the Bible presents us with a torrent of testimonies that unequivocally assert that the Scripture is inspired by God.

2. The Permanence of Scripture.

The Bible is an ancient book – parts of it are 3,500 years old. The fact that it has survived to this day is not especially miraculous; there are other old books still in existence. But no other book in the history of the world has been hated and attacked, banned or burned like the Bible. In the days of the Roman Empire's persecution of Christians, the Emperor Diocletian declared that he had rid the world of it. During the Reformation, the Roman Catholic Church put people to death for possessing Scripture, burning them at the stake with their Bibles tied around their necks. In the last few centuries, scholarly sceptics have assaulted it, claiming it is full of fables and fairytales, mistakes and contradictions. Yet the Bible has survived all attempts to destroy it, and has outlived the mightiest empires on earth committed to its destruction. Everything in this world seems to have its day, and then pass away – except the Bible. The Bible is indestructible. If the Bible were not God's Word, surely it would have perished, or remain today just a museum piece. But the Bible is 'the word of God which lives and abides forever' (1 Peter 1:23). Christ said that 'Heaven and earth will pass away, but My words will by no means pass away' (Matt. 24:35). Bernard Ramm has written, 'A thousand times over, the death knell of the Bible has been sounded, the funeral procession formed, the inscriptions cut on the tombstone, and the committal read. But somehow the corpse never stays put'[6].

> *A thousand times over, the death knell of the Bible has been sounded, the funeral procession formed, the inscriptions cut on the tombstone, and the committal read. But somehow the corpse never stays put*
>
> Bernard Ramm

3. The Popularity of the Bible.

Not only has the Bible survived all attempts to destroy it, but according to the *Guinness Book of Records*, it remains the world's best-selling book. In fact, it is specifically excluded from best-seller lists (like the *New York Times Bestsellers List*) because it would always win. The Bible, in part or whole, has been translated into more than 2500 languages, more than any other book. Charles Dickens wrote *The Life of Our Lord* so that his children would become familiar with Jesus Christ, and he often read the story to them. When his children left home, he gave each a New Testament and he wrote to one, 'I put a New Testament among your books, for the very same reasons, and with the very same hopes that made me write an easy account of it for you, when you were a little child; because it is the best book that ever was or will be known in the world'. Abraham Lincoln said, 'I believe the Bible is the best gift God has ever given to man. All the good from the Savior of the world is communicated to us through this book'. In Queen Elizabeth II's coronation ceremony, a Bible was placed in her hands, with the words: 'we present you with this Book, the most valuable thing that this world affords. Here is Wisdom; this is the Royal Law; these are the lively Oracles of God'.

Despite being written thousands of years ago, the Bible has

---

[6] Bernard Ramm, *Protestant Christian Evidences*, Chicago: Moody Press, 1957, p232

universal appeal. It is read and loved by millions of people of all countries, cultures, ages and classes. Why is the Bible so popular? The Bible is not a dry, old, dusty relic of another age – a dead letter; it is the living Word of God. The Bible's unparalleled popularity suggests that there is something more to it than any ordinary human book, ancient or modern.

4. The Unity of the Bible.

The sixty-six books of the Bible were written by more than 30 different human authors over a period of 1,500 years. Despite most of these authors never having met each other, despite living in different centuries, in different countries, and coming from different classes of society, the books these authors left to us in the Bible are a harmonious unity. Despite the fact that some books are long and others are very short, and that the books include all types of literature – history, biography, legal documents, poetry, proverbs, prophecy – the Bible is far more than a diverse collection of documents. 'There is a unity which binds the whole together'[7], despite the fact that no human editor compiled it. By comparison, if we were to ask ten different people today from just one culture – an artist, a politician, a farmer, a soldier, a teacher, a sportsman, a builder, a doctor, a mechanic and a scientist – to each independently write an essay about their religious beliefs, we would doubtless get a jumbled mess of contradictory ideas. We would hardly expect to launch a new religion that millions would follow.

The Bible tells us about the one same God in every book: eternal, all-powerful, all-knowing, holy and righteous, yet loving and kind. It tells us about one continuing story throughout: God's unfolding plan for the salvation of the world through His Son, Jesus Christ. It presents to us the same message wherever we look: we are lost sinners who have wandered far from God's ways, but He lovingly calls us to be reconciled to Him through repentance and faith in Christ. All Scripture is about Christ. W. H. Griffith-Thomas wrote that the Old Testament is full of unfulfilled prophecies, unexplained ceremonies and unsatisfied longings. But the prophecies are fulfilled in Jesus, the ceremonies are explained in Jesus and the longings are satisfied in Jesus. Augustine wrote about how the Old and New Testaments are related to each other in a famous statement: 'the New is in the Old concealed, the Old is in the New revealed'. The Old Testament anticipates the New and foresees the

---

[7] F. F. Bruce, *The Books and the Parchments*, Fleming H. Revell Co, 1963, p88

events recorded in it, while the New unlocks the meaning of the Old, and makes its puzzling parts clear. Everything in the Bible is woven together in a marvellous unity.

5. The Fulfilled Prophecies of the Bible.

Wilbur Smith wrote that the Bible 'is the only volume ever produced by man, or a group of men in which is to be found a large body of prophecies relating to individual nations, to Israel, to all the peoples of the earth, to certain cities, and to the coming of the one who was to be the Messiah. The ancient world had many different devices for determining the future, known as divination, but not in the entire gamut of Greek and Latin literature, even though they use the words prophet and prophecy, can we find any real specific prophecy of a great historic event to come in the distant future, nor any prophecy of a Saviour to arise in the human race. Mohammedanism cannot point to any prophecies of the coming of Mohammed uttered hundreds of years before his birth. Neither can the founders of any cult in this country rightly identify any ancient text specifically foretelling their appearance'[8].

There are over 300 different prophecies relating to the coming Messiah fulfilled in the life of Jesus Christ. Professor Peter Stoner studied eight of these prophecies – the Messiah would: be born in Bethlehem (Micah 5:2); be preceded by a messenger (Isa. 40:3); ride into Jerusalem on a donkey (Zech. 9:9); be betrayed by one of his friends (Psalm 41:9, 55:12-14); be sold for thirty pieces of silver (Zech. 11:12), the money being thrown down in the temple (Zech 11:13); be silent before accusers (Isa. 53:7); and be pierced in his hands and feet (Psalm 22:16). Stoner estimated the probability of someone fulfilling just eight of the prophecies at one in one hundred million billion[9]. That's the number 1 followed by 17 zeros.

Whatever the exact figure, we get the point: it's a big number. Stoner used an illustration to help people understand the probability: if someone dumped one hundred million billion silver coins into the state of Texas (or France, or New South Wales), the coins would cover the ground two feet deep. If a special mark were placed on one of those coins, and a blindfolded man was sent out to find this one special coin, the chances of him finding the one special coin out of the other

---

[8] Wilbur Smith, *The Incomparable Book*, Minneapolis, MN: Beacon Publications, 1961, pp9-10
[9] Peter W. Stoner, *Science Speaks*, Chicago: Moody Press, 1963, pp109-10

100,000,000,000,000,000 coins would be the same as the chances of one person fulfilling just eight of the prophecies about Christ.

The sceptic might protest that Jesus deliberately set out to fulfil all these prophecies. However, most of these prophecies refer to things which were done *to* Jesus by other people. The two most important Messianic prophecies are that He would be put to death despite being innocent, and rise again from the dead. Even if someone was able to fulfil these prophecies, who would want to put himself through all the suffering to make it look as if he were the Messiah? The fact that all three hundred of these prophecies were fulfilled by one person, Jesus of Nazareth, is beyond the possibility of human manipulation or coincidence. It points to a divine author behind the Bible's prophecies. In Isaiah 46:9-10, God said, 'I am God, and there is none like Me, declaring the end from the beginning, and from ancient times things that are not yet done'.

6. The Historical Accuracy of Scripture.

Sceptics claim the Bible is full of historical inaccuracies and fables, but fresh discoveries have repeatedly proven the Bible right and the sceptics wrong. The Bible is a book set in time and space, and this enables us to test whether its history is true or not. In the March/April 2014 issue of *Biblical Archaeological Review*, Professor Lawrence Mykytiuk of Purdue University wrote an article entitled, Archaeology Confirms Fifty Real People in the Bible. He listed people like Shishak king of Egypt, Tiglath-Pileser king of Assyria, Nebuchadnezzar king of Babylon, Mesha king of Moab, Ben-Hadad king of Syria, Hezekiah king of Judah, Ahab, Jehu and David kings of Israel.

In addition, hundreds of biblical locations have been excavated by archaeologists. Archaeological investigations of Ur of the Chaldees suggest it was the wealthiest and most populous city in the world when Abraham left it, the New York of the day. Proof of ancient writing was found in Ur, disproving the claim of sceptics that Moses could not have written the first five books of the Bible because writing had not yet been invented. In 1845, Nineveh was discovered, the capital of the mighty Assyrian empire where Jonah was sent. In the royal archives of King Ashurbanipal were found 22,000 cuneiform texts, confirming many biblical people and events, like Sargon's conquest of Israel (found in 2 Kings 17:6).

Another example of the Bible being proved correct concerns the book of Daniel, which says the last king of Babylon was Belshazzar, a name unknown to history outside of the Bible. However, the discovery of the *Nabonidus Cylinders* in 1854, and the *Nabonidus Chronicle*, translated in 1882, vindicated the Bible, showing that Belshazzar was the crown prince of Babylon who ruled in the long absence of his father and was in charge when the city fell.

Sir Frederick Kenyon of the British Museum wrote, 'It is therefore legitimate to say that, in respect of that part of the Old Testament against which the disintegrating criticism of the last half of the nineteenth century was chiefly directed, the evidence of archaeology has been to re-establish its authority, and likewise to augment its value by rendering it more intelligible through a fuller knowledge of its background and setting'[10]. William Albright, the greatest authority on biblical archaeology of his day, wrote: 'There can be no doubt that archaeology has confirmed the substantial historicity of Old Testament tradition'[11].

7. The Scientific Accuracy of the Bible

Sceptics claim that the Bible is full of pre-scientific myths and scientific absurdities. However, consider the difference between what the Bible teaches and what other ancient cultures believed. The ancient Hindus believed the earth rested on the back of an elephant, the ancient Japanese thought that it rested on the back of a catfish, the Greeks taught that it rested on the shoulders of a god called Atlas, and Muslims believed that it was suspended on the horns of a bull. By contrast, the Bible teaches that the earth hangs upon nothing (Job 26:7). Nor does the Bible teach that the earth is flat; rather, it tells us that the shape of the earth is spherical (Isaiah 40:22 speaks of the 'circle of the earth', Proverbs 8:27 says 'He prepared the heavens . . . He drew a circle on the face of the deep' and Job 26:10 says 'He drew a circular horizon on the face of the waters, at the boundary of light and darkness'). Ancient astronomers were only able to see a very limited number of stars with the naked eye, less than 5000, yet the Bible said in its first book that the number of the stars of heaven was comparable with the number of grains of sand on the seashore (Gen. 22:17, see also Jer. 33:22), and Hebrews 11:12 speaks of the stars as 'innumerable'. Scientists today tell us that in our Milky Way

---

[10] Sir Frederick Kenyon, *The Bible and Archaeology*, New York: Harper & Row, 1940, p279

[11] William F. Albright, *Archaeology and the Religions of Israel*, Baltimore: The Johns Hopkins University Press, 1968, p176

galaxy alone there are 400 billion stars and that there are about 170 billion other galaxies in the universe. These are estimates, of course, and the actual number of the stars is truly beyond the ability to definitively count, just as the Bible said long ago. How did the Bible manage to get these scientific facts correct without our modern scientific equipment and discoveries? Scripture's scientific accuracy suggests it is the Word of God.

There are many pagan creation myths, but they are all either absurd, childish, or grotesque. The ancient Chinese believed that P'an Ku was hatched from a giant egg, and half the shell above him became the sky, while the other half became the earth. After pushing heaven and earth apart, P'an Ku fell to pieces, his body becoming the mountains, his blood the rivers, his breath wind and his voice thunder. His two eyes became the sun and the moon, while the parasites on his body became mankind. The ancient Egyptians had a number of creation stories, but the most common involves Nun, the ocean, from which Amen, the sun, rises. Amen produces a divine son and daughter who gave birth to a race of gods, while his tears become mankind. Many pagan creation stories, like the Babylonian and Greek, involve gods breeding, fighting, and even eating each other until one god (usually the local deity) emerges as the chief. By contrast with these myths, the Bible teaches us that God created the heavens and the earth from nothing (Gen. 1:1, Heb. 11:3), a description that is both startling, simple, and yet perfectly up-to-date science. To borrow the words of the poet Cowper (writing about salvation): 'Oh, how unlike the complex works of man, Heaven's easy, artless, unencumbered plan . . . Majestic in its own simplicity'.

Some argue that the Bible cannot be the Word of God because it is full of miracles which are, by definition, violations of the laws of nature. However, if God created the universe from nothing and is its Supreme Governor, it stands to reason that He has the power to override the laws of nature He created whenever He wishes.

8. The Character of the Human Authors.
2 Peter 1:21 assures us that the human writers of Scriptures were 'holy men of God', which gives us three more reasons we can trust the Scriptures they wrote:
1. They were *holy* men, men of character and integrity, set apart from dishonesty or corruption. 2 Peter 1:16 assures us that the apostles 'did not follow cunningly-devised fables when we made known to you the power and coming of our Lord Jesus Christ, but were eyewitnesses of His majesty'. The apostles were not scheming

fraudsters who tried to pass off their own writings as God's words.
2. They were holy *men*, plural. It was not just one man who wrote the Bible, whose word we must take on trust (like Mohammed with the Koran, or Joseph Smith who wrote the book of Mormon), but many writers whose witness corroborates each other and whose teachings harmonise. Most cults are based on the writings of one man or woman, but in the Bible there is safety in multiple authors.
3. They were holy men *of God* – men devoted to God. Most of them suffered rejection and persecution for their message. The fact that most of the New Testament writers were prepared to die as martyrs for their faith shows that they themselves believed what they wrote. Why die for a lie?

The Bible does not hide the sins of its main characters but tells us about their faults in frank detail. A. W. Pink wrote, 'A forged history would have clothed friends with every virtue, and would not have ventured to mar the effect . . . by uncovering the vices of its most distinguished personages. Here then is displayed the uniqueness of Scripture history. Its characters are painted in the colours of truth and nature'[12].

9. Christ's Testimony to the Inspiration of Scripture

None of the arguments we have made so far – the claims the Bible makes for itself, its fulfilled prophecies, its scientific and historical accuracy, its unity, permanence and popularity – none are enough to prove that the Bible is God's Word. The most important reason why we should believe in the inspiration of the Scriptures is because the Lord Jesus Christ, the very Son of God, himself assures us of this truth. John Stott writes, 'What is the major reason why evangelical Christians believe that the Bible is God's Word written, inspired by his Spirit and authoritative over their lives? It is certainly not that we take a blindfold leap into the darkness and resolve to believe what we strongly suspect is incredible. Nor is it because the universal church consistently taught this for the first eighteen centuries of its life. . . . Nor is it because God's Word authenticates itself to us as we read it today – by the majesty of its themes, by the unity of its message and by the power of its influence (though it does all this and more). No. The overriding reason for accepting the divine inspiration and authority of Scripture is plain loyalty

---

[12] A. W. Pink, *Divine Inspiration of Scripture*, Grand Rapids, MI: Guardian Press, 1976, p23

to Jesus. We believe in Jesus. We are convinced that he came from heaven and spoke from God. . . . So we are prepared to believe what *he* taught for the simple reason that it is *he* who taught it. . . . Our understanding of *everything* is conditioned by what Jesus taught. And this *everything* means *every thing*: it includes his teaching about the Bible. . . . All Jesus' teaching was true. It is the teaching of none other than the Son of God'[13]. As Tim Keller writes: 'If Jesus rose from the dead, then you have to accept all that he said; if he didn't rise from the dead, then why worry about any of what he said? The issue on which everything hangs is not whether or not you like his teaching but whether or not he rose from the dead'[14].

Please notice: this is a very different argument from 'the Bible says the Bible is the Word of God'. It is possible to read the gospels and, without holding them to be anything more than ancient documents (and reading them at face value with the same level of open-minded inquiry as a newspaper), conclude that Jesus truly rose from the dead and is, therefore, the Son of God. The gospels do not start by insisting that they are inspired by God and then dictate some creed for us to believe. Instead, they present the story of Christ's life and death for us to investigate, so we may come to our own conclusions. The New Testament presents Christ's claims to be the Son of God, and the proof of those claims (in His resurrection), and urges us to evaluate them by the ordinary standards of eye-witness evidence. Thus, Christ's testimony that the Bible is the inspired Word of God is not a circular or self-referencing argument – it is more like a spiral staircase, built upon a solid historical fact, His resurrection. The argument is not dependent upon the doctrine of the inspiration of Scripture to start with; it is built on who Jesus Christ is and what He said.

Thus, for the Christian, the primary reason we believe the Bible is God's Word is because of the authority of Jesus Christ the Son of God. Norman Geisler and Ron Brooks write, 'We know that the Bible came from God for one very simple reason: Jesus tells us so. It is on His authority, as the God of the universe, that we are sure that the Bible is the Word of God. He confirmed the Old Testament's authority in His teaching, and He promised an authoritative New Testament through His

---

[13] John R. W. Stott, *The Authority of the Bible*, Downers Grove, IL: IVP, 1974, pp6-7
[14] Timothy Keller, *The Reason for God: Belief in an Age of Scepticism*, London: Hodder & Stoughton, 2009, p202

disciples. The Son of God Himself assures us that the Bible is the Word of God'[15].

> ## What Christ Said about the Bible
>
> Christ's use of the Bible shows that He regarded it as divinely inspired. The sheer volume of His references to it, His allusions to its characters, His endorsement of its historicity, His ability to repeatedly quote it from memory, the profound insights He showed in its interpretation and application, the authority He attached to its teachings, the criticism He heaped on the religious leaders for neglecting or disbelieving it, and the fact that He saw His mission as the divine fulfilment of it, show us in what esteem He held the Scriptures. His was a mind saturated in its truth and a life of complete obedience to its letter and spirit. The Scriptures were the constant reference point for all His teachings, and His confrontations with the Jews always sprung from His stand for their essential message. He sealed His dedication to them by dying so 'that the Scriptures of the prophets might be fulfilled' (Matt. 26:56).
>
> ### *Specific Instances in which Christ Taught Inspiration*
> In Matthew 4:4, Christ replied to Satan's temptation with a quotation from Deuteronomy 8:3, 'It is written, man shall not live by bread alone but by every word that proceeds from the mouth of God'. By quoting from a verse in Deuteronomy which refers back to earlier parts of the Law of Moses as the 'word of God', Christ is agreeing with Deuteronomy that the OT Scriptures are divinely inspired. Christ here confirms the verbal, plenary inspiration of Scripture: 'every (plenary) word (verbal) that proceeds from God's mouth (inspiration)'.
>
> In Matthew 22:43, Christ said to the Pharisees and Scribes, 'How then does David in the Spirit call him Lord saying, "The LORD said to my Lord, 'Sit at My right hand, till I make Your enemies Your footstool'"'? Christ here affirms the divine/human duality of Scripture and its method of inspiration: David, the human author, wrote under the influence of the Holy Spirit. W. E. Hoste writes, 'Could our Lord have proved more clearly His acceptance of verbal inspiration, especially as He specifically affirms that it was "in Spirit" (i.e., under the action of the Spirit that David was speaking)?'[16]

---

[15] Norman Geisler and Ron Brooks, *When Skeptics Ask*, Baker Books, 1990, p143
[16] W. E. Hoste, *Studies in Bible Doctrine*, p282

Christ affirms inspiration in Matthew 5:17-18, 'Do not think that I came to destroy the Law or the Prophets. I did not come to destroy but to fulfil. For assuredly, I say to you, till heaven and earth pass away, one jot or one tittle will by no means pass from the law till all is fulfilled'. Here Christ uses the description 'the Law and the Prophets', treating the books of Moses as God's law or instructions and the Prophets as God's mouthpieces. Christ declares the divine nature of Scripture by assuring us of its permanence (as God's Word, it will last till heaven and earth pass away, for 'the word of our God stands forever', Isaiah 40:8) and by assuring us that it contains predictive prophecy that will surely be fulfilled. Christ also affirms plenary inspiration, by treating the entire OT as a unity under the two conjoint categories of the Law and the Prophets. Lastly, Christ extends inspiration to the words, to the very smallest characters in the Hebrew text, the letter yod, and the tittle, a stroke that distinguished certain letters from each other.

Christ referred to the OT Scriptures as the Word of God in a number of other places. In Mark 7:6-13 Christ describes written Scripture as 'the word of God'. Quoting from Exodus 20:12 ('Honour your father and mother') and from Exodus 21:17 ('He who curses mother or father shall be put to death'), Christ proclaims these passages the 'word of God' ('making the word of God of no effect through your tradition which you have handed down, Mark 7:13). Similarly, in John 10:34-35, we read, 'Jesus answered them, "Is it not written in your law, 'I said, "You are gods"'? If He called them gods, to whom the word of God came (and the Scripture cannot be broken)"'. Here Christ quotes from Psalm 82:6 and uses the terms 'the word of God' and 'the Scripture' synonymously. Contrary to the claims of some, then, it is Christ Himself who refers to the Bible 'the Word of God'.

Christ quoted, not only from all of the five books of Moses, but from every part of the OT – from 'the law, the prophets and the psalms' (a description of the three parts of the Jewish Bible, Luke 24:44). In doing so, He put them all on the same level and footing, so we may say that Christ affirmed all of the OT writings as equally inspired by God. Hoste asks, 'Are we not then on sure and unassailable ground in accepting with the fullest assurance our Lord's Bible, and the New Testament, the product of His own Spirit and words. . . . It is at our eternal peril if we do less, for *to depart from the words of Christ is to depart from Christ Himself*'[17].

---

[17] Hoste, *Studies in Bible Doctrine*, p286-7, emphasis in original

Conclusion: For the person who believes that Jesus Christ is God's Son who died and rose again, the most powerful reason for believing in the inspiration of Scripture is Christ's testimony. Abraham Kuyper writes, 'If it appears that Christ attributed absolute authority to the Old Covenant as an organic whole, then the matter is settled for everyone who worships Him as his Lord and his God and confesses that He cannot err'[18].

10. The Living Power of the Bible.

> *I started reading the Bible not because I believed in Christianity, but because it was the best-selling book of all time. To my surprise it started to change me*
> Rosalind Picard

The Bible is the most powerful book in the world. People from all walks of life have had their lives changed by it, from kings and queens to humble miners and housewives, to cannibals and drug-addicts. This is what Rosalind Picard was talking about when she described how the Bible changed her, and she became a Christian. This is because it is the Word of God, and God speaks through it to us in living power; it is 'living and powerful, sharper than any two-edged sword' (Heb. 4:12).

Ultimately, no matter how much evidence is presented about the Bible, the only way people can find out if the Bible is the Word of God is to read it for themselves. This last reason for believing the Bible is a personal experience, not an intellectual argument. In one sense, it is the most powerful and important reason for believing that the Bible is God's Word. A person may read the Bible and realise (through the working of the Holy Spirit) that God is speaking from the Bible to them. No matter how much evidence may be presented about the Bible, we must take this step of reading the Bible for ourselves and allow God to speak to us through it. The Bible is thus self-authenticating, as some theologians have described it.

This is my personal story too. I grew up in a Christian family and was taught the Bible from a very young age. I became a Christian when I was 9 years old, putting my trust in the Lord Jesus Christ as my personal Saviour. As I continued to grow up, I thought I knew the Bible quite well – that is, I knew most of the Bible characters and a number of Bible verses (like John 3:16 and Romans 6:23). But I was ignorant of vast areas of the Bible. I had never read the Bible in a regular and systematic way.

---

[18] Abraham Kuyper, *Principles of Sacred Theology*, Grand Rapids, MI: Eerdmans, 1968, p429

When I was in my late teens, a friend challenged me to try to read the entire Bible through in a year, and after initially resisting the suggestion, I eventually decided to do this. As I read through the Bible, there were many things that I did not understand, but also many things that became much clearer in my mind. At the end of the year, I had enjoyed reading through the Bible so much that I decided I would have to do it again the next year. Around this time, however, a realisation dawned on me. I still remember sitting in a Sydney park during lunch one day when the thought occurred to me: 'I am a different person to what I was one year ago – reading the Bible has changed me'.

Wayne Grudem writes, 'It is helpful for us to learn that the Bible is historically accurate, that it is internally consistent, that it contains prophecies that have been fulfilled hundreds of years later, that it has influenced the course of human history more than any other book, that it has continued changing the lives of millions of individuals throughout its history, that through it people come to find salvation, that it has a majestic beauty and a profound depth of teaching unmatched by any other book, and that it claims hundreds of times over to be God's very words. All of these arguments and others are useful to us and remove obstacles (for) . . . believing. But (they) . . . cannot finally be convincing'[19]. Grudem goes on to quote the Westminster Confession of Faith: 'our full persuasion and assurance of the infallible truth and divine authority thereof, is from the inward work of the Holy Spirit bearing witness by and with the Word in our hearts' (WCF, 1.5).

We only really come to a deep acceptance that the Bible is God's Word when we experience the Bible itself speaking to us in its own divine energy and power. This is the ultimate reason for believing that the Bible is God's Word.

---

[19] Wayne Grudem, *Systematic Theology*, Leicester: IVP, 1994, p78

CHAPTER 2

What does it mean that the Bible is Inspired?

Billy Graham grew up on a dairy farm outside Charlotte, North Carolina. As a teenager, he was more interested in playing baseball, driving cars and taking girls on dates than going to hear the evangelist Mordecai Ham when he came to town in 1934. He only changed his mind when word got round that a high school group was going to cause a disturbance. Ham was famous for his graphic tirades against sin and had publicly accused some high school students of extra-curricular activities of an immoral nature. Billy Graham came to see a protest but left spellbound by the preaching. Rather than pointing out the sins of others, Graham thought Ham's message was directed at him. He continued attending, night after night, convicted of his own sinful rebelliousness. Although growing up in a church-going family, he realised that neither his parents' faith nor his church membership made him a genuine Christian, and his attempts at moral self-improvement had got him nowhere. Finally, one evening he responded to the preacher's invitation and accepted Jesus Christ as his Saviour. His conversion at the age of sixteen was the great turning point of his life.

Another turning point came as a young evangelist in 1949. Billy Graham's faith had come under attack from an unexpected direction – a fellow evangelist named Charles Templeton. Templeton had been having doubts about the Bible, and as he debated with Billy Graham over whether the Bible contained errors, Graham's faith in the Bible reached crisis-point. He studied what the Bible said about itself, pondered what Christ said about the Bible, and talked and prayed with other Christian leaders. But still, he was not sure whether he could trust the Bible.

In desperation one evening he went out into the woods. He laid his Bible on a tree stump, knelt down and prayed something like this: "O God! There are many things in this book I do not understand. There are many problems with it for which I have no solution. There are many seeming contradictions. There are some areas in it that do not seem to correlate with modern science. I can't answer some of the philosophical and psychological questions Chuck and others are raising". However, as he continued wrestling in prayer over the issue, he said, "Father, I am going to accept this as Thy Word – *by faith*! I'm going to allow faith to go beyond my intellectual questions and doubts, and I will believe this to be Your inspired Word". Graham said: 'When I got up from my knees . . . my eyes stung with tears. I sensed the presence and power of God as I had not sensed it in months. Not all my questions were answered, but a major bridge had been crossed. In my heart and mind, I knew a spiritual battle in my soul had been fought and won'[1].

Templeton took a different direction, leaving evangelistic ministry to wrestle with his intellectual doubts about the Bible at Princeton Theological Seminary. Some years later, he abandoned the faith. In his 1996 book, *Farewell to God*, he recounts a conversation with Graham: 'All our differences came to a head in a discussion which, better than anything I know, explains Billy Graham and his phenomenal success as an evangelist. In the course of our conversation I said, "But, Billy, it's simply not possible any longer to believe, for instance, the biblical account of creation. The world was not created over a period of days a few thousand years ago; it has evolved over millions of years. It's not a matter of speculation; it's a demonstrable fact"'.

Billy Graham replied, "I believe the Genesis account of creation because it's in the Bible. I've discovered something in my ministry: when I take the Bible literally, when I proclaim it as the word of God, my preaching has power. When I stand on the platform and say, 'God says', or 'the Bible says', the Holy Spirit uses me. There are results. Wiser men than you or I have been arguing questions like this for centuries. I don't have the time or the intellect to examine all sides of the theological dispute, so I've decided once for all to stop questioning and accept the Bible as God's word"[2].

. . .

---

[1] *Just As I Am: The Autobiography of Billy Graham*, New York: HarperPaperbacks, 1997, pp 163-4.
[2] Charles Templeton, *Farewell to God: My Reasons for Rejecting the Christian Faith*, Toronto: McClelland & Stewart, 1999, pp7-8

Billy Graham is hardly the only person to have ever struggled with the question of whether the Bible is God's Word. I once knew a Christian who had started to develop doubts about the Bible. We had an ongoing debate over a period of time about whether the Bible contained errors and contradictions. This person was being dragged in two directions. He still said he believed the Bible was God's Word, but he was also convinced it contained errors. He was not at all clear about how it was possible to reconcile these two ideas: that the Bible was the Word of God and yet it also contained mistakes. Many people argue that mistakes in the Bible show it cannot be from God; after all, how could a book with errors and mistakes come from God who knows all and never lies? My friend did not abandon his faith completely, but he was very vague about what it meant for the Bible to be God's Word.

In this chapter, we need to get something straight before we go any further: what do we mean when we say that the Bible is the Word of God? Another way of asking this question is, What does it mean for the Bible to be 'inspired'? Many people have all sorts of wrong ideas about what it means for the Bible to be the inspired Word of God. Such is the confusion that some Christians have even suggested we give up using the term 'inspiration' altogether[3].

Five Truths about the Inspiration of Scripture

One of the most common ways that people deny that the Bible is God's inspired Word is via slippery definitions. Some twist the term 'inspiration', changing its meaning to set out their own theories about the Bible. In this chapter, we are going to explain what it *really* means when we say that the Bible is the Word of God. Here are five truths that explain what the inspiration of Scripture means, as well as ten common errors people hold.

Five Truths about Inspiration	
Inspiration's Meaning	Inspiration means 'God-breathed'
Verbal Inspiration	The Bible's words are inspired
Plenary Inspiration	The entire Bible is inspired
Dual Authorship	The Bible is God's word and man's word
Autograph Inspiration	The text of original manuscripts is inspired

---

[3] Wayne Grudem, *Systematic Theology*, Leicester: IVP, 1994, p75

Truth No. 1: Inspired means 'God-breathed'

A Christian friend of mine recently mentioned in a group conversation that he was reading John Bunyan's *Pilgrim's Progress*. He was greatly impressed by it and said he felt the book must have been 'inspired'. I was surprised to hear a Christian say this and tried to gently correct his statement by saying that *Pilgrim's Progess* was not inspired in the same sense that the Bible is inspired. He seemed slightly taken aback at this, but agreed that *Pilgrim's Progess* is not inspired in the same way as Scripture. My friend's confusion is not surprising because there are lots of misunderstandings about what the word 'inspiration' means, particularly when it is used in relation to the Scriptures.

There are two important Bible verses which directly teach us about the meaning of the inspiration of Scripture. The first, in 2 Timothy 3:16, says that 'all Scripture is inspired by God and is profitable for doctrine, reproof, for correction, for instruction in righteousness'. The words 'inspired by God' are a translation of the single Greek word *theopneustos* which means 'God-breathed'. The idea behind 'God-breathed' is that the very words of Scripture are God's. Here is the meaning of inspiration: behind the human authors' written words were the breathed-out words of God's Spirit. Secondly, 2 Peter 1:20-21 says 'knowing this first, that no prophecy of Scripture is of any private interpretation (or, origin[4]), for prophecy never came by the will of man, but holy men of God spoke as they were moved by the Holy Spirit'. Peter tells us that Scripture did not originate with the human authors. It is ultimately the product of the Holy Spirit by whom the writers were 'carried along'. Like a sailing ship being propelled before the wind, the authors were driven and directed by the Holy Spirit as they wrote. The inspiration of Scripture means that the human writers were divinely 'carried-along' so that their words were 'God-breathed' Scripture.

all Scripture is inspired by God
2 Timothy 3:16

Error No. 1: Inspiration Refers to a 'Creative Spark'. When my father was at school, he had an English teacher who had been in the marines during

---

[4] See the NIV, NLT or NET, all of which translate verse 20 as saying that Scripture did not come from the prophet's own imagination, understanding or interpretation. The Greek word *epilusis* can mean 'release' (LSJ), and here likely refers to the 'sending forth' of the prophetic words, as verse 21 explains: 'prophecy never came by the will of man . . . but by the Holy Spirit'.

World War Two, and the boys gave him the nickname Dynamite. One day, one of the boys had not done his homework, and Dynamite asked him why. The boy replied, 'Sir, I didn't have any inspiration'. Dynamite said, 'I'll give you some inspiration', and with that, he punched the boy in the stomach. Needless to say, this is not what we mean by the inspiration of the Scriptures! To some people, 'inspiration' refers to a creative spark or influence that prompted an author, musician or poet to produce a great work of art or literature. However, when we use the word inspiration in relation to the Bible, we are not referring to a 'creative spark' that prompted the authors to write. Nor is it true, as some suggest, that God inspired the human authors of the Bible in the same the way a teacher inspires students; notice that 2 Timothy 3:16 speaks of the Bible's words as inspired, rather than the writers.

Error No. 2: Inspired Books are Works of Genius. Some people think the Bible is a work of natural genius, written without supernatural aid, just as Shakespeare's plays or Handel's music (or even Bunyan's *Pilgrim's Progress*) were works of creative brilliance. They gladly admit that the Bible is one of the world's great works of literature, although not perhaps the Word of God. However, inspiration does not refer to naturally talented, creative, brainy or brilliant authors writing books.

Error No. 3: Inspiration means Uplifting. Some people misunderstand the meaning of the word 'inspired' and think that it means that the Bible is 'uplifting' or 'thrilling' in its effect upon the readers. Thus, we sometimes hear people say (about secular works of literature, or even modern Christian books), 'I found that story very inspiring'. However, although the Bible can definitely have this effect upon us, the word 'inspired' does not mean thrilling, uplifting, exciting or inspirational when we use it in relation to Scripture.

Instead of referring to a 'creative spark' or a work of genius or something 'inspirational', the word 'inspired' has a special, technical meaning when we use it in relation to the Bible: it teaches that the Bible is God-breathed. It means that the Bible is *really* God's Word.

Truth No. 2: The Bible's Words are Inspired

Inspiration applies to the very words of Scripture, and not simply to the general truths it teaches. Another way of stating this is to speak of *verbal inspiration*. 2 Timothy 3:15-16 speak of the holy 'writings' (Greek: *grammata*) being God-breathed 'Scripture' (Greek: *graphe*). These verses identify the *written* words of the apostles and prophets (not merely their spoken oracles) as inspired. In Matthew 5:18, Christ said that the inspiration of 'the Law and the Prophets' applied to the 'jot or tittle', the jot being the smallest letter in the Hebrew alphabet, and the 'tittle' being the smallest pen-stroke that distinguished different letters. Proverbs 30:5 says 'Every word of God is pure; He is a shield to those who put their trust in Him'. J. I. Packer writes, 'Inspiration is a work of God terminating, not in the men who were to write Scripture (as if, having given them an idea of what to say, God left them to themselves to find a way of saying it), but in the actual written product. It is Scripture – *graphe*, the written text – that is God-breathed'[5].

Error No. 4: The Bible Contains the Word of God. When I was in my teens, a number of people came and joined my home church because of troubles in their denomination. Instead of saying that the Bible *was* the Word of God, certain denominational leaders were teaching that the Bible *contained* the Word of God. The word 'contained' expressed the fact that these leaders did not believe that everything in the Bible was true, or that all the words of the Bible were inspired by God. While they believed that the Bible contained the Word of God, they also believed that the Bible contained errors, which were not the Word of God.

One missionary to Vanuatu in the Pacific protested against the attempt by the (theologically liberal) parent denomination in his homeland to force a new constitution on the Christians in Vanuatu with the words, 'the Scriptures contain the Word of God'. He argued that the wording ought to be, 'the Scriptures are the Word of God'. To help the native Christians to understand the difference between the two expressions, he held up an old and worn-out Bible and starting solemnly ripping out one page here and another page there. The native Christians got the message and changed their constitution to state that all Scripture is the Word of God[6].

> *'I maintain that every book, and chapter, and verse, and syllable of the Bible, was given by inspiration by God'.*
> J. C. Ryle

---

[5] J. I. Packer, "Inspiration", *New Bible Dictionary*, Leicester: IVP, 1996, p507
[6] J. Graham Miller, *A Day's March Nearer Home: Autobiography of J. Graham Miller*, Edinburgh: Banner of Truth, 2010, pp96-100.

Error No. 5: The Bible's Concepts are Inspired, but Not its Words. Some argue that the inspiration of Scripture refers to the general concepts that the Bible conveys (God, the 'golden rule', etc.), rather than to the particular wording that the Bible uses. On this theory, God inspired the thoughts or ideas of Scripture, which are true, but not the words, which were left up to the human writers and may contain mistakes. However, we cannot clearly communicate concepts without words. Unless we use words carefully, concepts become so vague as to mean nothing. For example, if someone were to argue that we must not place our trust in the actual words of Scripture but instead simply believe in a Supreme Being, we would be unsure what sort of God to believe in (for there are all sorts of gods in our world).

William Hoste wrote, 'Some admit Inspiration in a general sense, but deny [that all the words are inspired]; but if nothing short of verbal accuracy satisfies men in their legal documents, Acts of Parliament, etc., would not God have His statute-book of the kingdom, our "title-deeds for eternity," accurately drawn up? How else could we be sure of its terms, or use it for our comfort or for contending for the faith? To deny the possibility of verbal accuracy in what claims to be God's Book, is to exalt man's work above God's'[7].

Those who deny the possibility of verbal inspiration obviously have a very low opinion of God, for they must either believe He was unable to reliably supervise the words His prophets and apostles wrote, or that He was only grudgingly interested in revealing the truth to us.

Truth No. 3: The Entire Bible is Inspired

The whole of Scripture is inspired by God, not just certain parts. A term sometimes used to express this truth is the *plenary inspiration* of Scripture ('plenary' means 'full, complete or entire'). Psalm 119:160 says 'the entirety of Your word is true, and every one of Your righteous judgments endures forever'. 2 Timothy 3:16 says that '*all* Scripture' is inspired by God. It is not just the stories of Jesus, or the New Testament letters, or certain comforting passages that are inspired. Even the Old Testament books were written for our benefit. Romans 15:4 says, 'For whatever things were written before were written for our learning, that we through the patience and comfort of the Scriptures might have hope'.

J. C. Ryle wrote, 'I maintain that every book, and chapter, and verse,

---

[7] William Hoste, *Studies in Bible Doctrine*, London: Pickering and Inglis, 1932, p260

and syllable of the Bible, was given by inspiration by God. I hold that not only the substance of the Bible, but its language, – not only the ideas of the Bible, but its words, – not only certain parts of the Bible, but every chapter of the book, – that all and each are of Divine authority. I hold that the Scripture not only *contains* the Word of God, but *is* the Word of God. I believe the narratives and statements of Genesis, and the catalogues in Chronicles, were just as truly written by inspiration as the Acts of the Apostles. . . . I do not say, be it remembered, that all these parts of the Bible are of equal importance to our souls. Nothing of the kind! But I do say they were all equally given by inspiration'[8].

Error No. 6: Inspiration only Applies to Spiritual Subjects. Some people have argued that the Scriptures are inspired in all they say about spiritual topics like salvation, but not in minor matters of history, geography, chronology or science. But this is to say that the Bible is a mixture of truth and error, of divine and human ideas. Christianity is a historical religion, and the Bible's spiritual message is based upon its historical record, so why should we believe that its spiritual message is true if we know that it contains errors or untruths in its reporting of history?

The Pope claims infallibility when speaking *ex cathedra* (that is, in his official capacity as Pope) on matters of faith, but not when speaking about mundane matters of life. But how can we trust the Pope to be right when speaking on spiritual matters (which we cannot test) if he gets ordinary matters (which we are able to check) wrong? Christ asked Nicodemus, 'If I have told you earthly things and you do not believe, how will you believe if I tell you heavenly things?' (John 3:8). Similarly, if the Bible were wrong about some matters – facts of history or science which we are able to check – how could we trust it about spiritual matters? And if it is possible that some of the Bible's spiritual teachings are wrong, how would we know which are true and which are false? How could we even be sure that John 3:16 is true? We must either believe that the Bible is God's inspired Word or accept that it is simply another human religious book groping for God in the dark, mixing truth and error in some unknown proportion. We would thus be left unable to determine the extent of the Bible's errors and, for all we know, no closer to God or the truth.

---

[8] J. C. Ryle, *Bible Inspiration: Its Reality and Nature*, London: William Hunt and Co., 1877, pp41-42

Error No. 7: Some Parts of the Bible are More Inspired than Others. Some people elevate certain parts of Scripture over others. For example, self-styled 'red-letter Christians' claim that the words of Jesus (printed in red in some Bibles) have a higher status than other writings in the Bible. Old Testament histories or teachings of New Testament letters are downplayed or disparaged, as if they are somehow less inspired. Some 'red-letter' Christians today argue that Jesus said nothing about issues like abortion, homosexuality or people of other religions going to Hell. Therefore they say that Christians should not mention such matters. Is this true? If so, other teachings of the Bible may be dismissed as 'just what Paul said, not Jesus'. But if someone says that they believe in Jesus, rather than the Bible, they need to remember that everything we know about Jesus comes from the Bible. Even the glorious message of the children's song, 'Jesus loves me, this I know', is grounded on the truth, 'for the Bible tells me so'. It is true that the gospels are the heart of the Christian faith, and that certain parts of the Bible are more relevant to us today than others. But because all Scripture is God-breathed, there is a sense in which every word should be in red letters. Once we start elevating some parts as specially inspired, there is little to stop us excluding other parts as not God's Word at all. Any system which picks-and-chooses certain bits of the Bible, which sets up 'a canon within the canon', is not accepting God's Word but trying to silence what it says.

Error No. 8: The Bible Becomes God's Word. Neo-orthodoxy (a mid-20th-century theological fad, promoted by Karl Barth) taught that the Bible is not the Word of God – Christ is. The Bible is only a witness to the Word (Christ), and even those parts of the Bible which tell us about Christ are not without errors and myths. Neo-orthodoxy taught that the Bible may *become* the Word of God if God speaks through it in a personal encounter with the reader. Thus, again, only certain parts of the Bible are inspired. Another neo-orthodox theologian, Emil Brunner, expressed it this way: what speaks to me in the Bible is the Word of God, and what does not speak to me is not the Word of God[9]. Neo-orthodoxy is true in that God speaks powerfully and personally to us through the Bible, but is wrong in claiming that the Bible is not the Word of God (see Mark 7:8-13 and John 10:35 where Jesus called the Scriptures 'the Word of God'). It is also wrong in claiming that the Bible

---

[9] This confuses inspiration with illumination (the Holy Spirit's enlightenment of us through Scripture).

only becomes the Word of God when we are in a fit state to hear it. The fact that we experience that the Bible is 'living and powerful' and speaks to our hearts should lead us to place our full confidence in it as 'the Word of God' (Hebrews 4:12).

Truth No. 4: The Bible has Dual Authorship

The Bible is both God's Word and Man's Word. The Bible is not part-human and part-Divine, but fully God's Word and fully man's words. God is the Bible's Author, but the human authors of its books were not mere machines, robots, secretaries or typewriters to whom God dictated the Bible. Some books were written by fishermen (like John) and some by doctors (like Luke), and the different personalities, interests, historical settings and writing styles of the various human authors shine through in their books. B. B. Warfield writes, 'The Bible is the Word of God in such a sense that its words, though written by men and bearing indelibly impressed upon them the marks of their human origin, were written, nevertheless, under such an influence of the Holy Ghost as to be also the words of God, the adequate expression of His mind and will'[10]. J. I. Packer writes, 'Scripture is not only man's word, the fruit of human thought, premeditation and art, but also, and equally, God's word, spoken through man's lips or written with man's pen. In other words, Scripture has a double authorship, and man is only the secondary author; the primary author, through whose initiative, prompting and enlightenment, and under whose superintendence, each human writer did his work, is God the Holy Spirit'[11].

Error No. 9: Dictation Inspiration. Some would argue that the Scriptures were dictated by God, just as Muslims believe the Koran was dictated from heaven in Arabic. Whilst parts of the Bible were dictated (see Rev. 2:1), and other parts were written by the very finger of God (the Ten Commandments), yet other parts were written as the result of research (see Luke 1:1-4) or recollection (see John 14:26). If the Bible were dictated by God, the different writers' styles would be identical. Instead, God used people from different backgrounds, cultures, classes and times, whose writings took different forms (histories, letters, poems). Therefore, the Bible is both God's words and man's words.

---

[10] B. B. Warfield, *The Inspiration and Authority of the Bible*, Philadelphia: Presbyterian and Reformed, 1948, p173
[11] J. I. Packer, "Inspiration", *New Bible Dictionary*, Leicester: IVP, 1996

E. W. Rogers writes, 'The Inspiration of Scripture is plainly affirmed therein, but its process will ever remain a mystery . . . The inspiration of Scripture is far different from that of a great poet or painter. Nor is it mere mechanical dictation. That would destroy 'the human element' which we discern throughout it. Like the Living Word, the Lord Jesus (who indeed is the very heart of the Scripture), the Bible is at once divine and human'[12].

Truth No. 5: The Text of the Original Manuscripts was Inspired

There is a joke (or maybe even a true story) about an old farmer who, hearing a preacher making reference to the meaning of a Greek word, said, 'If the King James Version was good enough for the apostle Paul, it is good enough for me'. However, we only have to read the title page of a King James Bible to learn that it is 'The Holy Bible, Containing the Old and New Testaments, translated out of the Original Tongues, and with the former translations diligently compared and revised . . . '. In other words, the King James Version (KJV) is not the original Bible, and it wasn't even the first English Bible. The Bible was translated into English out of the 'Original Tongues': Hebrew, Aramaic and Greek. None of the apostles or prophets spoke or wrote in (Elizabethan) English.

Inspiration applies only to the text of the Bible in its original manuscript (i.e. hand-written) autographs (i.e. those written by the apostles and prophets themselves), not to the work of later copyists, Bible translators, printers, or modern religious writers. We have ample evidence of copying errors in our Greek and Hebrew manuscripts, none of which are perfectly identical. Further, despite the great respect we have for all those who have translated the Bible into our mother tongue, some translators have used inexact language that does not clearly convey the original meaning in some places. Inspiration involved fallible men writing infallible words under God's supervision, but none of the later copying, printing or translating processes resulted in perfect or infallible Bible versions. (Nor does infallible Scripture prevent Christians misinterpreting it; as the Greek scholar A. T. Robertson joked, 'The greatest proof that the Bible is inspired is the fact that it has withstood so much bad preaching').

C. H. Mackintosh wrote, 'We believe that the Bible, as written in the original Hebrew and Greek languages, is the very word of the only

---

[12] E. W. Rogers, "The Scriptures of Truth", *Treasury of Bible Doctrine*, Precious Seed Publications, 1977, p20

wise and the only true God', and again, 'We could not say how much we prize the labours of those learned men who have consecrated their energies to the work of clearing the sacred text of the various errors and corruptions which, from age to age, had crept into it, through the carelessness or infirmity of copyists, taken advantage of by a crafty and malignant foe'[13].

Here is J. C. Ryle: 'In making this statement I ask the reader not to misunderstand my meaning. I do not forget that the Old Testament was written in Hebrew and the New Testament in Greek. The inspiration of every word, for which I contend, is the inspiration of every original Hebrew and Greek word as the Bible writers first wrote it down. I stand up for nothing more and nothing less than this. I do not say that those who wrote copies of the original Hebrew and Greek Scriptures were incapable of making mistakes, and never left out or added a word. I lay no claim to the inspiration of every word in the various versions and translations of God's Word. So far as those translations and versions are faithfully and correctly done so far they are, practically, of equal authority with the original Hebrew and Greek. We have reason to thank God that many of the translations are, in the main, faithful and accurate. At any rate our own English Bible, if not perfect, is so far correct that in reading it we have a right to believe that we are reading in our own tongue, not the word of man, but of God'[14].

Some would argue that 'inspiration can only be predicated of the original writings, not to copies or translations, however accurate they may be'[15]. However, it is better to say that our English (or other language) Bibles are inspired by God to the (very large) extent that they accurately correspond to and convey the original text of the Bible. The Chicago Statement on Biblical Inerrancy states, 'We affirm that inspiration, strictly speaking, applies to the autographic text of Scripture, which in the providence of God can be ascertained from available manuscripts with great accuracy. We further affirm that copies and translations of Scripture are the Word of God to the extent that they faithfully represent the original' (Article X).

---

[13] C. H. Mackintosh, "The Bible – Its Sufficiency and Supremacy", *The Mackintosh Treasury: Miscellaneous Writings*, Neptune, NJ: Loizeaux Brothers, 1976, p18
[14] J. C. Ryle, *Bible Inspiration*, p43
[15] Charles Ryrie, *Basic Theology*, Chicago: Moody Publishers, 1999, p82

Error No. 10: Only Certain Translations are Inspired. In 1993 Gail Riplinger, a lecturer in home economics, published a book called *New Age Bible Versions*, the general drift of which was that the editors of modern Bible versions were Satan worshippers in league with the New Age movement. The words of one competent reviewer pretty well sum up the book: '*NABV* is replete with logical, philosophical, theological, biblical, and technical errors'[16]. Leaving aside the scholarship (or lack thereof), perhaps the most interesting thing about the book is how the author claims it was written. In the January/February 1994 edition of *The End Times and Victorious Living* newsletter Riplinger wrote: 'Daily during the six years needed for this investigation, the Lord miraculously brought the needed materials and resources – much like the ravens fed Elijah. Each discovery was not the result of effort on my part, but of the directed hand of God – so much so that I hesitated to even put my name on the book. Consequently, I used G. A. Riplinger, which signifies to me, God and Riplinger – God as author and Riplinger as secretary'. However, the idea that God is authoring books or inspiring people as they write today is heresy and nonsense. Only the apostles and prophets were inspired by God to write Scripture.

Some would argue that only one particular Bible version (for example, the 'authorised' King James Version) was inspired by God. While we thank God for the KJV and the great blessing it has brought to many down through the centuries, it was neither the first English translation nor has it been without mistakes. The so-called 'Wicked Bible' (the 1631 KJV) read, 'Thou shalt commit adultery' (it left out the word 'not' in Exodus 20:14), the 1612 KJV read, 'Printers have persecuted me without cause', (instead of 'princes', Psalm 119:161), the 1682 KJV read, 'if the latter husband ate her' (instead of 'hate her', Deut. 24:3), and the 1795 KJV read, 'Let the children first be killed' (instead of 'filled', Mark 7:27). Thankfully, we are able to correct these mistakes because we have large numbers of original language manuscript copies of the Bible which we may compare against each other to identify the correct, original reading. And by learning the original languages, it is possible to understand more clearly the meaning of the Greek and Hebrew words. The current KJV is the 1769 Oxford Standard edition of the KJV which contains approximately 75,000 changes to the 1611 KJV.

---

[16] H. Wayne House, *A Summary Critique: New Age Bible Versions*, Christian Research Institute, http://www.equip.org/article/a-summary-critique-new-age-bible-versions/, viewed 29/4/2016

It still contains a misprint in Matthew 23:24 where it reads 'strain *at* a gnat' instead of 'strain *out* a gnat'.

If the KJV were the only true Bible, as KJV-Only proponents argue, then what was the pure Word of God, divinely-preserved for all time, before the KJV in 1611? Was it written in English or another language? Why did God take so long to give the world the only true Bible? To ask such questions is to silence the argument. As noted earlier, the KJV was not the first English Bible. Parts of the Bible were translated into Anglo-Saxon by Bede in the eighth century. John Wycliffe, the 'Morning Star of the Reformation', translated the entire Bible from Latin into English in 1382. William Tyndale translated the New Testament from Greek in 1526 and started translating the Old Testament from Hebrew before he was burned at the stake. Before the KJV, there was also Coverdale's Bible (1535), the Matthew Bible (1537), the Great Bible (1539), the Geneva Bible (1560), and the Bishop's Bible (1568). Even the KJV was attacked as a modern innovation, and its translators called 'damnable corrupters' of the Word of God. The translators themselves claimed that they were not trying 'to make a new translation, nor yet to make of a bad one a good one . . . but to make a good one better, or out of many good ones one principal good one'.

The Roman Catholic church claims that the Latin Vulgate is the 'authorized' version of the Bible. But God did not 'inspire' (i.e. infallibly supervise) any translators to produce a perfect translation, either 1600 years ago (in the case of the Latin Vulgate) or 400 years ago (the KJV). Nor does God inspire people today as they translate the Bible into foreign languages. These versions (the KJV in English or the Vulgate in Latin) are only translations from the original languages, and as anybody who has learnt a foreign language knows, there is no translation which perfectly captures the full meaning of any book in another language, nor does any language stand still. Translations of the Bible are only authoritative to the degree that they faithfully convey the originals.

Ten Errors about Inspiration	
Inspiration is a 'creative spark'	*Spiritual* Subjects are Inspired
Inspired means a 'work of genius'	Some Parts are *More* Inspired
Inspired means 'uplifting'	The Bible *Becomes* God's Word
The Bible *Contains* God's Word	*Dictation* Inspiration
The Bible's *Concepts* are Inspired	Only certain *Versions* are Inspired

A Definition of Inspiration

Let's pull all these different truths about inspiration together, and put them into a definition:

> **Definition**: *The Inspiration of Scripture means that the Bible is God's Word, and although its various books were written by human authors, yet their writing was infallibly supervised by the Holy Spirit in such a way that all the words in the original autographs are truly the words of God.*

The Result: We have the Word of God

The result of inspiration is that we have, in the Bible, the very Word of God. If the Bible is inspired by God, it is the most important book in the world. It is God's self-revelation, telling us who God is, and what He is like. Its unique message teaches us of God's plan of salvation through faith in Jesus Christ. We should therefore read it, meditate on it, memorise it, and obey it. It is 'the living and powerful Word of God'[17] (Heb. 4:12), which saves and sanctifies, converts and cleanses, regenerates and revives, illumines and instructs, builds up and blesses, warns, makes wise, and works powerfully in us; it is perfect and pure, 'true and righteous altogether'; it is our joy, our food, and our treasure[18].

God continues to speak to us through the Bible today. When we read the Bible, God is speaking. 'What Scripture says, God says' (B. B. Warfield). In Hebrews 3:7 we read, 'therefore, as the Holy Spirit says', going on to quote Psalm 95, and the fact that the Holy Spirit is said to be speaking (in the present tense) here means that, as a result of inspiration, God continues to speak to us through the Bible today. F. F. Bruce writes, 'the Holy Spirit is not only the Primary Author of Scripture, but also, in Abraham Kuyper's phrase, the Perpetual Author,

---

[17] Some might argue that the 'Word of God' in this verse does not refer to Scripture, however from Heb. 3:7 down to 4:11, the writer is expounding Psalm 95, and this is what he calls 'the Word of God' in 4:12.

[18] The Word of God saves (Jam. 1:21, 2 Tim. 3:15), sanctifies (John 17:17), converts (Ps. 19:7), cleanses (John 15:3, Eph. 5:26, Ps. 119:9), regenerates (Jam. 1:18, 1 Pet. 1:23), revives (Ps. 119:25, 107, 154), illumines (Ps. 119:105, 130), instructs (Rom. 15:4, 1 Cor. 10:11), builds up (Acts 20:32), blesses (Ps. 1:3, Luke 11:28, Jam. 1:25), warns (Ps. 19:11), makes wise (Ps. 19:7), and works in us (1 Thess. 2:13); it is perfect (Ps. 19:7), pure (Ps. 19:8), true (Dan. 10:21, Jam. 1:18), righteous (Ps. 19:9), our joy (Ps. 1:2, 19:8, 119:162), food (Job 23:12, Jer. 15:16), and treasure (Ps. 19:10, 119:72, 127).

continually speaking through the Word to the believing reader and unfolding fresh meaning from it'[19].

Conclusion

Whether by ignorance or design, many people hold wrong ideas about the inspiration of Scripture. Some misunderstand the meaning of the term, while others deliberately twist it to deny the truth of inspiration. The inspiration of Scripture means that the Bible really is the Word of God, and that all its words in the text of its original manuscripts were God-breathed, while also having been composed by human authors.

Charles Spurgeon, in one of his last sermons[20], spoke about the inspiration of Scripture and the attempts of some to change the meaning of the term: 'We are resolved, then, to use more fully than ever what God has provided for us in this Book, for we are sure of its inspiration. Let me say that over again. WE ARE SURE OF ITS INSPIRATION. You will notice that attacks are frequently made as against *verbal* inspiration. The form chosen is a mere pretext. Verbal inspiration is the verbal form of the assault, but the attack is really aimed at inspiration itself. You will not read far in the essay before you will find that the gentleman who started with contesting a theory of inspiration which none of us ever held, winds up by showing his hand, and that hand wages war with inspiration itself. There is the true point. We care little for any theory of inspiration: in fact, we have none. To us the plenary verbal inspiration of Holy Scripture is fact, and not hypothesis. . . . If you adopt theories which pare off a portion here, and deny authority to a passage there, you will at last have no inspiration left, worthy of the name'.

In this chapter we have looked at what the Bible says about its own inspiration. But if the Bible *really* is God's Word, what position should we give it in our lives?

---

[19] F. F. Bruce, "The Scriptures", *The Faith – A Symposium*, Kilmarnock: Ritchie, 1999, p18
[20] *The Greatest Fight in the World*, April 1891, published just before his death, emphasis in the original.

CHAPTER 3

The Highest Court of Appeal

Martin Luther was born in Germany in 1483. As a boy, he prayed to saints and Mary instead of God, because he thought of God as 'the Thunderer' – an angry Judge. His father, a hard-working miner, sent him to school and then to university, hoping for him to eventually become a lawyer. After one summer holiday, he was caught in a thunderstorm on his way back to university. As the lightning struck nearby, Luther fell to his knees and prayed to St. Anne to save him, promising to abandon his law studies and devote his life to God. Safely back at university, he kept his promise and became a monk, much to his father's displeasure.

As a monk, Luther took vows of poverty, chastity and obedience. He owned no money or clothes of his own, and had to beg for bread in the streets. He fasted for days at a time and attended seven chapel services every day. But all his religious activity and self-denial did not seem to bring God any closer. He increased his devotion, praying for hours, lying on the cold stone floor of his cell staring at a crucifix on the wall. He went on pilgrimage to Rome, where he prayed and viewed religious relics, but God still seemed a distant and angry God.

Luther's monastic superiors, worried about his spiritual, mental and physical condition, asked him to teach the Bible in the university. Studying the New Testament, he found no mention of obtaining forgiveness for sins through prayers, pilgrimages, penance or fasting. Instead, he discovered from Romans that 'faith alone justifies before God without works'. Luther believed he was forgiven – not because his works somehow appeased God – but through simple faith in Christ.

In 1512, Luther became professor of theology in the University of Wittenberg, and in 1517, nailed his famous 95 theses to the church door in Wittenberg. The 95 theses attacked the sale of 'indulgences', certificates by which the Pope sold forgiveness for sins and the release of souls from the fires of purgatory. This brought Luther into conflict with the Church authorities, and as a result, in 1520, the Pope condemned Luther's teachings and ordered him to recant. In 1521, Luther was offered safe conduct to travel to the Diet of Worms to stand trial before the Holy Roman Emperor, Charles V of Spain. Luther knew that the safe conduct meant little: one hundred years before, John Huss was offered a safe conduct to his trial, whereupon he was condemned as a heretic and burned at the stake. Luther was preaching the same gospel as Huss, and it seemed likely that he would share Huss' fate.

When Luther arrived he was shown a pile of his books and told to renounce them. Luther asked for time to consider his reply, and on the next day famously answered: 'Unless I am convinced by the testimony of the Scriptures or by clear reason (for I do not trust either in the pope or in councils alone, since it is well known that they have often erred and contradicted themselves), I am bound by the Scriptures I have quoted and my conscience is captive to the Word of God. I cannot and will not recant anything, since it is neither safe nor right to go against conscience. [Here I stand. I can do no other[1]] May God help me. Amen'.

Luther knew that the Bible taught that we are saved by faith in Christ's work, not by our own works, and he was willing to risk his life to argue the case. His challenge to the church authorities was this: show me from the Bible where I am wrong and I will admit it. The Church authorities refused to debate the Bible with Luther; instead, they condemned him to death for refusing to bow before their authority.

Luther's 'stand' raises a question: is the Bible or the Church our highest court of appeal, our ultimate authority in the matter of salvation? Luther rightly believed that because the Bible is the Word of God, it is the supreme authority in the matter of salvation.

Marriage and Other Matters

The Bible deals with other matters besides salvation. A few years ago, I was involved in a Facebook 'debate' over homosexual marriage with a lady who I had once known as a Christian. As surprised as I was to hear her arguing for homosexual marriage, I was more troubled by something she wrote in the middle of her arguments: she did not believe that the Bible was 'our final or only authority'. In effect, she was saying that any arguments from the Bible carried little weight with her. This was an eye-opening admission – far more significant than her support for

---

[1] It is not clear whether Luther actually said these last words.

homosexual marriage. It seemed to me that this lady no longer claimed to believe in the Bible, for once people deny the Bible as our final authority, they have in effect denied it is God's Word. Either the Bible is God's Word – the supreme authority, or we deny its divine origin and reduce it to just another voice in the noisy marketplace of human ideas, lacking any special authority.

> *Let the Bible, the whole Bible and nothing but the Bible be the rule of our faith and practice.*
>
> J. C. Ryle

There is a story about a tourist walking around an art gallery in Europe loudly criticizing the masterpieces on display. Eventually one of the staff at the gallery could stand it no longer and told the man that it was not the pieces of art that were on trial; rather, the artwork was judging the visitors. It is the same with us. We may either submit to the authority of scripture, or, in effect, we arrogantly assert that we know better than God. Either God sits on the throne of our lives, or we have taken back control for ourselves. The Bible is not only our supreme authority in matters of salvation, or marriage, but in every area of life: church life, Christian service, family, business, and leisure.

We cannot take a pick-and-mix approach to the Bible, a form of cafeteria Christianity, a designer version of our own devising. If we accept some things that the Bible teaches but ignore others that make us uncomfortable, or 'feel led' to do things that contradict the Bible because we 'have peace about it', or if we compromise on biblical issues for the sake of consensus or to preserve relationships at all costs, then we have watered-down the real thing. As Augustine wrote, 'If you believe what you like in the gospel, and reject what you don't like, it is not the gospel you believe, but yourself'.

...

In this chapter we are going to look at another way we can deny that the Bible is really God's Word. We have already seen in previous chapters that it is possible to deny that the Bible is God's Word by redefining the meaning of inspiration, or by outright rejection of the idea. But here is a third way to deny the Bible is really God's Word: by ignoring what it says, believing what we choose and living our own way. This is a danger for all Christians: it is possible for us, even though we claim to believe that the Bible is God's Word, to deny it by our actions. However, if the

Bible is God's Word, then we must believe and obey what it says. The Bible must be our highest court of appeal.

The Authority of Scripture

> **Definition**: *The Authority of Scripture means that God's Word should govern our lives. We should believe it, obey it, and let it determine our doctrine and practice.*

As Christians, there are four main ways we can live. There are four different sources of authority to guide our beliefs and lifestyles.

The Four Main Sources of Authority
1. Tradition
2. Reason
3. Experience
4. Scripture

1. Tradition

Some Christians consider tradition to be the ultimate authority. By tradition, we mean what has been handed down from one generation to another. The Roman Catholic Church claims that church tradition must be placed alongside Scripture on an equal footing. The Roman Catholic catechism states: 'the Church, to whom the transmission and interpretation of revelation is entrusted, does not derive her certainty about all revealed truths from the holy Scriptures alone. Both Scripture and Tradition must be accepted and honoured with equal sentiments of devotion and reverence' (Section 81).

Despite the fact that the Roman Catholic church says that Scripture and Tradition are equal in authority, since the Church claims that it alone can infallibly interpret Scripture, in practice the Church makes itself the final authority on matters of faith. One Roman Catholic scholar said that he believed the Bible was the inspired Word of God because his Church told him so, and if the Church were to teach that Aesop's Fables were inspired by God, he would believe that too[2].

---

[2] Quoted by John H. Gerstner, "The Contributions of Charles Hodge, B. B. Warfield and J. Gresham Machen to the Doctrine of Inspiration" in *Challenges to Inerrancy: a Theological Response*, eds. Gordon Lewis and Bruce Demarest, Chicago: Moody Press, 1984, p370

Further, despite the fact that the Roman Catholic Church claims that it is *semper eadem* ('always the same') and that it has handed down unchanged the traditions of the apostles from the beginning, the facts prove otherwise. The Roman Catholic Church has not remained the same; it has added many doctrines down through the years: indulgences (that is, forgiveness of sins through paying money to the church or going on pilgrimage), prayers to the saints, purgatory and papal infallibility. These teachings not only add to Scripture, they undermine its message about salvation by grace through faith in the finished work of Christ.

Reliance upon tradition is not limited to the Roman Catholic Church. Some Christians, when confronted by a particular issue, appeal to tradition by using phrases like 'we've never done that before'. Or, if change is suggested, ask, 'Do you mean that we have been wrong all these years?' Any churches which have a long or glorious history (and even some which do not) tend to take pride in their spiritual inheritance. Someone has said, 'It is possible to reject traditions a thousand years old and yet be slaves to traditions of scarcely fifty years standing'. A. W. Tozer wrote in *The Crucified Life*, 'As great and wonderful as moves of God are, it does not take long to drift slowly back into externalism. Once externalism gets a good hold, institutionalism begins to take over. Then follows form, ceremony and tradition – and the church begins to celebrate what once was and those who once were. An external ceremony replaces the inner fire of the Holy Spirit'.

We see Christ's attitude towards tradition when He was criticized by the Pharisees for not keeping 'the tradition of the elders' about hand-washing (Mark 7:1-13). Christ replied by quoting from Isaiah: 'in vain they worship Me, teaching as doctrines the commandments of men' (Mark 7:7). Christ said that, by their tradition, the Jews had 'laid aside the commandment of God' (verse 8), 'rejected the commandment of God' (verse 9), and 'made the Word of God of no effect' (verse 13). Thus, for Christ, God's commandments in His Word were of greater authority than human traditions.

2. Reason

Some people give reason the ultimate place of authority. Liberal theologians reject supernatural events or predictive prophecy in Scripture, as well as many of the most important doctrines of the Bible. Rudolf Bultmann wrote 'It is impossible to use electric light and the wireless and to avail ourselves of modern medical and surgical discoveries, and at the same time to believe in the New Testament world of spirits and miracles'. Thomas Jefferson cut out all the miracles in the gospels with scissors. Other people reject Biblical doctrines that they cannot fathom; for example, the Jehovah's Witnesses reject the doctrine of the Trinity.

It is not just liberal theologians who rely on human reason. Modern evangelical Christianity is increasingly characterized by expedience and pragmatism. Instead of asking, 'What does the Bible say?' the instinctive reaction of many today is to have a 'brainstorming' session to try to think what might work the best. Ignoring the uncomfortable parts of Scripture, we try to keep up with other churches by following the latest fads. We love to quote Proverbs 3:5-6 ('Trust in the Lord with all your heart, and lean not on your own understanding. In all your ways acknowledge Him and He shall direct your paths'). But all too often we give in to the temptation of leaning on our own 'common sense' rather than relying on God's wisdom in Scripture.

The problem with giving human reason the ultimate place of authority is that there are many things about God that we cannot understand (how He can be without beginning, how He can be Triune, how He can create from nothing, or even how He can hear the prayers of His people from all over the world at the same time). To claim that our intelligence is the judge of all truth claims or the highest authority is to usurp God's place as the Lord of all things. Bruce Demarest writes, 'Experience proves that there are upper limits to what can be known about God from nature and reason. Natural reason cannot fathom the hidden character or secret councils of God. It cannot inform man what God demands to render the sinner acceptable to Himself. And reason can never break the dominion of indwelling sin. Arrogant reason, which falsely usurps the function of faith, Luther described as 'blind and poor' and as the 'arch-prostitute and Devils' bride'[3].

We see Christ's attitude towards reason in His confrontation with the Sadducees, the equivalent of today's liberal theologians, who did not believe in the resurrection or angels or spirits. Christ condemned their unbelief saying, 'You are mistaken, not knowing the Scriptures nor the power of God' (Matthew 22:29). He condemned their denial of resurrection by pointing to Scripture as the ultimate authority: 'concerning the resurrection of the dead, have you not read what was spoken to you by God?' (verse 31).

---

[3] Bruce Demarest, "The Bible in the Enlightenment Era", in *Challenges to Inerrancy*, p33

3. Experience

Some Christians place experience alongside Scripture as their ultimate authority. They base their faith upon some event they experienced – perhaps they had a dream or enjoyed some fortunate coincidence. Some rely on intuitions, emotions and gut feelings in following God. Charismatic Christianity is heavily experience-based, arguing that experiences (e.g. speaking in tongues, healing, prophecies, etc.) are manifestations of the Holy Spirit that confirm faith and encourage us to follow Christ. Whatever we think of such experiences (this is not the place to evaluate them), at least they are found in Scripture. The same cannot be said for the increasing number of experiences charismatics have added to the list of manifestations of the Holy Spirit over the last few decades, like being 'slain in the Spirit' (falling backwards on the ground), the 'Toronto Blessing' (making animal noises like lions roaring, monkeys chattering, dogs barking or roosters screeching), 'holy laughter', alternately described as 'getting drunk on the Holy Spirit' (breaking out spontaneously into laughter at inappropriate times during church services), and even violent shaking – as if having an epileptic fit.

None of these experiences are found in the Bible, nor are they even supernatural. A friend of mine, when he was a young Christian, was taken along to a charismatic church where, as one person was 'slain in the Spirit', others arrived to catch her. My friend thought this a very fortunate coincidence, and was impressed by the way God had prompted the 'catchers' to arrive at the same time as the 'slain' fell. Eventually he realised that it was all humanly orchestrated. Charismatics resemble the Jews of Christ's and Paul's day with their constant craving for 'signs and wonders' (Matt. 12: 38, 16:4, 1 Cor. 1:22), an attitude not encouraged by Christ Himself (John 4:48). At their best, charismatics energetically live out their faith and spread the gospel, but all too often many are very quick to believe sensational stories, some of which turn out to be untrue.

In 2008, Todd Bentley's 'revival' in Lakeland, Florida, drew crowds from all over the charismatic world while many others watched the continuous live coverage on GOD TV. Covered in tattoos and body piercings, and wearing black skeleton t-shirts, Bentley shrieked, shook, shouted "Sheeka Boomba" and even punched and kicked people who came for prayer. He claimed to have healed many people and even raised dozens from the dead (later attempts to verify these miracles were unsuccessful). After the revival ended abruptly with the news that Bentley was leaving his wife for a staff member, the charismatic magazine *Charisma* carried an editorial which read: 'I'm sad. I'm disappointed. And I'm angry. Here are a few of my many, many questions about this fiasco: Why did so many people flock to Lakeland from around the world to rally behind an evangelist who had serious credibility issues from the beginning? To put it bluntly, we're just plain gullible. . . . discernment was discouraged. They were expected to swallow and follow. The message was clear: "This is God. Don't question". . . . I blame this lack of discernment, partly, on raw zeal for God. We're spiritually hungry – which can be a good thing. But sometimes hungry people will eat anything . . . Our adolescent craving for the wild and crazy makes us do stupid things. It's way past time for us to grow up'[4].

Charismatic Christianity has typically (but unofficially) held to two sources of authority: Scripture plus 'signs and wonders'. Increasingly, however, the belief in the power of the Word of God – the sword of the Spirit (Eph. 6:17), the hammer that breaks the rock in pieces (Jer. 23:29) – seems to have been displaced. Instead, and not just in charismatic circles, it is all about the power of money, music and motivational talks: money to build huge auditoriums, music to keep the mood upbeat, and motivational talks – no Bible needed – so everyone feels good about themselves. Instead of the teaching of the Scriptures, it is all about what excites the emotions.

However, we should never allow our feelings or experiences (a 'tingle in our fingers, a tingle in our toes') to be our authority-source, for not all feelings or 'spiritual experiences' are from God. We must test all claims by the Word of God. We cannot claim something is from the Holy Spirit if it is not found in Scripture, for as John Knox said to Queen Mary, the Spirit in the Word 'is never contrarious to Himself'. The Holy Spirit will never deny the Scriptures He has written, or 'go beyond' (Num. 22: 18, 24:13, 1 Cor. 4:6, ESV) what is written in them.

The Christian faith is based on facts, not feelings. Non-Christians today say that we should follow our heart, but the Bible says that 'the heart is deceitful above all things, and desperately wicked – who can know it?' (Jer. 17:9). Our feelings will go up and down; we may experience elation or suffer hardships. We cannot place our trust in feelings as any guide or anchor for the soul, nor can we allow our experiences to be the ultimate authority for our faith.

Peter showed that Scripture is a higher authority than experience

---

[4] J. Lee Grady, "Life after Lakeland: Sorting out the Confusion", *Charisma*, Aug 14, 2008

when he said that, despite his experience as an eyewitness of Christ's majesty when he was with Him on the Mount of Transfiguration, the prophetic Scriptures are an even *'more sure'* word (2 Pet. 1:19, KJV), 'which you do well to heed'. Christ also showed that Scripture has greater authority than experience in His story of the rich man and Lazarus. The rich man in Hades asked for Lazarus to be sent to his brothers, arguing that his brothers would believe and repent if they saw someone raised from the dead. But Christ's words, 'they have Moses and the prophets' (Luke 16:29-31), show that Scripture has more authority than human experience, even that of a person rising from the dead.

4. Scripture

Scripture must be given the place of ultimate authority. What the Bible says is better than the most profound experience, the cleverest human reasoning or the noblest human tradition. The reason for this is simple: if the Bible is God's Word, then it carries God's authority, and this divine authority trumps any human authority, whether human tradition, human reasoning, human experiences or any other human claims. Isaiah 8:20 says, 'To the law and to the testimony! If they do not speak according to this word, it is because there is no light in them'. The Westminster Confession of Faith says, 'The supreme judge by which all controversies of religion are to be determined, and all decrees of councils, opinions of ancient writers, doctrines of men, and private spirits, are to be examined and in whose sentence we are to rest, can be no other but the Holy Spirit speaking in the Scripture' (1.10).

As C. H. Mackintosh wrote: Men must either deny that the Bible is the Word of God, or admit its sufficiency and supremacy in all ages. . . . Neither tradition nor expediency will do for the servant of Christ. The all-important inquiry is, "What saith the Scriptures." This settles everything. From the decision of the Word of God there must be no appeal. When God speaks man must bow. It is not by any means a question of obstinate adherence to a man's own notions. Quite the opposite. It is a reverent adherence to the Word of God. Let the reader distinctly mark this. It often happens that, when one is determined, through grace, to abide by Scripture, he will be pronounced dogmatic, intolerant, and imperious; and, no doubt, one has to watch over his temper, spirit, and style, even when seeking to abide by the Word of God. But, be it well remembered, that obedience to Christ's commandments is the very opposite of imperiousness, dogmatism, and intolerance. It is not a little strange that when a man tamely consents to place his conscience in the keeping of his fellow, and to bow down his understanding to the opinions of men, he is considered meek, modest, and liberal; but let him reverently bow to the authority of the Holy Scripture, and he will be looked upon as self-confident, dogmatic, and narrow-minded. Be it so. The time is rapidly approaching when obedience shall be called by its right name, and meet its recognition and reward.[5]

Interestingly, Job's three 'comforters' appear to present the three main alternative authority sources to Scripture. Eliphaz argues from experience – his dream in the night (Job 4:12-16), Bildad argues from tradition ('inquire, please, of the former age, and consider the things discovered by their fathers', Job 8:8-10), while Zophar argues arrogantly based on reason, intelligence and understanding (11:3, 6, 20:2, and compare Job's reply to Zophar in 12:1-2). The answer to Job's problems does not come from human tradition, reason or experience, but from divine revelation, when God finally speaks (Job chapters 38-41).

J. C. Ryle, commenting on the story of the lawyer who asked Christ about how to have eternal life in Luke 10:25, wrote: 'We should notice, second, in this passage the great honour that our Lord Jesus Christ gives to the Bible. He refers the expert in the law immediately to the Scriptures as the only rule of faith and practice. He does not say in answering his question, "What does the Jewish church say about eternal life? What do the scribes and Pharisees think? What do the traditions of the elders say on this subject?" He takes a far simpler and more direct course. He sends his questioner at once to the writings of the Old Testament: "What is written in the Law? How do you read it?" (verse 26). We see in this verse one of the foundational principles of our Christianity. Let the Bible, the whole Bible and nothing but the Bible be the rule of our faith and practice. It is of no consequence what human beings say about religion, whether it is an ancient Father or a modern bishop or a learned divine. Is it in the Bible? Can it be proved by the Bible? If not, it is not to be believed. It does not matter how beautiful and clever sermons and religious books may seem to be. Do they deviate at all from Scripture? If they do, they are no good as guides. What does the Scripture say? This is the only rule and yardstick to measure religious truth.[6]

---

[5] C. H. Mackintosh, "The Bible: Its Sufficiency and Supremacy" in *The Mackintosh Treasury: Miscellaneous Writings*, Neptune, NJ: Loizeaux Brothers, 1976, p17, 20.
[6] J. C. Ryle, *Luke*, Nottingham: Crossway, 1977, p144

Biblical Basis for the Authority of Scripture

The main reason for believing in the authority of Scripture is because, being inspired and inerrant, it is God's Word. Because God is the supreme Governor of the Universe, His Word is the ultimate authority, and is superior to any human opinions.

The Lord Jesus Christ and the Authority of Scripture. We believe in the authority of Scripture because Jesus Christ the Son of God taught this truth, not only in his words but also by his life. Thus, when Christ was tempted in the wilderness He replied to Satan's temptation with the words, 'It is written', followed by a quote from Deuteronomy 8:3, 'Man shall not live by bread alone, but by every word that proceeds from the mouth of God'. The fact that Christ appealed to Scripture to silence Satan indicates that the words of Scripture are the supreme authority, for only God has greater authority than Satan: if Scripture was sufficient to silence Satan, it must be God's Word. Here we see that Christ attributed ultimate and final authority to Scripture as 'the word of God'.

Christ turned to Scripture to settle any question; it was His highest court of appeal. Christ quoted the OT profusely: there are about forty separate quotes in the gospels (seventy in total) in addition to many biblical allusions. Christ repeatedly used expressions like 'Have you not read' (Matt. 12:3, 5; 19:4, 22:31, Mark 12:26), 'have you never read' (Matt. 21:16, 42, Mark 2:25), 'Go and learn what this means' (Matt. 9:13), and 'If you had known what this means' (Matt. 12:7) when debating with the Pharisees, mocking not just their familiarity with the Scriptures, but also their submission to it as God's Word.

The Apostles and the Authority of Scripture. We see the authority of Scripture in the epistles, particularly in the way the apostles prove a point or make an argument by quoting Scripture. They use expressions such as 'for it is written' or 'as it is written' or 'For the Scripture says' or 'what says the Scripture?' Various NT books appeal to the authority of Scripture to establish their arguments. For example, in Romans 3, Paul quotes seven OT verses to prove the sinfulness of man, while in Galatians 3, he uses seven quotes to establish that justification is by faith not works, and Hebrews 1 gives seven verses to prove the superiority of Christ over angels.

The apostles considered the NT writings to be equally authoritative alongside the OT. Thus, 1 Timothy 5:18 quotes Luke 10:7 alongside Deuteronomy 25:4 and calls both 'Scripture' (a word always used to

> indicate the God-inspired writings). 2 Peter 3:15-16 refer to Paul's writings alongside 'the rest of the Scriptures'.

The Bible is our Ultimate (but not our Only) Authority

On the other hand, it is a mistake to say that Scripture is our only authority. All Christians acknowledge a debt to tradition, reason and experience. It is better to say that the Bible is our final, supreme, or ultimate authority.

Tradition: There are some things that have been handed down to us by tradition that we gladly accept. We did not invent the word Trinity, nor is it found in Scripture, but we are happy to agree that the word sums up what the Bible teaches us about the Godhead. The fact that the Bible places so much emphasis on teaching the next generation the truth means that Christians should have an inbuilt respect for what has been handed down to us. Note that there are good, biblical traditions as well as humanly devised traditions; good traditions are truths passed down in Scripture from the apostles (see 1 Cor. 11:2 and 2 Thess. 3:6).

Reason, too, has its place. Thus, Paul reasoned in the synagogues as he preached the gospel (Acts 17:17, 18:4, etc.). God said, 'come, let us reason together' (Isa. 1:18). We need to meditate on Scripture, that is, to turn it over in our minds and think about it. Four times Christ said, 'What do you think?' (Matt. 17:25, 18:12, 21:28, 22:42). Martin Luther appealed to reason as well as Scripture in his famous words at the Diet of Worms: Unless I am convinced by the testimony of the Scriptures or by *clear reason* (for I do not trust either in the pope or in councils alone, since it is well known that they have often erred and contradicted themselves), I am bound by the Scriptures I have quoted and my conscience is captive to the Word of God'. John Wesley, in a letter to a critic of the Methodists named Rev. Dr. Rutherford, wrote: 'You go on, "It is a fundamental principle in the Methodist school that all who come into it must renounce their reason". Sir, are you awake? Unless you are talking in your sleep, how can you utter so gross an untruth? It is fundamental with us that to renounce reason is to renounce religion, that religion and reason go hand in hand, and that all irrational religion is false-religion'[7].

---

[7] *The Works of the Rev. John Wesley*, Vol. 8, J&J Harper, New York, 1827, p558

Experience is not to be despised either. The Bible itself say, 'Oh, taste and see that the Lord is good, blessed is the man who trusts in Him' (Psalm 34:8). John Wesley was converted through hearing the Preface to Luther's translation of the epistle to the Romans. He spoke of his heart being *'strangely warmed* – I felt I did trust in Christ, Christ alone for my salvation; and an assurance was given me that He had taken away my sins, even mine and saved me from the law of sin and death'. We, too, should feel our heart warmed if we have believed the love that God has towards us (Rom. 5:5), and the joy of salvation from sin's judgment through Christ. Christians should be a joyful, singing people.

Experience is a good schoolmaster. The failure of Communism in the late 20th century showed that Marxist economic theory was flawed – because it failed the test of experience and did not work in practice. There is a group of charismatic Christians in the United States called The Church of God with Signs Following, who practice snake-handling and poison drinking in their church services (based on Mark 16:17-18). In May 2012, a snake handler was bitten by his snake and died, a fact made even more tragic when we learn that his father suffered the same fate. A. W. Tozer wrote: 'Facts are glorious, tough, stubborn things, and they are fine criteria against which to measure our beliefs. Wesley taught that any doctrine which was found untenable in practice should come under suspicion of being erroneous and should be carefully re-examined in the light of Scripture. If it would not *work* in real life it was not likely to be the true teaching of the Bible[8]. The Lord Jesus himself said, 'Wisdom is justified by her children' (Matthew 11:19, Luke 7:35); that is, the evidence of the wisdom (or otherwise) of some course of action is seen in its results.

> *Facts are glorious, tough, stubborn things, and they are fine criteria against which to measure our beliefs . . . If it would not* work *in real life it was not likely to be the true teaching of the Bible*
> A. W. Tozer

Other Sources of Authority. Tradition, reason, experience and Scripture are not the only bases of authority. Some Christians appeal to biblical scholarship or celebrity preachers or favourite commentaries or creeds or confessions ('paper popes'). These sources of authority are only

---

[8] A. W. Tozer, *Wingspread: A. B. Simpson: a Study in Spiritual Altitude*, Camp Hill, PA: Christian Publications, 1943, p80, emphasis in original

dependable insofar as they follow Scripture. We must not treat the teachings of men as if they were the inspired divine revelation.

There are also a number of other authorities which have legitimate but limited authority. Church elders have authority, given by Scripture itself. This does not licence elders to act as lords or dictators over the church; their authority is dependent upon, derived from and limited to what Scripture teaches and allows. Similarly, earthly governments and parents in a family have divinely-delegated authority.

Non-Christians have various sources of authority: some hold scientific pronouncements to be their ultimate authority, while others are heavily influenced by the media and peer pressure. The Bible describes contemporary culture as being ultimately under 'the authority of darkness' (Col. 1:13), that is, under Satan's control (see Eph. 2:2). People in primitive cultures are even more directly under the power of idolatry, superstition, spirits, witch-doctors and the occult.

Conclusion

Tradition, reason and experience have some validity, and we are all influenced to some degree by them. We must not simply throw out everything that has been passed down to us (tradition), nor suspend our critical faculties (reason), nor should we be without a personal experience of God in our lives. However, if the Bible is God's inspired Word, it must be our final or ultimate authority. Scripture must have the last word. It is by Scripture that we test all traditions, arguments or experiences. The Bereans 'searched the Scriptures daily to find out if these things were so' (Acts 17:11).

CHAPTER 4

Isn't the Bible Full of Mistakes and Contradictions?

When I was in my early twenties, I went through a crisis of faith similar to Billy Graham's described in a previous chapter. What troubled me was a Bible problem, the story of Judas' death. Matthew's Gospel tells us that Judas hanged himself (27:5), while the book of Acts tells us that 'falling headlong, he burst open in the middle and all his entrails gushed out' (Acts 1:18). This seemed to be a contradiction; honesty prevented me describing it any other way. I had heard attempts to resolve the problem, but I was not convinced; they seemed forced.

The reason this problem disturbed me so much was the stark realization of the logical consequences that it opened up: if the Bible contained mistakes or contradictions, then it could not really be the Word of God, for God does not make mistakes or lie. If the Bible is not true in some details, then maybe many parts are false, but either way, it cannot be God's Word. As John Wesley wrote, 'Nay, if there be any mistakes in the Bible there may as well be a thousand. If there be one falsehood in that book it did not come from the God of truth'[1]. And, as my line of reasoning continued, if there is no God behind the Bible, maybe there is no God at all. This was the dark fog of despair that settled upon me.

Many people argue that the Bible cannot be the Word of God because it is full of contradictions and mistakes. The liberal theologian David Edwards wrote of 'innumerable passages' which are 'contradicted either by other passages in the Christian Bible or by the proofs or probabilities of modern historical knowledge'[2]. How can the Bible really

---

[1] John Wesley, *Journal*, VI, p117
[2] David L. Edwards with John Stott, *Essentials: A Liberal-Evangelical Dialogue*, London: Hodder and Stoughton, 1988, p73

be the Word of God if it is full of such errors?

It was coming up to Christmas when my doubts about the Bible over Judas' death reached their peak, and for some reason Christmas Day that year was very quiet. Nothing much was happening during the afternoon, so I settled down to study this problem, praying with quiet desperation that God would help me understand what was going on. It turned out to be one of the most memorable Christmas Days in my life. What I learned was not simply a little more about Judas' death, but a lot more about how to understand the Bible. We will return later to what I learned from Judas' death.

...

In this chapter, we face up to the contradictions and mistakes of Scripture. My argument here is that most of the alleged contradictions and errors in the Bible spring from a failure to understand the human side of Scripture. Please don't misunderstand me: some people argue that because the Bible is a human book, and 'to err is human', there must be errors in Scripture. However, I am not making this argument. For one thing, this is not necessarily true – humans can also carefully avoid error.

Instead, what I am arguing here is that the Bible is written by human authors, not in the language of heaven, but using ordinary human language. Human language is full of all sorts of fascinating and funny ways of saying things. Think about a few strange things we say in English: a pineapple is not an apple nor does it grow on pine trees, a guinea pig is neither a pig nor does it come from Guinea, and a boxing ring is not round but square. But nobody argues that people using these words are making mistakes; this is just the way language works.

Human literature has its peculiarities too. Ever since I was at school, I have enjoyed reading books about modern history. But a history book is a very different form of communication to a sermon, and they both have different purposes. While most Christians know that some sermons are strange, many people are unaware that history books have peculiar features too. (We will learn more about the difference between historical narratives and sermons when we return to the story of Judas' death). Bible sceptics like to say that the Bible is full of errors and contradictions, as if it was the most hopelessly muddled nonsense ever written. But we are going to see that it is not the Bible that is blundering. It is rather the sceptics who repeatedly fail to appreciate the human side of Scripture and the way that human language and literature operate in the real world.

Furthermore, the Bible is usually (although not always) written from a human, rather than heavenly, viewpoint. Although the Bible's human writers were inspired by God, they were not all-knowing, nor do they write exhaustively about their characters or events. Instead, the biblical authors write sparingly about what they experienced from their own individual perspective, so that when we have multiple accounts of the same events (as in the gospels) we hear the same story being told by different people with different personalities and different backgrounds, for different reasons. Even the prophets, to whom God revealed things beyond ordinary means of human understanding, only report what they saw and heard. The Bible is thus divinely-inspired and perfectly true, but nevertheless very human and down-to-earth.

Eighteen Misunderstandings about Scripture

Eighteen Misunderstandings about Scripture	
Reporting of Falsehoods	Translation Issues
Recording of Evil	Copying Mistakes
Language of Appearance	Multiple Motives
Figurative Language	Double Trouble
Hyperbole	Selective Reporting
Approximations	Abbreviation
Broken Grammar	Logical Versus Chronological
Reported Speech	Author's Intention
Free Quotes	Discrepancies

1. Reporting of Falsehoods

At first sight, it might seem that the most Christian position to take on the question of mistakes and contradictions in the Bible would be to affirm that every word of the Bible is true in everything it says. However, we must not take everything in the Bible as true, without any qualifications. For one thing, sometimes the Bible will report sayings that are not true, like 'There is no God' (Psalm 14:1). This verse accurately reports what a fool says, although the statement itself is not true. We cannot rip sentences like this out of their context to make the Bible contradict itself; this is to abuse the way literature works. Sometimes the Bible reports the lies that people told, for example, Rahab's lie about the spies in Joshua 2:4-5 or the lie of the Hebrew midwives in Exodus 1:19. Satan's lie in the Garden of Eden ('you will not surely die', Genesis 3:4) is not true, although accurately recorded.

2. Recording of Evil

The same applies to some events that the Bible records. The fact that the Bible records some evil deeds does not mean that it approves of them; for example, Abraham's marriage to Hagar, or Solomon's polygamy (700 wives), or Moses's murder, or David's adultery. Sometimes the Bible reports events without offering any commentary upon the morality of what happened, neither holding them up as examples to follow nor specifically condemning them. Often the biblical writer simply narrates the history and allows the dreadful consequences of such evil deeds to teach us that sin produces a bitter harvest.

3. The Language of Appearance

Sometimes the Bible will use the language of appearance, 'phenomenological language', describing things in everyday terms rather than using technical jargon. For example, 'the sun rises' (Psalm 104:22) is not strictly true in a scientific sense (because the earth spins on its axis). Yet it is true in terms of what we see. It is simply ordinary human language; even scientifically-trained meteorologists and weather reporters speak this way. Some people argue that the resurrection accounts contradict each other because some mention 'men' (Luke 24:4) while others mention 'angels' (John 20:12) at the tomb. However, the language of observation is describing how the angels appeared – as men.

4. Figurative Language

The Bible often uses figurative language which is not strictly true. However, any reader recognizes that the Bible uses figures of speech that are not meant to be taken literally. For example, Jesus criticized the scribes and Pharisees because they 'devour widows' houses' (Matt. 23:14), but this does not mean that the Jews actually ate houses. On another occasion, Jesus warned his followers about false prophets who were 'ravenous wolves' (Matt. 7:15), but there are few people so dull as to understand this literally. Psalm 19:5 speaks poetically about the sun, 'which is like a bridegroom coming out of his chamber, and rejoices like a strong man to run his race', but this is simply figurative language – the Bible is not teaching that the sun is actually a bridegroom or a runner.

Sometimes the Bible uses figurative descriptions of nature, which involve poetic license. Thus, the expression, 'the pillars of the earth' (1 Sam. 2:8, Job 9:6) does not literally mean that the earth is built on pillars, for Job 26:7 says, 'He hangs the earth on nothing' (indicating that the earth hangs in space). The expressions, 'the ends of the earth' (Deut.

33:17, Acts 13:47) or the 'four corners of the earth' (Isa. 11:12, Rev. 7:1) are colloquialisms, and do not teach a 'flat earth', for the Bible speaks about the earth being spherical ('He who sits above the circle of the earth', Isa. 40:22, cf. Job 26:10 and Prov. 8:27). Similarly, the 'windows of heaven being opened' (Gen. 7:11, 8:2) is a poetic description of rain, as can be seen from the way the Bible speaks about the hydrological cycle elsewhere: 'He causes the vapours to ascend from the ends of the earth; He makes lightning for the rain; He brings the wind out of His treasuries' (Psa. 135:7; see also Eccles. 1:6-7). Therefore, in the Bible we encounter a variety of ways in which nature is described: sometimes poetic language is used, sometimes phenomenological language, and sometimes the Bible's statements are factual and 'scientific'.

5. Hyperbole

In real life, we sometimes exaggerate to make a point; this is called hyperbole. Thus we may say that it is freezing cold or boiling hot today, or that someone won a race by 'miles'. Similarly, Jesus spoke of mustard as 'smaller than all the seeds on earth' (Mark 4:31). This is not strictly true, but neither was Jesus attempting to make a scientific statement; it is simply a picturesque, figurative use of language. Neither was Jesus literally insisting that we must hate our father and mother (Luke 14:26), or gouge out our eyes (Matt. 5:29).

6. Approximations

Sometimes the Bible will use approximations. For example, we need not believe that there were exactly 5000 men fed by the five loaves and two fish. This is just the normal way we speak – we talk about the size of a crowd in round numbers. Similarly, the bronze sea in Solomon's Temple is described as having a circumference of 30 cubits (13.5m), while the diameter is 10 cubits, 4.5m (2 Chron. 4:2). However, we know that a circle with a diameter of 4.5m multiplied by *pi* (3.14159) would have a circumference of 14.14m. Actually, *pi* does not exactly equal 3.14159, for *pi* is an infinite, non-repeating decimal, so it is a mathematical necessity to approximate *pi*. The Bible approximates the dimensions of Solomon's 'sea' at the nearest whole numbers, and for most purposes this is acceptable; biblical truthfulness does not depend on technical precision.

This might also be the reason for a discrepancy between two Bible passages which record the numbers of people who died in a particular incident: Numbers 25:9 (24,000) and 1 Cor. 10:8 (23,000). Presumably, the number of people who died was not exactly 23,000 or 24,000; it is likely that these numbers are round figures. But why the difference? Perhaps a modern day situation provides a parallel. If we buy something at the shops costing somewhere between $23 and $24, we might generalize this figure up (if it is closer to $24), but sometimes we might round the figure down to $23, particularly if we are trying to justify spending the money (which is why shops price items at $23.99, not $24). Any amount between $23 and $24 can either be rounded up or down. We do not know the exact number of people who died, however we know from experience that we use language in the very same way.

7. Breaking the Rules of Grammar

Sometimes Bible writers are accused of breaking the rules of grammar. The book of Revelation is pointed to as a book with 'bad Greek', especially the expression in Rev. 1:4, 'from Him who is and who was and who is to come'. Some scholars reply that this is evidence of a Hebraism, the form of the writer's native Jewish language affecting his Greek. To use an analogy, it would be similar to an Italian saying, 'from da one who is and who was and who is to come'. The English purist might tell the Italian to speak properly, but we understand him perfectly and there are no errors of fact in which he has said. In real life, some people speak in a less educated and grammatically polished way than others, but using clumsy wording is not the same as telling lies. On the other hand, we have the expression in John 8:58, 'Before Abraham was, I am', in which the Lord deliberately breaks all the rules of grammar to make the astonishing claim that He is God, using the divine name, I AM.

8. Reported Speech

The Bible does not necessarily report what someone said, word for word. In written English we sometimes use "quotation marks" to indicate that we are quoting what someone said verbatim. However, particularly in spoken English, we usually paraphrase or summarize what another person said, giving the content in such a way that (hopefully) our report is true to what was originally stated. Thus, in the book of Acts we are given summaries of the speeches made by the apostles in their preaching, not every word they said. This is seen in the first major speech in the book of Acts (thereby setting a precedent), where at the conclusion of the speech we read, 'And with many other words he testified and exhorted them, saying, "Be saved from this perverse generation"' (Acts 2:40). The same qualification also applies to the speeches of Christ in the Gospels, all of which were originally spoken in Aramaic (and later translated into

Greek, the language of our New Testament). In the gospels, we sometimes have the *ipsissima vox* (lit. 'the very voice') of people speaking, not necessarily the *ipsissima verba* (lit. 'the very words').

9. Free Quotes

Similarly, the New Testament does not always quote the Old Testament word for word, but sometimes gives a free quotation of it. Thus, Psalm 40:6 says 'My ears You have opened', but this verse is quoted in Hebrews 10:5 as 'a body You have prepared for Me'. In fact, a literal translation of the Psalm reads 'My ears You have dug'. This seems to be saying that God created the ear-canal of Christ, so that (as the following verses state) He could obediently do God's will (Psalm 40:8, Heb. 10:7). But not only was the ear-canal prepared to hear God's voice but (as Hebrews 10:5 tells us), Christ's whole body was also prepared so that He would obey God's will. This is what we mean by a free quote; it is a quote which gives the same sense and meaning rather than the exact wording. We do this all the time when we try to quote something from memory. Similarly, Psalm 68:18 says, 'You have ascended on high, You have led captivity captive; You have received gifts among men', but in Ephesians 4:8 these words are quoted as 'When He ascended on high, He led captivity captive and gave gifts to men'. Notice how Paul amends the quote by changing 'You' to 'He', so that, while originally, the psalm was addressed to God ('You'), yet in the New Testament the verse takes the same words and refers them to Christ ('He'). This suggests something about how Paul views Christ – as the God of the Psalmist.

10. Translation Issues

Sometimes the Bible appears to have an error or a contradiction, but the problem is really in the translation. One example of this is a discrepancy in the story of Saul's conversion. In Acts 9:7, we read that the men who accompanied Saul were 'speechless, *hearing a voice* but seeing no one', while in Acts 22:9, Paul recounted the story of his conversion as follows: those with him 'saw the light . . . but *they did not hear the voice* of Him who spoke to me'. One passage seems to contradict the other. However, the Greek word used for 'voice' in both these verses is *phone* (from which we get 'telephone' in English), and this Greek word covers a range of different meanings; depending on the context it can mean either 'sound' or 'voice'. Thus, we read about the 'sound' of the wind in John 3:8, of a trumpet in 1 Corinthians 14:8, and of wings (Rev. 9:9), while we have the 'voice' of one crying in the wilderness (Mark 1:3), of God speaking from heaven (Mark 1:11), and of Jesus crying out with a loud 'voice' (Mark 15:37). The apparent difficulty in the story of Saul's conversion disappears: the men heard the sound of someone speaking to Saul but did not hear what was being said. We experience the same thing when a person calls out to someone in another room in the house, only to get the reply, 'I can't hear you'. What they mean is that they can hear that someone is calling, but can't make out the words[3].

The English preacher Harold St. John told the story of meeting a man who said he could no longer believe the Bible because he had read in Galatians 6:2 that we are to 'bear one another's burdens', while a few verses later in Galatians 6:5, we read, 'for each one shall bear his own burden'. St. John pointed out to the man that there are two different Greek words for 'burden' here, the first (*baros*) referring to a weight or burden, but the second word (*phortion*) referring to a load or cargo that a ship carries. As Christians, we are to help each other with burdens that weigh us down (Gal. 6:2), but we should also be carrying home to heaven a cargo of harvest from our labours for the Master (Gal. 6:5).

11. Copying Mistakes

Only the text of the original biblical autographs is without error, because only the original text was inspired by God. Some mistakes in our modern Bibles are the result of errors made by scribes during the many years that the Bible was copied out by hand. Thus, we read that Solomon had 4,000 stalls for horses (2 Chron. 9:25), but in another passage we read that he had 40,000 stalls for horses (1 Kings 4:26). Or, in 2 Chronicles 22:2 we read that Ahaziah was forty-two years old when he became king (even though his own father Ahaziah died at age forty, 2 Chron. 21:20, and a son cannot be older than his father at the same time). The parallel passage in 2 Kings 8:26 tells us that Ahaziah was twenty-two years old when he became king. The reality is that it was much easier for scribes to make mistakes when copying numbers (e.g. I once saw an internet page setting out some of these discrepancies, in which the author had made a mistake in the verse number in the Bible reference relating to Ahaziah's age). Similarly, we see some differences in the spelling of obscure people's names in genealogical lists, because this is another kind of

---

[3] Further, the book of Acts uses two different Greek constructions in the two passages. In Acts 9:7 it uses the word 'to hear' with the genitive case, which means to hear something, whereas in Acts 22:9 it uses 'to hear' with the accusative case, which means to apprehend what is said.

copying error that is easy to make, particularly when some Hebrew letters, like ד (d) and ר (r) are so similar. Mistakes in numbers and spelling of names are the easiest of all copying mistakes to make, but there are other copying mistakes that have made their way into our Bible. Thankfully, we have ways of working out what the correct reading is – from the internal logic of a Bible passage, and from the abundance of ancient manuscripts, early translations into other languages, and quotations from early Christian writers which show us which reading is more likely. These sorts of copying mistakes do not undermine our belief in the inerrancy of Scripture, for the Bible's inspiration applies to the text of the autographs, not to any later copies or translations.

12. Multiple Motives

I once had a friend who argued that Matthew 14:13 contradicted Mark 6:30-31. In the first passage, we read that Jesus and the disciples departed to the other side of the lake after Jesus heard the news of the death of John the Baptist. In the second passage, we read that Jesus and the disciples departed to the other side of the lake because the disciples needed a break from ministering to the crowds: 'Come aside by yourselves to a deserted place and rest awhile'.

The reason I think this is a useful example to mention is because we have all gone on holidays at some point in our lives, and know a little about the subject. There are usually multiple reasons we decide to go on holidays at a certain time to a certain place. For example, we may have wanted to visit a place for a long time, or we may have been invited to spend some time together with friends, or now may be the best time to enjoy some seasonal holiday, or we may only now have saved up enough money to be able to afford a particular holiday, or we may just need a rest (like the disciples). The possible reasons for a holiday are many and varied. Sometimes we cannot take a holiday until a certain number of criteria are fulfilled, so there are multiple, simultaneous reasons why we take a break. These reasons do not contradict each other; they coincide. The idea that there must only be one solitary motive for someone wanting to take a holiday is unrealistic. Here in this passage, Jesus and the disciples have a number of different reasons for taking a break.

There are a number of other cases of multiple reasons behind certain events in the Bible. For example, Saul lost his kingdom because (a) he disobeyed God by offering sacrifices and in the matter of the Amalekites (1 Sam. 13, 15) and (b) because he went over to the 'dark side' by visiting the witch of Endor (1 Chron. 10:13). David was unable to build the temple because (a) he was too busy fighting wars (1 Kings 5:3) and (b) he was not allowed to build the temple because he had shed much blood (1 Chron. 22:8). The spies were sent into the land of Canaan (a) because the people in unbelief asked Moses for spies to be sent (Deut. 1:12), and (b) because God told Moses to send spies (Numbers 13:2). All of these reasons for various events are true; the idea that these different perspectives contradict each other is baseless.

13. Double Trouble

When my two sons were young, I was once driving in our car with them in the back seat, and I asked my younger son what book he was reading. Before he could speak, my older son answered, 'Granny Guru'. A split second later, my younger son answered, 'Granny the Great Inventor'. Puzzled by the discrepancy, I repeated my question. The boys explained that the answer given by my older son was correct: this was the name of the book. However, the book contained two stories, and my younger son's answer was the name of the second story in the book. (For those curious, the name of the first story was 'Granny joins the Gym'). There was no contradiction between what my boys said, although at first it sounded like one. Or, imagine if I went to my children's school and happened to speak to the school principal who was standing with one of my children's class teachers. If I later told my child that I had spoken to the principal, and then told my wife that I had spoken to the teacher, would I have contradicted myself? Of course not. Real life is complex and these sorts of situations happen in the Bible too.

I was once preaching on Mark 8, a chapter which includes the story of the feeding of the 4000. Afterwards, a lady came up to me puzzled and perplexed, with her Bible still open at the page. She pointed out to me that the Bible said that Jesus had fed the 4000, but she was sure that somewhere else the Bible said that Jesus had fed 5000. This looked to her like a Bible contradiction. This lady only attended our church occasionally, and had not been present a few weeks previously when we looked at Mark 6, where we read about the feeding of the 5000. The Bible actually tells us about two cases of Jesus feeding large crowds of people, one of 5000 (in Mark 6) and one of 4000 (in Mark 8).

Nobody who knows the Bible well would argue that we have a contradiction here; we just have a similar event that occurs twice. But, other cases of similar accounts that occur twice prompt some people to claim that the Bible contradicts itself. For example, John's Gospel tells us that Jesus cleansed the Temple at the beginning of His public ministry, whereas the other gospels tell us that Jesus cleansed the Temple at the end of His public ministry. Why this should be counted a contradiction is unclear, for if (a) Jesus' ministry lasted over three years, (b) He visited Jerusalem and its Temple on multiple occasions, and (c) He was very angry about the money-grubbing going on in the Temple, it would seem strange for Him *not* to have reacted to the corrupt practices on more than one visit.

Another example is that Matthew and Luke give us two different genealogies of Christ. The idea that this is a contradiction is again strange, for anybody with two parents will have two genealogies, one on their mother's side and one on their father's, and if we go back another generation, there will be four genealogies, one for each grandparent. There is nothing more natural in the world than multiple genealogical lines. Moreover, in Jesus' case, we have the extra factor that Joseph (through whom a genealogy would naturally be traced) was not His true father. It seems highly likely that Matthew gives us Joseph's ancestry while Luke gives us Jesus' ancestry through Mary. This is in line with the fact that Matthew explores Jesus' birth from Joseph's perspective: (a) an angel appears to Joseph telling him not to divorce Mary his betrothed wife, Matthew 1:20, (b) telling Joseph to take Mary and Jesus down into Egypt, Matthew 2:13, and (c) telling Joseph to return from Egypt to the land of Israel, Matthew 2:19. Luke, on the other hand, explores Jesus' birth from Mary's perspective: (a) an angel was sent to tell Mary about Christ's birth, Luke 1:26-38, (b) Mary visits her relative Elizabeth where she prophesies about Mary and her child, Luke 1:39-45, and (c) after the birth, Simeon prophesies about Mary and her child, Luke 2:34-35. Matthew thus traces the royal line of David's descendants, while Luke traces Jesus human ancestry all the way back to Adam.

14. Selective Use of Material

Historical narratives (biblical as well as secular) selectively focus on certain details and omit others. My pre-teenage son was asked to write his autobiography for English homework. When I heard about this, I feared that he might write a long tedious narrative of incidents, one after another. But he showed me the teacher's instructions detailing the importance of the '*selection*, organisation and synthesis of information and ideas'. At the beginning of the Bible's history, after the story of Cain killing Abel, we read about Cain's wife giving birth (Gen. 4:17). Where did Cain get his wife from? Quite obviously, Cain didn't marry a Martian or a monkey – he had to marry a woman. What women were available for him to marry? There was his mother Eve (who he couldn't marry), but if we keep on reading, we see in Genesis 5:4 that Adam had 'sons and daughters'. By a process of elimination, then, we are left with the conclusion that Cain must have married one of his sisters. This seems the only sensible answer, but notice: the Bible does not tell us this detail. To expect the Bible to give exhaustive information, explain all minor details, and tie off all the loose ends of history is unreasonable.

Similarly, in the gospels, John tells us that there were many other things that Jesus did that he has not written about, 'but these are written that you might believe that Jesus is the Christ, the Son of God' (John 20:30-31). It is the same with the other gospels. For example, the Gospel of Mark does not include the story of the centurion whose servant was healed by Jesus, even though Matthew and Luke do. This omission should not surprise us, nor does it contradict anything else in the Bible, for a writer must be allowed to focus on the stories he wishes to emphasize. The four gospels do not all tell the same stories; some stories are unique to just one gospel.

Perhaps the most surprising example of a Bible story that deliberately leaves out information is the paralyzed man who was not able to get to Jesus because of the crowds at the house where Jesus was teaching. The most interesting detail about this story is the fact that his friends broke up the roof to lower him to Jesus. However, Matthew's Gospel completely omits any reference to the roof being broken up, or to the man being lowered down into the room. All Matthew says is 'they brought to Him a paralytic lying on a bed' (Matt. 9:2). Mark and Luke both give us the details about the roof being broken up and the man being lowered down. Strictly speaking, this is not a contradiction on Matthew's part because historians regularly have to skip over details to get to their point. Very few historians give a minute by minute, blow by blow, account that includes every single detail involved in an event.

15. Abbreviation

Not only is it perfectly natural for historians to selectively omit details; they also abbreviate accounts they do not wish to enlarge upon. How do we know Matthew has deliberately omitted the details about the roof being broken up and the man being lowered down? We know because of a pattern that points to Matthew consistently shortening miracle stories. Thus, if we look at the following miracles, Matthew consistently gives us the shortest account, and sometimes his accounts are only one-half or one-third the length of other gospels.

Miracle Story	Matthew	Mark	Luke
Leper Cleansed	3 verses (8:2-4)	6 verses (1:40-45)	4 verses (5:12-15)
Centurion's Servant	9 verses (8:5-13)	*Not Included*	10 verses (7:1-10)
Paralysed Man	7 verses (9:2-8)	10 verses (2:3-12)	9 verses (5:18-26)
Jairus' Daughter	9 verses (9:18-26)	22 verses (5:22-43)	16 verses (8:41-56)
Gadarene Demoniac	7 verses (8:28-34)	20 verses (5:1-20)	14 verses (8:26-39)

One notable example of abbreviation is Matthew and Mark's account of the call of the four fishermen (Matt. 4:18-22, Mark 1:16-20). We read that Jesus, walking by the Sea of Galilee, called them to 'follow me', and they immediately left all. This seems strange until we read Luke 5:1-11, where we learn that Jesus' miracle of the great catch of fish compelled the disciples to leave all and follow Him.

Biblical narratives will sometimes give a shorter version of an incident, on the principle that 'a little simplification saves tons of explanation'. In real life, wind-bags weary us by with their much talking; we sometimes wish they would give us less detailed versions of their stories. Matthew's gospel, particularly, shortens stories by simplifying details. Thus, in the story of the centurion's servant, there are two surprising differences between Matthew's and Luke's accounts.

Matt. 8:5-9	Luke 7:3-8
The Centurion asks Jesus to come and heal his servant; Jesus says He will come and heal him, but the Centurion tells Jesus he is unworthy to have him come under his roof: 'only speak a word and my servant will be healed'. So Jesus healed the servant with a word.	The Centurion sends *Jewish elders* to ask Jesus to heal his servant; Jesus went with them, but as He neared the house, the Centurion sent *friends* to Jesus saying he was unworthy to have Jesus enter his house: 'say the word and my servant will be healed'. So Jesus healed the servant.

In Matthew the centurion comes and speaks to Jesus, while in Luke two sets of messengers from the centurion speak to Jesus – the Jewish elders and then some of the centurion's friends. For a second difference, in

Matthew there is only one conversation, while in Luke there are two. Matthew is not contradicting Luke here, he is compressing him; Matthew has combined the two conversations into one, placing all the words in the mouth of the centurion instead of the two sets of messengers he sent. Notice, however, even in Luke's Gospel, that the centurion's messengers use the centurion's own words: 'say the word and *my* servant will be healed'. It is as if the Centurion himself is speaking to Jesus through the messengers; all the words (whatever way we look at it) were the centurion's. There is no contradiction here, but rather condensation.

We see a similar thing happening in the story of the raising of Jairus' daughter (Matt. 9:18-26, Mark 5:22-43), and in the story of the cursing of the fig tree (Matt. 21:18-20, Mark 11:12-14, 20-21). Matthew consistently abbreviates and simplifies these miracle stories by merging details together. Some people accuse the different gospels of disagreeing with each other but this accusation fails to allow Matthew the editorial freedom that we would gladly grant any modern historian.

16. Logical versus Chronological Order of Events

Sometimes the gospels arrange certain incidents in a different order to each other. Consider the order of the following miracles in Matthew, Mark and Luke:

Matthew	Mark	Luke
Leper (8:2-4)	Peter's Mother-in-law (1:29-31)	Peter's Mother-in-law (4:38-39)
Centurion (8:5-13)	Leper (1:40-45)	Leper (5:12-15)
Peter's Mother-in-law (8:14-15)	Paralytic (2:3-12)	Paralytic (5:18-26)
Storm (8:23-27)	[*Centurion*]	Centurion (7:1-10)
Gadarene (8:28-34)	Storm (4:35-41)	Storm (8:22-25)
Paralytic (9:2-8)	Gadarene (5:1-20)	Gadarene (8:26-39)
Jairus (9:18-26)	Jairus (5:22-43)	Jairus (8:41-56)

Mark and Luke follow the same order of events (except that Mark does not include the story of the Centurion's servant), but Matthew's order of events differs radically from the other two gospels. Matthew also places all these miracles in two chapters of his gospel (Chs. 8 and 9), whereas Mark and Luke spread them out over five chapters, interspersed with other stories. It seems that Matthew has grouped all the miracles together in one section of his gospel, not based on a chronological order of events, but rather grouping incidents together because they have topical or thematic similarities (i.e. they are all miracles).

In fact, Matthew groups together similar incidents in Jesus' life all the way through his gospel. For example, Matthew groups together Jesus' teachings on various subjects into five main 'sermons', on a topical rather than chronological basis, whereas Luke has the different parts of these sermons in different chapters of his gospel, where they are placed according to the setting which prompted the teaching.

Jesus' Teachings	Matthew	Luke
Sermon on the Mount	Chs. 5-7	Chs. 6, 11, 12
Evangelistic Instructions	Ch. 10	Chs. 9, 10, 12
Parables of the Kingdom	Ch. 13	Chs. 8, 13
Fellowship Teachings	Ch. 18	Chs. 9, 17
Olivet Discourse	Ch. 23-24	Chs. 12, 17, 21

17. Author's Intention

All authors have a message they wish to present, and it is important that readers try to understand what it is. When my son was asked to write the autobiography mentioned above, the teacher emphasized the word *'theme'* in the assignment hand-out by making the students underline it multiple times; the essay had to have a point, a moral, a lesson.

As readers, we naturally bring our concerns and questions to the Bible as we read it, looking for the Bible's answer to our problems. In my case, the problem was the puzzle over Judas' death. However, while the Bible will often answer our questions, our first priority must be to try to listen to what Scripture itself is saying. John Goldingay writes, 'By imposing our questions on a passage we may miss the questions it intended to raise'[4].

One of the peculiarities of biblical historical narratives is that the authors do not normally tell us the point of an incident. Instead they let the narrative tell its own story, and leave us clues to work out the author's point for ourselves. These clues involve selectively emphasising certain facts, or repeating important themes, or by contrasting ideas found in neighbouring incidents. Here are three examples:

---

[4] John Goldingay, "Expounding the New Testament" in *New Testament Interpretation*, ed. I. H. Marshall, Carlisle: Paternoster Press, 1992 reprint, p353.

Firstly, why does Matthew cram so many miracle stories into chapters 8 and 9 as a block, when they did not happen chronologically straight after each other? The reason seems to be partly for emphasis. Matthew arranges these incidents so that the cumulative effect of all these short accounts of miracles emphasizes how numerous, how varied and how amazing Christ's miracles were.

Secondly, in Mark 10, after little children were brought to Jesus to be blessed, the 'rich young ruler' came to Jesus but went away unblessed. Both stories teach that those who are prepared to humble themselves and trust in Christ, not in their own self-sufficiency, will enter God's kingdom. Mark places these stories next to each other to suggest a comparison.

Thirdly, in Mark 14 we have the story of the woman who poured the expensive ointment on Jesus. After this Mark tells us how Judas went to the chief priests to bargain with them to betray Jesus. It seems that the disciples' displeasure at the waste of the ointment helped prompt Judas to betray Jesus. Mark appears to tell these stories one after another to illustrate cause and effect; that is, to show, to some degree, how the first story explains the second.

Thus, it is important for us, when reading the Bible, to try to understand the author's intention or purpose in telling us about various incidents. Sometimes an author will do this by selectively mentioning (or omitting) certain details, or by repeatedly mentioning some theme in his writing, or by arranging incidents next to each other for thematic or logical reasons.

18. Discrepancies

J. Warner Wallace was an atheist until the age of thirty-five, when he started to look at the gospels. As a police detective, it was his job to investigate real-life murders and other crimes. As a specialist in the examination of witness statements, he describes his approach to discrepancies in his book, *Cold-Case Christianity*: 'If there's one thing my experience as a detective has revealed, however, it's that witnesses often make conflicting and inconsistent statements when describing what they saw at a crime scene . . . but that is the natural result of a witness's past experience, perspective, and worldview. I can deal with inconsistencies; I expect them. . . . The apparent contradictions are usually easy to explain once I learn something about the witnesses and their perspectives (both visually and personally) at the time of the crime'[5].

We find discrepancies among the gospel records. For example, a discrepancy exists in relation to the women who came to the tomb: was it 'Mary Magdalene and the other Mary' (Matt. 28:1), 'Mary Magdalene, Mary the mother of James and Salome' (Mark 16:1), 'Mary Magdalene, Joanna, Mary the mother of James, and other women with them' (Luke 24:10), or 'Mary Magdalene' (John 20:1)? John mentions one woman, Matthew two, Mark three and Luke five or more. Actually, John's Gospel gives us a clue; after Mary Magdalene's visit to the tomb (20:1), we read her saying to Peter and John: 'They have taken away the Lord out of the tomb, and *we* do not know where they have laid him' (20:2). While John only mentions Mary, her words show that there were others involved. None of the gospel accounts claim to provide exhaustive information: they do not state the total number of the women or say that *only* two (or three) women went to the tomb. The gospels do not contradict each other here; some gospels just provide more information.

The very fact that the Bible contains apparent discrepancies is thus, strangely enough, a reason for us to trust it. This is because real life is complex and messy. If everything in the Bible was as neat and straightforward as some fictional storylines we would have every reason to suspect a fabrication. As Gregory Boyd has written, 'The Gospels present a consistent portrait of who Jesus is and what He did, as well as of the events which surrounded His life. If the four accounts were individually fabricated, where did this consistency come from? But there are also significant differences in each account, showing the relative differences of their perspectives. If they were all fabricated together, the consistency would be greater than we find'[6].

Judas' Death

It's time to return to Judas' death, and what I learned about the Bible from my study of this story. There was only one thing I noticed as I read about Judas' death in Matthew 27:3-9: Matthew interrupts the story of Jesus' Roman trial to tell us about Judas' death. This seemed slightly strange and untidy: would it not have been more natural to finish the more important story of Jesus' trial (and crucifixion) before Matthew told

---

[5] J. Warner Wallace, *Cold-Case Christianity: a Homicide Detective Investigates the Claims of the Gospels*, Colorado Springs, CO: David C. Cook, 2013, pp74-75

[6] Gregory Boyd, *Letters from a Skeptic*, Colorado Springs, CO: Cook Communication Ministries, 2003, p84

us about Judas death? But then I realized that maybe Matthew was deliberately presenting a comparison between the deaths of Judas and Jesus. Both of them died virtually the same way: Judas hanged himself, while Jesus was crucified (which the apostles sometimes equated with 'hanging on a tree', Acts 5:30, 10:39). In the Old Testament we learn that a person who was hanged on a tree was cursed by God' (Deut. 21:23). Maybe this explained why Matthew told us about Judas' death – to point out the similarity yet significant difference between Christ (who was cursed by God for our sin, Gal. 3:13), and Judas who was cursed by God for his own sins. But this still did not explain the puzzle of why Judas's death in Matthew was different from how Acts says he died.

When I turned to study the book of Acts, there were three surprising and very interesting things I noticed. Firstly, it seemed obvious once I read the passage carefully that Peter was not announcing Judas' death to the other disciples at all, for the following reasons: (1) in Acts 1:15-22, Peter was speaking to the other disciples about six weeks after Judas' death (see Acts 1:3), (2) Peter said that Judas' death was well known to 'all those dwelling in Jerusalem' (Acts 1:19), and (3) both Matthew and Luke tell us the people living in Jerusalem had already given Judas' field a nickname – 'the field of blood' (Matt. 27:8, Acts 1:19). If everybody else in Jerusalem had heard of Judas' death, it is hardly likely that Judas' closest companions, the other disciples, did not yet know of his death six weeks after the event. Peter's purpose was obviously not to break the news of Judas' death to the other Christians.

So, what was Peter's purpose in talking about Judas' death? The second thing I noticed as I studied Peter's speech in Acts 1 was that it was a *sermon* in which he seemed to be making a sophisticated wordplay on the words 'lot' and 'place'. He uses the word 'lot' three times:

- 'for he was numbered with us and obtained a *part* (Gk. *kleros*, meaning 'lot') in this ministry' (v17).
- the apostles chose two possible replacements for Judas, and prayed to the Lord to show which of the two He had 'chosen to take *part* (Gk. *kleros*, 'lot') in this ministry and apostleship' (vs24-25)
- the apostles chose Judas' replacement by casting *lots* (verse 26).

Peter was making a play on the word 'lot', exploiting the fact that a 'lot' can refer to three things: (1) a share or part of something (in this case, the position Judas held as an apostle of Christ, just as we still speak of 'someone's lot in life'), (2) lots in the sense of 'casting lots', and (3) to describe a parcel of ground (we still use the word this way today). Peter continues his 'lot' word-play by talking about Judas' 'field' (v18), the field of blood (v19), his 'place' (v20), and his own 'place' in verse 25. Peter's speech is full of talk about real-estate.

What all these sophisticated word-plays suggested was that Peter was not breaking the news of Judas' death, but was rather sermonizing. A sermon is very different from a historical narrative. A sermon teaches moral and spiritual lessons, and is sometimes extremely selective in the text (or events) the lessons are based upon. Peter's message here was that Judas had a 'lot', or part, in the apostolic ministry, but he had decided to sell it for a 'lot', a block of ground, bought with blood money, but Judas had now left this earthly scene to go to 'his own place' (Hell). Peter was tracing Judas' moral journey downwards – he traded the highest possible 'lot' in life, as an apostle of the Messiah, for a parcel of land, motivated by greed, and finally ended up going to the worst possible destination.

Peter was not simply drawing moral lessons from Judas' property dealings, but also from the events surrounding Judas' 'fall'. Judas' physical fall mirrored his spiritual descent (a 'fall from grace', we might say). His fall involved all his bowels bursting out, and this taught a moral too: Jews used to refer to the bowels in the same way we talk about the 'heart', to signify the love and compassion of a person (see Phil. 2:1 or 1 John 3:17 in the KJV). Peter's point seems to be that whatever little humanity Judas once possessed had burst out of his body and spilled on the ground. How fitting: Judas, the cold-hearted betrayer, ended up without any 'heart'.

It was clear to me that Peter was not breaking the news of Judas' death, recounting the gory details in case anyone had not heard, but was instead teaching spiritual lessons from Judas' career. Judas' spiritual 'fall' is the main moral of Peter's sermon, and he uses Judas' physical fall to illustrate its poetic justice.

The third thing I noticed, the more I studied, was how vague Peter was in his sermon about the details of Judas' death. Peter gives us very limited reporting of the event. In fact, Peter does not actually mention the 'death' of Judas at all. Let me explain the significance.

My wife for her birthday once received a box of brain-teasers and IQ questions. One of the puzzles read: 'A man has a blazing argument with his wife one morning. He goes out and throws himself headlong off a sheer rock face. Later in the evening he returns home unharmed. Explain.' This seemed difficult to explain until the card was turned over to reveal the answer: 'The man did a bungee jump'. Actually, the more we thought about it, there were a number of possible answers: he could have dived into a lake, jumped into a net, used a parachute, or a hang-glider, or cheated death another way. By withholding some information, the brain teaser made the situation seem puzzling, just as Judas' death seems puzzling because neither Matthew nor Peter (in Acts) give us all the possible information we might wish to have.

The reality of the Judas situation (like the case of the bungee-jumping husband) is that it is possible to think of ways to harmonize Matthew's and Luke's accounts once we notice the limited information Matthew and Acts provide. For example, Judas could have hanged himself and some time later his body was cut down, falling to the ground and bursting open, or perhaps Judas hanged himself and some time later the rope (or branch) broke and Judas' body fell to the ground and burst open. The story of Judas' death is far from a clear-cut case of contradiction for the simple reason that Peter did not specify when or how Judas fell, or whether he had already died.

I came away from my study of Judas' death with a much better understanding of what the story of Judas' death was really all about. In addition, I had stumbled upon some of the most important lessons of Bible study: the need to read the Bible carefully for ourselves, looking to God in faith for help in understanding His Word, the need to investigate Bible words, and the need to determine the original author's intention or purpose in writing. Instead of coming to the Bible with our questions, problems and needs, we instead need to listen to the point the Bible is trying to make. The result was that my faith was greatly confirmed – not only in the Bible's trustworthiness, but in the way God answered prayer and had given me light and understanding as I studied His Word.

How to Deal with Difficulties in the Bible

What should we do if we come up against a problem in the Bible that we think is insoluble? We should firstly pray for the Spirit of God's help to us. After all, He is the One who wrote the book! Then we should patiently wait on Him to open up the passage for us as we continue to read and study. Sometimes, passages elsewhere in the Bible will explain the difficulty we are worrying over because Scripture is its own interpreter.

Sometimes it is we who need to grow more spiritually before we can understand the things that God is saying in His Word. In 2 Peter 3:16, Peter says that Paul's writings contain some hard things to understand: 'as also in all his epistles, speaking in them of these things, in which are some things hard to understand, which untaught and unstable people twist to their own destruction, as they do also the rest of the Scriptures'. Notice that people who struggle with Bible difficulties are described as having two problems: they are lacking in knowledge and understanding ('untaught'), as well as lacking in faith ('unstable').

Often with a little more knowledge or understanding, Bible problems become easy to understand. Sometimes this may involve a clearer knowledge of the original languages the Bible was written in. Sometimes, the answer to our problem is found elsewhere in the Bible, and it is only our lack of acquaintance with the entire Bible that causes the problem. On other occasions, an alleged 'contradiction' rests upon the very limited reporting of an event in the Bible – not all events in the Bible are given in-depth coverage. Just as in the case of the bungee jumper we discussed earlier, were a little more information available, it might satisfactorily clear up a detail that troubles us.

We also need to remember how important faith is in understanding the Bible. The Lord continually said things that tested the disciples' faith, sometimes provoking unbelieving reactions. For example, before the feeding of the 5000, when Jesus saw the crowds coming, He asked Philip, 'Where shall we buy bread that these may eat?' (John 6:5), but the next verse says, 'But this He said to test him, for He Himself know what He would do'. Similarly, Jesus asked His disciples 'Who touched my clothes?', when the woman touched the hem of His garment (Mark 5:30). God wants us to believe Him and to trust His Word, even when we do not have all the answers to some Bible problems.

The Inerrancy of Scripture

Judas' death helped me to understand, from personal experience, the inerrancy of Scripture. The word inerrant means that the Bible is 'without error'. It is similar in meaning to the word infallible which means the Bible is 'unable to err or to lead us astray'. Both words have been used interchangeably to refer to Scripture's truthfulness.

Biblical Evidence for Inerrancy

Because God can neither lie (Numbers 23:19, Titus 1:2) nor make errors (for He understands all things, Psalm 147:5, Isaiah 40:28), it logically follows that His Word would similarly be without error.

Christ affirms the inerrancy of Scripture by saying, 'Sanctify them by the truth, *Your word is truth*' (John 17:17). Notice, Scripture is not simply true, but truth; Matthew Henry, commenting on this verse, writes that in the counsel of God, 'it was settled and agreed . . . that all needful truth should be comprised and summed up in the word of God. Divine revelation, as it now stands in the written word, is not only pure truth

> without mixture, but entire truth without deficiency'. Christ also affirmed the inerrancy of Scripture by saying that 'Scripture cannot be broken' (John 10:35, which means that the words of Scripture cannot be wrong). Christ constantly appealed to Scripture as the arbiter of truth, and never once criticized, contradicted or cast doubt on any part of the Bible.
>
> The Bible itself claims to be without error. Thus, Psalm 12:6 says 'the words of the LORD are pure words, like silver . . . purified seven times'. The Bible here is compared to a precious metal which has its impurities removed seven times, so as to be perfectly free from corruption (see also Psalm 119:140, which says 'very pure'). Proverbs 30:5 says 'every word of God is pure', and the ESV translates this as 'every word of God proves true'. 2 Samuel 22:31 says, 'As for God, His way is perfect, the word of the Lord is proven'. Psalm 19:7 says 'the law of the LORD is perfect' and verse 9b says 'the judgments of the LORD are true and righteous altogether'. Psalm 119:160 says 'the entirety of Your word is truth' (KJV: 'Your word is true from the beginning'). Psalm 119:142 says 'Your law is truth' and verse 151 says 'all Your commandments are truth'. Daniel 10:21 calls the Bible the 'Scriptures of truth'.

The inerrancy of Scripture is the corollary, the flip-side, of the inspiration of Scripture. If the inspiration of Scripture is true, then so is the inerrancy of Scripture; if the Bible is God's Word, then it must be without error. As J. I. Packer writes, 'To assert biblical inerrancy and infallibility is just to confess faith in (i) the divine origin of the Bible and the (ii) truthfulness and trustworthiness of God'[7]. On the other hand, if the Bible contains errors, then the inspiration of Scripture is not true. These truths stand or fall together. Although there are difficulties in Scripture, there are good reasons to believe that Scripture is inerrant. As we have seen, most of the so-called contradictions and mistakes in the Bible are the result of not understanding and allowing for the normal ways that human language and literature work.

The *Chicago Statement on Biblical Inerrancy* describes the situation well, in Clause XIII: 'We deny that it is proper to evaluate Scripture according to standards of truth and error that are alien to its usage or purpose. We further deny that inerrancy is negated by Biblical phenomena such as a lack of modern technical precision, irregularities of

---

[7] J. I. Packer, *Fundamentalism and the Word of God*, Grand Rapids, MI: Eerdmans, 1958, p96

grammar or spelling, observational descriptions of nature, the reporting of falsehoods, the use of hyperbole and round numbers, the topical arrangement of material, variant selection of material in parallel accounts, or the use of free citations'.

Having taken into account some of the qualifications we made for the human nature of Scripture, we can define inerrancy as follows:

Definition: *The inerrancy of Scripture means that the Bible is true and without error in what it teaches, not only about salvation but in all matters, and even though in places we encounter difficulties, yet the fault lies not with Scripture but with our misunderstanding of its nature or meaning, or our own ignorance or lack of faith.*

Wrong Ideas about Inerrancy

Absolute Inerrancy: the idea that every word of the Bible is true in everything it says. The fact that the Bible reports untruths shows this idea is unsatisfactory; some qualifications and clarifications are necessary.

Limited Inerrancy: the idea that the Bible is inerrant in what it says about spiritual and doctrinal matters, but it may contain mistakes in relation to scientific or historical matters. Another way this idea is sometimes stated is that the Bible is inerrant in its purpose, in describing how people can be saved through Christ, but seeing it was not written as a scientific or history textbook, it may contain errors in these matters.

Infallible but not Inerrant. Although historically the terms inerrant and infallible have been used interchangeably, more recently, some evangelicals have preferred to say that the Bible is infallible, by which they mean that the biblical writers did not lie or deliberately deceive us, although they may have inadvertently written things containing mistakes or inaccuracies. Thus, the Bible does not lead us astray in matters of faith or practice, but we should not require factual perfection of it.

Accommodation: Some argue that Christ accommodated Himself to the prevailing ideas of His day. Thus, it is claimed that although much of the Old Testament is mythical, unhistorical or unscientific, Christ quietly acquiesced with its stories rather than stir up unnecessary trouble for Himself. However, Christ consistently attacked error, hypocrisy, corruption and human traditions not based on Scripture. If Christ wished to, He could have ignored 'mythical' Bible stories like Creation (Mark 10:6, 13:19), Adam and Eve (Mark 10:6-9), Noah's flood and Sodom's judgment (Luke 17:26-27, 29), Abraham (John 8:56), Moses

> (John 5:46), Jonah (Matt. 12:39-41), and Daniel (Matt. 24:15), but instead He affirmed them, and based spiritual truths like marriage, future judgment, and His resurrection upon them. Christ did not accommodate the errors of His day to please His enemies. He was 'the truth' (John 14:6) and God's 'faithful witness' (Rev. 1:5). He constantly appealed to Scripture as the test by which truth was determined. We believe in the inerrancy of Scripture primarily because Christ, the Son of God, attested to the verbal, plenary inspiration of Scripture.

Augustine wrote, 'I have learnt, I confess, to pay such deference to the books of Scripture, and to them alone, that I most firmly believe that none of their writers has ever fallen into any error in writing. And if I meet with anything in them which seems to me to be contrary to truth, I doubt not that either the manuscript is in fault, or that the translator has missed the sense, or that I myself have not rightly apprehended it' (*Letters*, 82.1.3).

CHAPTER 5

The Best Way to Start a New Religion

Joseph Smith was born in 1805 in the United States of America. As a young man he was a treasure-hunter, and was even put on trial in 1826 as 'a disorderly person and an imposter' for falsely advertising to be able to help people find buried treasure using a 'peep-stone'.

Smith claimed that when he was fifteen he had a vision of God the Father and Jesus Christ, who appeared to him and told him not to join any of the existing Christian denominations, since they were all wrong. Then, in a second vision in 1823, the angel Moroni appeared to him and told him about a book, written on gold plates, which was buried on a certain hill, which told the history of the original inhabitants of America. In addition, there were two special stones, the Urim and the Thummim, which could be used to translate the book. Moroni showed him where the book was buried, but it was not until four years later in 1827 that he was allowed to take the book and translate it out of the 'reformed Egyptian' language it was written in. After this, Smith was told to give back the gold plates and the two stones, and the angel sadly took them all back to heaven, never to be seen again.

Smith officially formed his new Church of Jesus Christ of Latter-Day Saints in 1830. As his band of followers grew, Smith had to keep on moving his flock to avoid persecution. Eventually, he was arrested and put in prison after a local newspaper published material against his new religion and he retaliated by destroying the printing press and burning all the copies. On June 27, 1844, the jail was stormed by about 200 people. Smith was shot and killed, but not before he himself had shot several of the attackers with his own gun.

People who belong to the Church of Jesus Christ of Latter-Day Saints are called Mormons, not only because the name is shorter and easier to say, but also because of the *Book of Mormon* which Joseph Smith translated from the gold plates with the help of the two magic stones. The *Book of Mormon* tells the story of how the American Indians were the descendants of various Jewish immigrants who travelled to America, first at the time of the Tower of Babel around 2000 BC (using saucer-shaped submarines to cross the Pacific ocean), and then again in later migrations. Christ also visited the American Indians (i.e. Jews) after his resurrection and preached the gospel to them. One branch of these Jews were the Nephites, God's chosen people, but they were unfaithful and were destroyed by another group called the Lamanites. The last of the Nephite prophets, called Mormon, was told to engrave a record of these histories on gold plates, and his son Moroni buried these plates in AD 420. After this, Moroni became an angel, and in due time revealed all to Joseph Smith.

Mormons believe some things that are very different from what the Bible teaches. They believe that God the Father was once a man who lived on earth but has been elevated to Godhood. God the Father is not a Spirit, but has a body of flesh and today lives on a planet near the star Kolob. Just as God the Father was once a man, so men will one day be exalted to be gods, if they work hard at perfecting themselves. To be prepared for godhood, Mormons go to a special Temple where they receive special holy underwear and receive special passwords and signs that they have to memorize to be able to get into Heaven.

What was the master-stroke of the Mormon religion? Someone might argue that Mormonism was the product of the fertile imagination of the founder Joseph Smith. This would be true, but it does not explain Mormonism's continued appeal. The central feature of Mormonism, and the fact that explains its staying power, is that it placed another book, the Book of Mormon, alongside the Bible. 'We believe the Bible to be the Word of God in so far as it is translated accurately . . . We also believe the Book of Mormon to be the Word of God'[1]. By adding another book alongside the Bible, Mormons were able to incorporate all the unique new strange ideas into their religion and continue to teach them down through the years.

Here is the best way to start a new religion: not by denying that the Bible is God's Word, but by adding another new book alongside it that subtly undermines the Bible's teachings. By adding another book to the Bible, or by adding other teachings to it, we deny that the Bible is complete and sufficient. In so doing, we again deny that the Bible is

---

[1] Mormon Articles of Faith, Section 8

really God's Word.

...

The Sufficiency of Scripture

In this chapter, we are going to look at the question of whether the Bible is enough for us, or whether we need something more. Is the Bible sufficient, or are we free to add to it? Various people down through the centuries have argued that the Scriptures are not enough for us as Christians. As a result, they have tried to add other books or other teachings to the Bible. However, because the Bible is God's Word, it is sufficient for all our needs as Christians. This is what we mean by the sufficiency of Scripture.

> **Definition**: *The Sufficiency of Scripture means that the Bible provides all that we need for faith and conduct as Christians*

The Scriptures are a complete and final revelation from God. There are no deficiencies in the Scriptures that require the addition of other writings or doctrines. The Westminster Confession of Faith says, 'The whole counsel of God concerning all things necessary for his own glory, man's salvation, faith and life, is either expressly set down in Scripture, or by good and necessary consequence may be deduced from Scripture: unto which nothing at any time is to be added, whether by new revelations of the Spirit, or traditions of men' (WCF 1.6). The 1561 Belgic Confession states, 'we believe that the Holy Scriptures fully contain the will of God and that whatsoever man ought to believe unto salvation is sufficiently taught therein'. John Piper writes, 'the Scriptures are sufficient in the sense that they are the only ("once for all") inspired and (therefore) inerrant words of God that we need, in order to know the way of salvation ("make you wise unto salvation") and the way of obedience ("equipped for every good work")'[2].

C. H. Mackintosh writes, 'We believe that the Bible . . . is the very word of the only wise and the only true God, with whom one day is as a thousand years, and a thousand years as one day, who saw the end from the beginning, and not only the end, but every stage of the way. We therefore hold it to be nothing short of positive blasphemy to assert that we have arrived at a stage of our career in which the Bible is not

---

[2] John Piper, "Thoughts on the Sufficiency of Scripture", Feb. 9, 2005, http://www.desiringgod.org/articles/thoughts-on-the-sufficiency-of-Scripture

sufficient, or that we are compelled to travel outside its covers to find ample guidance and instruction for the present moment, and for every moment of our earthly pilgrimage. . . . All the need of the Church of God, its members, and its ministers, has been most fully provided for. How could it be otherwise, if we admit the Bible to be the Word of God? Could the mind of God have devised, or His finger sketched an imperfect chart? Impossible. We must either deny the divinity or admit the sufficiency of *The Book*. We are absolutely shut up to this alternative. There is not so much as a single point between these two positions. If the book is incomplete, it cannot be of God; if it be of God it must be perfect'[3].

Biblical Basis

Jude 1:3 speaks about 'the faith *once for all* delivered to the saints'. In John 16:13, Christ said that 'when He, the Spirit of truth, has come, He will guide you into *all* truth'. Paul could speak about how he had declared 'the whole counsel of God' (Acts 20:27). 2 Peter 1:3-4 tell us that God's 'divine power has given to us *all* things that pertain to life and godliness, through the knowledge of Him who called us by glory and virtue, by which have been given to us exceedingly great and precious promises, that through these you may be partakers of the divine nature, having escaped the corruption that is in the world through lust'. 2 Timothy 3:16-17 says that 'All Scripture is given by inspiration of God' so that 'the man of God may be *complete, thoroughly equipped* for every good work'.

Other verses warn us against adding to, or taking away from, Scripture. After Moses had reminded Israel of the Ten Commandments he said, 'These words the LORD spoke to all your assembly, in the mountain from the midst of the fire, the cloud, and the thick darkness, with a loud voice; *and He added no more*. And He wrote them on two tablets of stone and gave them to me' (Deut. 5:22). The implication is that we are not to add any more words to the Ten Commandments God gave us. We should not try to improve upon Scripture or suggest it is lacking in any way. Deuteronomy 4:2 says, 'You shall not add to the word which I command you, nor take from it, that you may keep the commandments of the LORD your God which I command you'.

---

[3] C. H. Mackintosh, "The Bible – Its Sufficiency and Supremacy", *The Mackintosh Treasury: Miscellaneous Writings*, Neptune, NJ: Loizeaux Brothers, 1976, p18

> Deuteronomy 12:32 says, 'Whatever I command you, be careful to observe it; you shall not add to it nor take away from it'. Proverbs 30:5-6 say, 'Every word of God is pure; He is a shield to those who put their trust in Him. Do not add to His words, lest He rebuke you, and you be found a liar'. The Bible concludes with the words of Revelation 22:18-19 which say, 'For I testify to everyone who hears the words of the prophecy of this book: If anyone adds to these things, God will add to him the plagues that are written in this book; and if anyone takes away from the words of the book of this prophecy, God shall take away his part from the Book of Life, from the holy city, and from the things which are written in this book'.

Denials of the Sufficiency of Scripture

Very rarely have any religious groups openly denied the doctrine of the sufficiency of Scripture, or brazenly stated that the Bible is not enough for us. Instead, by the more crafty policy of adding other writings to the Bible, or by advocating teachings that add to what the Bible says, they have subtly undermined this principle.

Denials of the Sufficiency of Scripture
Adding books to Scripture
Adding new doctrines to Scripture
The 'doctrine of development'
'Words from the Lord'

Adding Books to Scripture: Non-Christian cults which deny the fundamental truths of the faith have usually insisted upon adding new writings to those found in the Bible. The Church of Jesus Christ of Latter-Day Saints (with the *Book of Mormon*) is not the only example of this. Mary Baker Eddy's book, *Science and Health with a Key to the Scriptures*, became the basis for the religion called Christian Science (which was neither Christian nor scientific). She wrote, 'I should blush to write of *Science and Health with Key to the Scriptures* as I have, were it of human origin and I apart from God its author, but as I was only a scribe echoing the harmonies of heaven in divine metaphysics, I cannot be super-modest of the Christ Science Textbook'[4].

The founder of the Jehovah's Witnesses organisation, Charles Taze Russell, wrote six volumes of *Scripture Studies*, and made the following

---

[4] Mary Baker Eddy, *Christian Science Journal*, Jan. 1901

comment: 'Not only do we find that people cannot see the divine plan in studying the Bible by itself, but we see, also, that if anyone lays the *Scripture Studies* aside, even after . . . he has read them for ten years – if he then lays them aside and ignores them and goes to the Bible alone, though he has understood his Bible for ten years, our experience shows that within two years he goes into darkness. On the other hand, if he had merely read the *Scripture Studies* with their references and had not read a page of the Bible as such, he would be in the light at the end of two years'[5]. In other words, the Jehovah's Witnesses believe that the Bible on its own is not sufficient, but their own writings are.

By far the most dreadful attempt (in terms of its effect) to add to Scripture was Mohammed's claim to have received the Koran from the angel Gabriel, thus to supplement the Bible.

It is significant that none of these people tried to launch their own new religions by 'starting from scratch'. Instead, while professing to revere Christian Scripture, and borrowing many of their ideas from it, they added to Scripture a new holy book, whose heresies undermined, contradicted and were diametrically opposed to biblical Christianity.

Adding New Doctrines to Scripture: It is not just books that have been added to Scripture. Just like the Pharisees in Christ's time, many groups have added new teachings to Scripture. The Roman Catholic church has added many extra doctrines:
- Prayers for the dead (AD 300)
- Worship of Mary (AD 431)
- Worship of images and relics (AD 786)
- Celibacy of clergy (AD 1079)
- Transubstantiation (the bread and wine turn into Christ's body and blood, AD 1215)
- Bible forbidden to laity (AD 1229)
- Cup forbidden to laity (AD 1414)
- Purgatory (AD 1439)
- Apocryphal books added to Bible (AD 1546)
- Mary's Immaculate Conception (i.e. sinlessness, AD 1854)
- Papal infallibility (AD 1870)
- Assumption of Mary (bodily ascent into heaven, AD 1950).

---

[5] Charles Taze Russell, *The Watchtower*, September 15, 1910, p298

These doctrines not only add to Scripture, but contradict what it teaches.

Charismatic Denials of the Sufficiency of Scripture: Some charismatic preachers and writers have gone as far as to openly deny the doctrine of the sufficiency of Scripture. Henry Frost wrote, 'It may confidently be anticipated, as the present apostasy increases, that Christ will manifest His deity and lordship in increasing measure through miracle-signs, including healings. We are not to say, therefore, that the word is sufficient. It is so to those who know and believe it; but it is not so to those who have never heard of it or who, having heard, have disbelieved it. To these persons a dramatic appeal may have to be made, and on the plane where such will be most easily be understood, the physical'[6].

Jack Deere, preaching at a 'Spiritual Warfare' conference, said: 'In order to fulfil God's highest purposes for our lives, we must be able to hear his voice, both in the written word and in the Word freshly spoken from heaven . . . Satan understands the strategic importance of Christians hearing God's voice, so he has launched various attacks against us in this area . . . ultimately this doctrine (the sufficiency of Scripture) is demonic even though Christian theologians have been used to perfect it'[7]. Peter Wagner, speaking at an American Association of Bible Colleges convention in 1985 said, 'The simple gospel is no longer adequate without signs and wonders'[8].

'The Lord told me': Charismatic Christians often claim that they have a word from the Lord, or that God has spoken to them in some way. John MacArthur writes: '"God told me . . ." has become the anthem of the Charismatic Movement. Strange private prophecies are proclaimed by all kinds of people who evidently believe God speaks to them. Surely the most infamous is Oral Roberts' preposterous death-threat prophecy. In 1987 Roberts told his nationwide audience that God had threatened to "call him home" if he couldn't raise eight million dollars by his creditors'

---

[6] Henry Frost, *Miraculous Healing*, New York: Revell, 1939, pp109-110

[7] Printed notes from the 1990 Spiritual Warfare Conference, Sydney, cited in Mark Thompson, "Spiritual Warfare: What Happens when I Contradict Myself", *The Briefing*, No. 45/46, (April 24, 1990), p11, also cited by Deere in his essay "Vineyard Position Paper #2: The Vineyard's Response to The Briefing", Anaheim, CA: Association of Vineyard Churches, 1992, pp22-23.

[8] As reported by John MacArthur, Jr. in a sermon, *The Sufficiency of Scripture*, 29 December, 1985, see www.gty.org/resources/sermons/80-18/The-Sufficiency-of-Scripture-Pt-1

deadline. Whether and how that threat might have been carried out, the world will never know; Roberts received a last-minute reprieve in the form of a large check from a Florida dog-track owner'[9]. Joyce Meyer, another charismatic preacher, regularly says "the Lord told me"; in one sermon ("Confidence to be Yourself") she used words to this effect eighteen times[10]. Why do some Christians constantly talk about what the Lord has told them? The common denominator, apart from God talking to them, is how much such people talk about themselves. They use the 'God told me' trick to appear super-spiritual, promote their ministry and garner a greater following. The divine 'name-dropping' is used, not to glorify God, but rather for self-promotion. These presumptuous prophetic claims usually fall into the following categories:

a. Words from their own Heart: I was travelling with a Christian once who told me about going into a certain church, where he was greeted by someone who said, "God has told me you are going to marry a beautiful woman". My friend replied, "So what do I do with the wife I already have?" False-prophecies like these are exactly what God was speaking to Jeremiah about: 'Do not listen to the words of the prophets who prophesy to you. They make you worthless; they speak *a vision of their own heart,* not from the mouth of the LORD. They continually say to those who despise Me, 'The LORD has said, "You shall have peace"'; and to everyone who walks according to the dictates of his own heart, they say, "No evil shall come upon you". . . . I have not sent these prophets, yet they ran. I have not spoken to them, yet they prophesied. But if they had stood in My counsel, and had caused My people to hear My words, then they would have turned them from their evil way and from the evil of their doings' (Jer. 23:16-22).

b. Dreams and Visions: God said to Jeremiah, 'I have heard what the prophets have said who prophesy lies in My name, saying: 'I have dreamed, I have dreamed!' How long will this be in the heart of the prophets who prophesy lies? Indeed, they are prophets of the deceit of their own heart, who try to make My people forget My name by their dreams which everyone tells his neighbour, as their fathers

---

[9] John MacArthur, *Does God Still give Revelation?* www.gty.org/resources/articles/A366, 13th July, 2009

[10] Tracy Hasley Frederick, *Feminizing the Pulpit: Feminine Style and the Rhetoric of Joyce Meyer,* Ph.D. dissertation, Regent University, 2009, p99

forgot My name for Baal. The prophet who has a dream, let him tell a dream; and he who has My word, let him speak My word faithfully. What is the chaff to the wheat?' says the Lord. 'Is not My word like a fire?' says the LORD, 'and like a hammer that breaks the rock in pieces?' (Jer. 23:25-29). Dreams are not a 'word from the Lord', nor are gut feelings, hunches or intuitions. We do not know where a dream comes from – from God, from some other spiritual source, or from 'much activity' (Eccles. 5:3). We must test all things by Scripture, and we need to call a dream by what it is: a dream, not a word from the Lord.

c. Natural Analogies: Charismatics often use illustrative object lessons in their 'prophesying'. A friend of our family in England was visiting a charismatic church where various people started 'prophesying' about how Christians should be like tea-bags. The first said we should diffuse the fragrance of Christ into the society around us. A second talked about how the boiling water (of persecution) causes the flavour of the tea to spread. A third spoke about how the tea-bag keeps the tea-leaves together and thus teaches us a lesson about Christian unity. Another charismatic church leader in the town in England where we once lived prophesied using the illustration of a half-time team-talk in a football game, to encourage members that although good things were happening, there was still much to be done for the Lord. These platitudes are not prophecies or 'words from the Lord'. They are motivational talks using ordinary preachers' illustrations.

d. Vague Generalities: Charismatics sometimes offer mystical, cryptic and flexible predictions. A relative of our family once went along to a charismatic 'prophetic art' group, where participants were encouraged to pray and then draw a picture as they sat opposite someone else. This picture was then interpreted to be a 'word' for the person sitting opposite. The lady opposite our relative drew a picture of a flower with multi-coloured petals, which was interpreted to mean 'You are a special person with unique qualities'. Our relative, in turn, presented the lady opposite with a picture of a cow with a big toothy smile. The toothy smile was interpreted to mean that the lady was rejoicing; the cow was left unexplained. Similarly, attempts to 'interpret tongues' in charismatic circles often involve vague generalities summing up 'the sense of the meeting'. Nothing here seems to fit the description of a 'word from the Lord'.

It is amazing how such nonsense passes for genuine Christianity nowadays. Ezekiel described such religious charlatans in his day as follows: 'And the word of the LORD came to me, saying, "Son of man, prophesy against the prophets of Israel who prophesy, and say to those who prophesy out of their own heart, 'Hear the word of the LORD!'" Thus says the Lord GOD: "Woe to the foolish prophets, who follow their own spirit and have seen nothing"' (Ezek. 13:1-2). Some charismatics admit that Christians should be cautious about accepting such 'words from the Lord'. Thus, Wayne Grudem, a prominent charismatic, quotes a series of other charismatic leaders to this effect, including Michael Harper who wrote, 'Prophecies which tell other people what they are to do – are to be regarded with great suspicion'[11]. But even genuine Christian experiences only derive their authority from Scripture. To quote W. H. Griffith-Thomas: 'Protestantism is careful to emphasize the written Word as against any dominion of ecclesiastical institution, or of subjective impressions of *even genuine religious experiences*'[12] (emphasis added).

The Doctrine of Development: The famous English convert to Roman Catholicism, John Henry Newman, coined the term 'the doctrine of development' in his 1845 book, *An Essay on the Development of Christian Doctrine*, in which he argued that the early church represented the church in its primitive, infant state, and that just as a child outgrows its clothing, so later doctrinal developments were natural and to be expected. This justified Catholic teachings not found in the New Testament. Protestants, by contrast, while accepting that biblical doctrine has been clarified down through history (because some doctrines are never properly defined until they are attacked), argue that the 'whole counsel of God' (Acts 20:27) has been 'once for all delivered to the saints' (Jude 3). In the first few centuries, the doctrines of the Deity of Christ and the Trinity were clarified through controversy, and in the 16th Century the Reformers reclaimed the Scriptural doctrine of salvation by grace through faith in the face of Roman Catholic corruptions and abuses.

---

[11] See various quotes in Wayne Grudem, *Systematic Theology*, Leicester: IVP, 1994, pp1040-1.
[12] W. H. Griffith-Thomas, *The Principles of Theology: An Introduction to the Thirty-Nine Articles*, London: Church Book Room Press, 1956, p105

However, these were not doctrinal developments, but instead refinements and recoveries of biblical truth.

Anglican writers argue for a doctrine of development in relation to church government, conceding that in the New Testament elders, bishops (overseers) and pastors (shepherds) refer to the same one office, but justifying the second-century practice of monarchical bishops as a natural development. J. B. Lightfoot, a 19th Century Anglican Bishop, admitted in his essay, *The Christian Ministry*, that in the New Testament, overseers (or, bishops) and elders (presbyters) were equivalent and interchangeable titles for the same office. He writes, 'as late therefore as the year 70 no distinct signs of the episcopal government [i.e. government by bishops] have hitherto appeared in Gentile Christendom'. 'Yet', he continues, 'unless we have recourse to a sweeping condemnation of received documents, it seems vain to deny that early in the second century the episcopal office was firmly and widely established. . . . So important an institution, developed in a Christian community of which St. John was the living centre and guide, could hardly have grown up without his sanction: and, as will be seen presently, early *tradition* very distinctly connects his name with the appointment of bishops in these parts'[13]. Lightfoot's argument for monarchical bishops rests, not on the Bible, but instead on early non-biblical history and, as he himself admits, tradition.

W. E. Vine wrote: 'The question arises whether what is therein revealed [in the NT] was intended to be complete and permanent, or simply introductory and subject to modification . . . The Scriptures themselves testify to their completeness and finality, as a divine revelation. "The faith," the body of Scripture doctrine, was "once for all delivered to the saints" (Jude 3 R.V.). That "once for all" is a plain statement. A confirmatory intimation is provided in the apostle Paul's exhortation to Timothy to guard the good deposit of the truth and to commit what he had received to faithful men that they might in their turn be able to teach others the same (2 Tim. 1:13; 2:1-2). . . . In church matters, as in other respects, the teaching of the New Testament is complete as a revelation of the will of God. While no ecclesiastical code, no list of doctrines, no formal set of regulations were issued, what is presented in the Word of God is uniform and consistent throughout, in matters both of doctrine and of practice, and has been proved sufficient

---

[13] J. B. Lightfoot, *The Epistles of St. Paul: Philippians*, 4th Ed., London: Macmillan and Co., 1879, pp201, 206, emphasis added.

under all conditions, however varied they may be, whether from the racial or any other point of view'[14].

Scripture is Not the Only Way that God Speaks Today

Having seen that Scripture is sufficient, it is important that we balance this by saying that Scripture is not the only way God reveals Himself today. Some evangelicals argue that because Scripture is sufficient, therefore God only speaks through Scripture today. This has been called Bible-Only-ism or Evangelical Deism (Deism is the belief that there is a God, but that He does not intervene in His creation). However, the idea that God only reveals Himself through Scripture today is false, for:

- The Bible tells us that God speaks to all people through Creation. Psalm 19:1-2 tell us that 'the heavens declare the glory of God and the firmament shows His handiwork. Day unto day utters speech, and night unto night reveals knowledge'. Romans 1:19-20 tell us that, 'because what may be known of God is manifest in them, for God has shown it to them. For since the creation of the world His invisible attributes are clearly seen, being understood by the things that are made, even His eternal power and Godhead, so that they are without excuse'.
- Paul, preaching in Lystra, said that God has testified to all people through His care for creation: 'Nevertheless He did not leave Himself without witness, in that He did good, gave us rain from heaven and fruitful seasons, filling our hearts with food and gladness' (Act 14:17).
- God speaks to us through conscience. Romans 2:14-15 say, 'for when Gentiles, who do not have the law, by nature do the things in the law, these, although not having the law, are a law to themselves, who show the work of the law written in their hearts, their conscience also bearing witness'. Seeing God wrote the Law, the conscience is God's Word written in our hearts.
- God the Holy Spirit speaks through the preaching of the gospel message today (John 15:26, 16:8-11, 1 Pet. 1:12), and through the teaching of Scripture. No one argues that we should just read Scripture in church, without comment.

---

[14] W. E. Vine, "The Origin and Rise of Ecclesiasticism and the Papal System", *The Collected Writings of W. E. Vine*, Vol. 4, Nashville, TN: Thomas Nelson Publishers, 1996, p356

- God reveals Himself through acts of history, or miracles. English Christians have long taken the defeat of the Spanish Armada and the Evacuation of Dunkirk in WW2 as divine interventions in history in response to prayer (national days of prayer were held).
- In the Old Testament, God sometimes spoke in the most unusual of ways, for example, through Balaam's donkey (Num. 22:28-30), or through an ungodly pagan king (e.g. Pharaoh Necho in 2 Chron. 35:20-22). There is nothing, in principle, to stop God speaking in extraordinary ways today. Muslims report having come to Christ through dreams which prompted them to seek the Lord. I once heard of a man being converted, in part, through hearing the name Jesus mentioned on the irreverent TV cartoon, *The Simpsons*.
- God guides His people (Psalm 48:14, 73:24, Isa. 58:11, Acts 16:6, Rom. 1:10, Col 1:9). He does this through Scripture, wisdom, advice from other Christians and through circumstances.
- The idea that God does not 'reveal' truth today, but only 'illumines' truth is not only a case of splitting hairs; even the terminology is debatable, for the normal word Scripture uses for what some people call 'illumination' is 'revelation' (e.g. Matt. 11:27, 16:16-17, Rom. 1:17, Eph. 1:17, Phil. 3:15).

What shall we say to all of these different ways that God 'speaks' today? How do they relate to the sufficiency of Scripture? Scripture is different to these other ways God speaks in three ways. Firstly, Scripture is clear and definite, in contrast with the general and vague revelation found in nature, providence and conscience. Thus, nature tells us there is a God, but it does not tell us much about what He is like. Secondly, Scripture is a certain Word from God, in contrast to the sometimes mistaken and misleading guidance we can take from circumstances, history, preachers, and human wisdom. Scripture is the only infallible Word from God. Thirdly, Scripture is our ultimate authority, the standard by which we test all other claimed 'messages' from God. Wayne Grudem quotes Edmund Clowney on the subject of the reliability of divine guidance as follows: 'the degree of certainty we have with regard to God's will in a situation is directly proportional to the degree of clarity we have as to how the Word of God applies to the situation'[15]. The sufficiency of Scripture does not deny the possibility of God intervening in the world or revealing Himself in some other way. It just means 'that we don't need

---

[15] Wayne Grudem, *Systematic Theology*, Leicester: IVP, 1994, p128, footnote 1

any more special revelation. We don't need any more inspired, inerrant words. In the Bible God has given us, we have the perfect standard for judging all other knowledge' (John Piper)[16].

Conclusion
The doctrine of the sufficiency of Scripture means that 'nothing is required of us by God that is not commanded in Scripture either explicitly or by implication. . . . we should emphasise what Scripture emphasises and be content with what God has told us in the Scriptures'[17]. Or, to put it another way, we must speak where Scripture speaks, and we must remain silent where Scripture remains silent. We must continue to test all things by Scripture, our ultimate and only infallible authority.

---

[16] John Piper, "Thoughts on the Sufficiency of Scripture", Feb. 9, 2005, http://www.desiringgod.org/articles/thoughts-on-the-sufficiency-of-Scripture.
[17] Wayne Grudem, *Systematic Theology*, 134

CHAPTER 6

Where is Your Scripture for That?

Isaac Watts was born in England in 1674 to a family of Dissenting or Non-Conformist Christians, which meant they did not belong to the Church of England because they felt it did not follow the Bible closely enough. Watts' father was imprisoned twice during his son's early years for his religious views. Isaac was educated at a grammar school in Southampton, where he learned Latin, Hebrew and Greek, as well as teaching himself French so he could speak with refugees. As a boy he showed great poetic ability. Once, during family prayers, he began to laugh. His father asked him why and he replied that he had heard a sound and opened his eyes to see a mouse climbing a rope in a corner. Isaac told his father that, seeing the mouse, he had immediately thought:

A little mouse for want of stairs, ran up a rope to say its prayers.

He would have been wiser not to have shared this rhyme with his father, who began to discipline him. As he was being beaten, young Isaac pleaded for mercy:

Father, father, pity take, and I will no more verses make.

Before Isaac Watts, most hymns sung in English-speaking churches were metrical versions of the Psalms. Some of them were of very poor quality (Watts called them 'ugly hymns' and 'cheap doggerel'). In his family's church, the clerk would read out the Psalm line by line, with the congregation singing after him. Watts complained about this to his father, but his father was not sympathetic. "Isaac", he said, "if you cannot be reverent, you can at least keep your mouth shut about things which do not concern you". When Isaac and his brother Enoch announced that they hoped to prepare their own hymns, their father laughed and said, "That old hymnal was good enough for your grandfather, and your father, and so I reckon it will have to be good enough for you!"[1].

Because he refused to join the Church of England, Watts was unable to go to university at Oxford or Cambridge, and went instead to a Dissenting Academy in Stoke Newington, London. After graduating there in 1694, he spent two years at home. During these two years, incredibly, he wrote the majority of his 800 hymns. These included not only the first real English hymns, but also some of the greatest hymns ever written in English, including *Joy to the World* (based on Psalm 98), *Jesus shall Reign where'er the Sun* (based on Psalm 72), *O God, Our Help in Ages Past* (based on Psalm 90), *When I survey the Wondrous Cross*, and *Alas! and did my Saviour Bleed*.

His hymns met with great approval, but also opposition. One critic protested, 'Christian congregations have shut out divinely inspired psalms and taken in Watts's flights of fancy'. In 1789, a Rev. Adam Rankin spoke in Philadelphia at the General Assembly of the Presbyterian Church in the United States: 'I have ridden on horseback all the way from my home in Kentucky to ask this august body to refuse to allow the great and pernicious error of adopting the use of Isaac Watts' hymns in public worship in preference to Rouse's versifications of the Psalms of David'[2]. The objectors were not complaining about the quality of Isaac Watts' poetry. Their protest was that Watts' hymns were undermining the divinely-inspired songbook we have been given, the book of Psalms, by adding other uninspired and humanly-devised songs to those found in the Word of God. Still today there are a small proportion of churches which practise 'exclusive-psalmody'[3].

On the other hand, most Christians would argue that the Bible does not forbid us composing new hymns and songs. In fact, nine times in the

---

[1] N. A. Woychuk, *Singing Psalms with Isaac Watts and a Biography of the Author*, Dallas, TX: SMF Press, 2004

[2] Clint Bonner, *A Hymn is Born*, Nashville, TN: Broadman, 1959, p8

[3] They argue that the 'psalms and hymns and spiritual songs' of Eph. 5:19 and Col. 3:16 are all referring to the Psalms, (e.g. Psalms are called 'songs', see Psalm 30, 65-68, 120-134, etc.; Psalms are also called 'hymns' in the Greek translation of the OT, see the titles of Psalms 6, 54, 55, 61, 76 and in Psalms 40:3; 65:1; 100:4, etc.). In the New Testament, Christ sung a 'hymn' with the disciples (Matt. 26:30, Mark 14:26) and this was probably a psalm, possibly Psalm 118.

Bible we are told to sing a 'new song' to the Lord. Which position is correct? More significantly, why doesn't the New Testament state whether we are must only use psalms or whether we are allowed to compose new hymns and songs?

Or, to take another issue, Christians in the 'house-church' movement believe that we should only meet in homes, like the early Christians (we do not read about dedicated church buildings in the New Testament, e.g. 'the church in their/his/your house', Rom. 16:5, 1 Cor. 16:19, Col. 4:15, Philemon 2). Does this mean that we must do likewise? Or is the Bible simply silent on some matters, allowing a degree of flexibility? The New Testament does not say we *must* meet in homes, nor does it forbid us meeting in other places at other times. There may have been good reasons why the early Christians met in this way, but there does not seem to be any rule about it.

If the Bible is sufficient and provides all we need for faith and conduct, as we saw in the previous chapter, then why does it appear to be silent on some issues? Can we do anything it does not specifically forbid, or can we only do what it specifically allows?

Think of some other areas where the New Testament appears to be silent. The English preacher Harold St. John was once walking across the campus of an American Bible college sometime around the middle of the 20th Century (a time of great social change) when he noticed about fifteen young people arguing animatedly. One of them called him over. 'Mr. St. John, do you think a young Christian should dance?' He replied that this was a hard question, and that he wished they had asked him about something easy like Ezekiel's wheels or the wings of a seraphim. Instead of giving his opinion, he drew a vertical line on a piece of paper and wrote on one side, BC and on the other side, AD and asked the students whether they thought certain things were more appropriate for the days before they became Christians or the days after. St. John said, 'I began throwing out words very quickly – sport for exercise, prayer meetings, this and that; and about the twelfth thing I threw out was dancing, and like a flash they all signaled the left side. When the question was put suddenly, they knew, instinctively'[4].

Harold St. John was a very highly-regarded Bible teacher, not only for his expository prowess (Professor F. F. Bruce referred to him as 'the maestro') but also his godliness, yet despite his great Bible knowledge, St.

---

[4] Patricia St. John, *Harold St. John: a Portrait by his Daughter*, London: Pickering and Inglis, 1961, p78-9

John was reluctant to give a straight answer to the question. Some Christians might point to the example of Miriam (Exod. 15:20) or David, who 'danced before the LORD' (2 Sam. 6:14), while others in reply might point to Herodias' daughter whose sensuous dancing at Herod's birthday party led to the beheading of John the Baptist (Mark 6:22). But the Bible does not directly tell us whether Christians should dance or not.

Another English Bible teacher of the same era, J. B. Watson, was a very good cricketer, but gave it up after his conversion. Is there anything wrong with playing competitive sport? Paul mentions various sports to illustrate the Christian life in his letters (boxing, running, etc.), but there is nothing stated in these passages about whether a Christian can (or cannot) participate in them. In Watson's biography, the answer given was 'If you do not wish to win the prize in the Christian race there is nothing wrong in this or that; but if you do, then it becomes wrong to you'[5]. Again, despite being highly regarded for his ability as a Bible teacher, Watson did not offer a Bible verse that directly settled the question. Upon other matters, like drunkenness or sexual relations outside of marriage, we can be sure that these preachers would have immediately pointed to Scriptures that dealt clearly and directly with the issues.

If the Bible is God's Word, sufficient and complete, then why does it not address these issues relevant to life in our day and age? If we want to follow the Bible, then how should we live when faced with questions which it does not directly answer? If the Bible is our ultimate authority, then why does it not clearly settle all these questions about 'gray areas' for us? Are we free to do anything that the Bible does not explicitly forbid, or are we only able to do those things that the Bible allows? Some Christians feel that they can do certain things, while others feel they should not, and the result is sometimes ugly arguments and divisions. What shall our rule of life be?

...

Scripture is Sufficient, but not Exhaustive

In the previous chapter, we saw that the Bible is sufficient, yet it does not seem to provide exhaustive information on how we should live as Christians. The Bible does not tell us everything on every subject.

---

[5] Robert Rendall, *J. B. Watson: a Memoir and Selected Writings*, London: Pickering and Inglis, 1957, p23

Consider the four following areas in which the Bible does not provide exhaustive information.

Firstly, the Scriptures are not sufficient for life in general. They do not teach us how to build a house, cook a meal, farm land, fix a car, or survive on a deserted island. The Bible might tell us about a Christian attitude that applies while we are doing these things, but this is not the same as giving us instructions about the actual task. Some religious groups, like the Amish people in the USA, have withdrawn from society and refuse to use motor cars, radios, televisions, computers or even buttons on their clothes. Their primary reason for not using these modern conveniences is social rather than biblical; these rules promote a group identity, and therefore their people do not integrate with the rest of society and leave the Amish. Someone could argue that Christians should not use modern conveniences because they are not found in the Bible, but if we were to do so, we would also have to stop using a whole host of other things, like modern medicines, and go back to an agricultural lifestyle. The reality, however, is that even the Amish use some modern devices that are not found in the Bible. Most Christians, therefore, believe that the Bible was never intended to provide exhaustive information about how we are to live.

Secondly, the Scriptures are not exhaustive in what they teach us about God. If they were, then we could know everything about God and be like God. God has not revealed everything about Himself. Deuteronomy 29:29 says 'The secret things belong to the LORD our God, but those things which are revealed belong to us and to our children forever, that we may do all the words of this law'. Paul said, 'If anyone thinks that he knows anything, he knows nothing yet as he ought to know' (1 Cor. 8:2).

Thirdly, Scripture does not give exhaustive teaching about our individual Christian lives. The Bible does not directly answer the question of what career or job an individual Christian should take. Nor will the Bible tell a Christian the name of the person he or she should marry. Nor will the Bible tell a Christian where to go on holiday. Some of these sorts of decisions will have an important influence over our Christian growth and life, but the Bible only gives general principles.

Nor, fourthly, does the New Testament provide exhaustive information about church life. The Bible does not tell us whether we should we have a Sunday School for children, or whether to have it before the main church gathering or after, or perhaps during the week instead. It will not tell us what hymn book to use (if we choose to have a hymn book), nor what to call our dedicated church building (if we choose to meet in one), nor what time to meet together. I once mentioned to a friend that the reason why Christians should meet together at 11am on Sunday morning is because it allows the dairy farmers time to finish the milking. This person thought I was being serious, and replied in a puzzled tone, 'But there are no dairy farmers in our church'. My point was precisely that most churches haven't had dairy farmers in their congregations for many years now, and there are certainly no Bible verses which lay down a rule about 11am meeting times. There are many other areas which the New Testament does not legislate upon in relation to church life.

The Regulative Principle: 'Scripture Says'
Many Presbyterian and Reformed churches hold to what is called the Regulative Principle, but we will call it the 'Scripture Says' rule. It is best expressed in the Westminster Confession of Faith (WCF): 'The acceptable way of worshipping the true God is instituted by Himself and so limited by his own revealed will that He may not be worshipped according to the imaginations or devices or men or the suggestions of Satan under any visible representation or any other way not prescribed in the Holy Scriptures' (WCF, 21.1). In practice, what this means is that anything not commanded or encouraged in Scripture is forbidden. This is the basis upon which some people objected to Watt's hymns.

However, the 'Scripture Says' rule throws up some problems. If we follow the 'Scripture Says' rule and prohibit anything in worship which is not mentioned in the New Testament, we would not meet in special church buildings – we would meet in homes. Nor should we have clocks on the walls by which to start or finish our meetings, or microphones for sound, or printed Bibles (these were all hand-written in apostolic times), and it would be debatable whether we should even sit on seats. Nor should we have musical accompaniment of singing in church because it is not mentioned in New Testament worship. My grandfather, when he was dying of cancer, was conducting a series of meetings preaching through the book of Revelation. Someone asked if it might be possible to record these meetings in view of the preacher's declining health, but was told that 'anything in a black box comes from the Devil'.

The Scottish Presbyterian Reformer John Knox was once challenged in a debate with a Roman Catholic over the fact that there was no scriptural support for him taking a drink from a glass of water while he was preaching. Some might argue that the principle of mercy allows the preacher to have a drink, but once we appeal to general 'principles' rather than direct scriptural evidence, we have changed the argument and abandoned the 'Scripture Says' rule altogether. We could similarly appeal to the principle of mercy for almost anything: microphones (for the deaf to hear better), printed Bibles (so that we do not have to spend long hours hand-copying Scripture), as well as musical instruments (in some places where the unaccompanied singing is not so tuneful).

Some churches also contravene their own Regulative Principle by baptising infants, a practice not mentioned in the New Testament. They defend this by arguing that 'the New Testament prescribes no repeal of the Old Testament command to give the covenant sign to covenant children'[6]. Leaving aside the fact that the New Testament does not repeal the Old Covenant item by item but rather as a whole, notice how, instead of arguing that 'what is not commanded in Scripture is forbidden' (the Regulative Principle), the exact opposite position is argued, 'what is not expressly forbidden is permissible', a principle normally rejected.

These are the some of the difficulties and contradictions that the 'Scripture Says' rule runs up against when taken to its natural and logical conclusion. Just as the Lord refuted the Pharisees by pointing out the inconsistency and hypocrisy of their practices (condemning Him for healing on the Sabbath, but happy to pull their animals out of pits on the same day, Matt. 12:11-12, Luke 14:5), so the inconsistencies of those holding to the 'Scripture Says' rule show that it is as much honoured in its breach as in its observance. Its advocates feel free to pick and choose when to obey it, and when to ignore it.

The main problem with the Regulative Principle is that while Scripture is sufficient, it is not exhaustive. The Bible is not full of checklists telling us what we can and cannot do. Ironically, the Regulative Principle is not found in the New Testament itself. It is a man-made addition to Scripture. As such, it stands self-condemned, falling under its own ban.

The Normative Principle: 'Anything Goes'

The opposite of the Regulative principle is sometimes called the Normative Principle, but we will call it the 'Anything Goes' Rule. It is generally held by Anglicans, Methodists and Evangelicals. It is best summarised in Article VI of the Church of England's Thirty-Nine

---

[6] Robert Reymond, *A New Systematic Theology of the Christian Faith*, Nashville, TN: Thomas Nelson Publishers, 1998, p870, footnote 8

Articles: 'Holy Scripture containeth all things necessary to salvation; so that whatsoever is not read therein, nor may be proved thereby is not to be required of any man that it should be believed as an article of the faith'. Whereas the Regulative principle states that Christians are only allowed to do what the Bible states, the Normative principle allows Christians to do whatever is not prohibited by the Bible (and also, in practice, not disruptive of Christian unity and fellowship).

However, this principle is even more problematic than the 'Scripture Says' rule because, as we have seen, the New Testament is not written as a legal document, spelling out what we must and must not do, in exhaustive detail. The result is that there is plenty of scope for people to add their own innovations to what the Bible teaches. I know of a church, for example, which started one of its Sunday services with the 1946 feel-good Disney song, *'Zipp a dee do dah, zipp a dee ay, My oh my, what a wonderful day, Plenty of sunshine headed my way, Zipp a dee do dah, zipp a dee ay'*. There are other churches which invite people to bring an animal to church to have it blessed, or even baptised. Or there is 'Messy Church', which turns Sunday services into something resembling a toddler playgroup where everyone plays games, makes craft, does some cooking, and generally has a lot of noisy fun together. Messy (or even Sweaty) Church might be a novel way to evangelise unbelievers, but it is questionable whether it is really 'church' by any biblical description.

Some people from a more traditional church background might find these practices irreverent or juvenile, but there are plenty of ancient Christian traditions which are not found or encouraged in the New Testament, like 'holy water' for protection against evil, praying with rosaries or prayer beads, fasting for Lent, and dressing clergymen up in bright and gaudy costumes. From such evidences of superstition and spiritual infantilism there is a graduated, ascending scale of extra-biblical innovation all the way up to full-blown Roman Catholicism with its worship of Mary, lighting candles for the dead, prayers to the saints, paying money for forgiveness of sins and papal infallibility.

In practice, the Normative Principle seems to provide less protection against the creeping corruption of Christianity. Its main problem seems to be a more relaxed and careless approach to what the Bible says about any issue. Instead of asking, 'What does the Scripture say?', the Normative Principle almost encourages us to ignore Scripture as our ultimate authority. Instead, everyone does what is right in his own eyes.

Once we stop taking Scripture seriously as God's Word, and stop allowing it to define Christian faith and practice, we are left with an 'anything goes' free for all (denominational politics permitting). Interestingly, while churches from the 'Anything Goes' tradition have been foremost in accepting homosexuality, there are also churches from the opposite Reformed, 'Scripture Says', tradition which have followed their lead. The common denominator is that all these churches have abandoned belief in the inspiration of Scripture and its supreme authority over faith and conduct.

Christian groups which follow the 'Anything Goes' Normative Principle tend to be a 'broad church', with wings as far separated as charismatic, liberal (i.e. functionally atheistic) and High-Church (i.e. functionally Roman Catholic). Churches following the 'Scripture Says' Regulative Principle tend to be divisive and fractious, continually splintering over minor matters. While church unity is more easily preserved under the 'Anything Goes' model, the gospel often is not. While the 'Anything Goes' principle unites true Christians and non-Christians underneath the one 'big-tent', the 'Scripture Says' principle often produces sectarian strife and Pharisaical pettiness. Is there a better way than these two principles?

A biblical approach should steer a middle course between the extreme positions of the Regulative and Normative principles. The Scriptures are sufficient but not exhaustive; they are neither lacking in any way nor are they legalistic or laboriously comprehensive. The New Testament does not provide us with lengthy lists of do's and don'ts (the error of the Regulative Principle), but on the other hand, neither are the Scriptures deficient in such a way as to leave us free to do whatever we wish (the danger of the Normative Principle).

A Biblical Approach

How do the Scriptures guide us as Christians? How do we live as Christians when we are faced with difficult issues? If the Scriptures provide all that we need for 'life (i.e. eternal life, salvation) and godliness' (2 Pet. 1:3), how do they show us the right way to live? The New Testament guides us in five ways:

1. Direct Commands

Firstly, the New Testament contains many direct commands. Some Christians from a legalistic background, having discovered that the New Testament teaches that we are not under law but grace, swing to the opposite extreme, and adopt an anti-authoritarian attitude. They cry 'legalistic' when anyone says that Christians should not use off-colour language, or drink to excess or watch films that are frankly pornographic in parts. They mistakenly think that the New Testament either does not issue commands, or that if it does they are somehow optional. However, the New Testament is hardly lacking in the language of authoritative command. We have, of course, the over-arching command to 'love one another' (John 13:34). Then there is the command to be holy: 'as obedient children, not conforming yourselves to the former lusts, as in your ignorance, but as He who called you is holy, you also be holy in all your conduct, because it is written, 'Be holy, for I am holy' (1 Pet. 1:14-16). There are commands to be fully devoted to Christ and to not love the world: 'present your bodies a living sacrifice, holy, acceptable to God, which is your reasonable service. And do not be conformed to this world, but be transformed by the renewing of your mind' (Romans 12:1-2). There are also many moralising commands, denouncing specific sins: 'But fornication and all uncleanness or covetousness, let it not even be named among you, as is fitting for saints; neither filthiness, nor foolish talking, nor coarse jesting, which are not fitting, but rather giving of thanks' (Eph. 5:3-4). Paul even gives detailed instructions about how the church gatherings should be conducted and leaves us in no doubt about their authoritative nature: 'the things which I write to you are the commandments of the Lord (1 Cor. 14:37).

2. Doctrines with Consequences

Secondly, the New Testament teaches us by its doctrines. This sounds strange because we tend to think of doctrines as abstract theological ideas, without practical consequences. However, all New Testament letters are a mixture of doctrine and its practical implications. Thus, Romans explains the doctrine of salvation, but a substantial section of the letter is devoted to the way the life of a believer is to be 'transformed' (Rom. 12:2) by the gospel. Doctrines have implications even though they are not always explicitly spelled out. For example, Christ is the head of the church (Eph. 1:22, 5:23, Col. 1:18), so it is hard to see how a church could appoint a human as its supreme ruler (such as the Pope, or the Queen of England) without undermining the truth of Christ's position. Flowing from this, the New Testament presents a consistent picture of individual congregations governed, not by a minister or other local figurehead, but by the shared pastoral oversight of elders (Acts 11:30, 14:23, 15:2, 20:17-28, Phil. 1:1, Tit. 1:5-7, James 5:14, 1 Pet. 5:1-4, etc.). 'The New Testament does not give the slightest hint that the eldership is to be presided over by a pastor' (Strauch[7]).

3. Apostolic Examples
Thirdly, the New Testament gives us apostolic examples. As disciples, we are to imitate Christ, and this also includes imitating the first disciples. This is because the apostles were ideally placed to show us what following Christ looked like in practice. Thus, Paul says, 'imitate me, just as I also imitate Christ' (1 Cor. 11:1). This not only applies to matters of discipleship and morality but also in relation to church life. Thus, take the fact that the early Christians met together on the first day of the week (John 20:1, 19, 26, Acts 2:1[8], 20:7, 1 Cor. 16:2, Rev. 1:10). We are nowhere *commanded* to meet together on Resurrection day, the first day of the week, but the apostolic pattern sets a precedent. We have not been asked to reinvent the Christian wheel in every age, but to follow the authoritative example of the apostles and the early believers.

4. Promises and Warnings
Fourthly, the New Testament gives us promises and warnings which we should act on. For example, 'if any of you lacks wisdom, let him ask of God, who gives to all liberally and without reproach, and it will be given to him' (James 1:5). Again, 'if anyone among you thinks he is religious, and does not bridle his tongue but deceives his own heart, this one's religion is useless' (James 1:26).

5. Wisdom Issues
Fifthly, there are matters upon which the New Testament is silent, and issues over which Christians hold differing opinions. Some complicated issues involve the interplay of competing principles, and we will need wisdom from God. Paul gives some examples from his day: eating meat or vegetables, and observing (or not observing) certain 'holy days', (Rom. 14:1-6, and see 1 Cor. 8-10). The New Testament gives us freedom of conscience in some matters. Paul gives a 'command' to the married wife not to depart from her husband (1 Cor. 7:10), but notice that he does not say 'I command' about whether a Christian should get married or stay single (he says, 'I give my judgment', 1 Cor. 7:25). He again gives his judgment in relation to whether a widow should remarry (7:40). I, too,

---

[7] Alexander Strauch, *Biblical Eldership: An Urgent Call to Restore Biblical Church Leadership*, Littleton, CO: Lewis & Roth, 1988, p12-13
[8] Pentecost was the day after the Sabbath, Lev. 23:16

have given my judgment about some matters in this chapter, and other people may have a different opinion. This is the inevitable result of the fact that, on some issues, the New Testament does not offer definitive judgments. Here, we need to respect other people's freedom of conscience. Even when we feel we have Scripture on our side, we need to adopt a humble, loving spirit when trying to show others the right way.

When we come, therefore, to matters upon which the New Testament is silent, we may be sure that Scripture will help us to navigate these difficult cases, even if it does not speak directly about the particular issue we face. There will always be underlying principles we can find to help us. The New Testament is thus necessary, as well as sufficient. It is to the Word of God that we must turn for help. We must not neglect it. Let's look at two examples of the way the Bible helps us when facing issues upon which it seems to be silent.

Gambling

Take the question of whether it is right for a Christian to be involved in gambling. We may instinctively feel that it is wrong for a Christian to gamble, however, the word 'gambling' is not mentioned in the Bible at all. It is true that the Roman soldiers gambled for Christ's clothing at the foot of the cross, but it could be argued that they were only following the wise guidance of Proverbs 18:18: 'casting lots causes contentions to cease and keeps the mighty apart'. What principles do we find that address the question of gambling? The Lord Himself warns against covetousness (i.e. materialistic greed, Mark 7:22, Luke 12:15), which the New Testament lists as a sin comparable with sexual immorality (Rom. 1:29, Eph. 5:3), likens to idolatry (Eph. 5:5, Col. 3:5), and warns Christians against: 'let your conduct be without covetousness; be content with such things as you have' (Heb. 13:5). The New Testament also teaches us to work hard for our own bread (1 Thess. 4:11, 2 Thess. 3:6-12), which is the opposite of trying to win the lottery. It also warns us against addictions which bring us under the control of forces other than the Holy Spirit (1 Cor. 6:12 says, 'All things are lawful for me, but I will not be brought under the power of any'). There may not be anything wrong with tossing a coin to settle a dispute, but the New Testament discourages the sort of greed that drives people to gamble.

Instead of providing us with simplistic diktats, we are forced to study the New Testament carefully to understand the underlying moral and spiritual issues involved. We are not treated like immature infants or slaves, and given lists of rules which govern our every movement. Instead, we have been adopted as the sons and daughters of the Living God; He wants us to develop spiritual intelligence and maturity. Just like the two Bible teachers reluctant to give direct answers about dancing and playing sport, the New Testament is interested in educating us about deeper spiritual principles. While not spelling out exhaustive lists of rules, the New Testament is far from silent on the subject of how Christians should live, and gives us sufficient principles to govern our conduct.

Church Life

Similarly, with Church life, there are things which the New Testament does not clearly command or forbid, and which we need Scriptural wisdom to evaluate. For example, while the New Testament does not mention Sunday Schools for children, yet the Lord's own example of receiving children (Matt. 19:13-15), using a child as an object lesson of the need for conversion and humility (Matt. 18:1-4), and his words, 'let the little children come to me and do not forbid them' (Matt. 19:14, Mark 10:14, Luke 18:16) show that the Saviour wants us to try to reach children with the gospel.

Or take the issue of musical accompaniment to church singing, which the New Testament never mentions. Some would defend this on the basis of Old Testament practices (e.g. Psalm 150:3-5), but claiming an Old Testament precedent is problematic, for we should still be sacrificing pigeons in church if we were to follow the Old Testament. If Psalm 149 tells us to praise God with the timbrel and harp (v3), it also tells us to wage 'holy war': we are to have a two-edged sword in our hand to execute vengeance on the nations (vs6-7). While the New Testament nowhere mentions music in church, some might reply that Revelation 5:8, 14:2, and 15:2 mention harps in heaven. It would seem inconsistent for Christians in a church which forbids musical accompaniment to sing hymns which mention heavenly harps. Even singing psalms which mention musical accompaniment can become a sensitive or subversive practice in such churches. The Bible does not seem to have a problem with musical accompaniment in itself. However, the fact that the New Testament places no stress upon music in church is noteworthy; it aligns with the deeper principle that God wants us to 'worship in spirit' (John 4:23-24) and that we are to 'make melody in [our] *hearts* to the Lord' (Eph. 5:19). A culture in which church becomes a concert, where musical performances encourage an entertainment mentality, where God's people are spectators rather than participants in worship, or where songs are more highly rated for their music than for any meaning in their words, is not only missing the point; it represents the aestheticization of religion – the triumph of art over substance. It is a failure to understand what it means to worship God in spirit and in truth.

The Necessity of Scripture

Everything the Bible teaches is important for our spiritual prosperity and progress. Psalm 119:128 says, 'Therefore *all* Your precepts concerning *all* things I consider to be right; I hate *every* false way'. This is the doctrine of the necessity of Scripture.

> **Definition**: *the Necessity of Scripture means that the Bible is essential for our salvation and spiritual blessing, for living a life that pleases God and for our fellowship with other Christians in the church; we cannot do without anything it teaches.*

There is nothing the Bible teaches that we can safely ignore. Everything in the Bible has been given to us for our spiritual good. Although there are difficult questions we face as Christians that the Bible does not directly address, an understanding of the great variety of ways that Scripture speaks to us – through doctrines, examples, promises, warnings and commands – should encourage us to be more dependent upon God's Word instead of abandoning it and doing whatever we wish. We might think that some things are not important, or that following them today is optional, or that they are only minor matters which can be disregarded. However, while we should not major on minors, nevertheless if God has told us to do something, we should obey. Read carefully what Christ said when criticizing the Pharisees: 'Woe to you, scribes and Pharisees, hypocrites! For you pay tithe of mint and anise and cummin, and have neglected the weightier matters of the law: justice and mercy and faith. These you ought to have done, *without leaving the others undone*' (Matt. 23:23). Christ said that the Pharisees ought to have kept the weightier matters of the law *as well as* tithing their herbs. All Scripture is necessary, and it is at our peril if we treat anything as unimportant.

Think about justice, which Christ mentioned in the verse above, and consider its relation to church discipline. Some churches ignore church discipline altogether, keen to avoid controversy or offence, while other churches cast people out for any cause, like Diotrephes did (2 John 10). Other churches excommunicate people, but finding it distasteful, cut corners and ignore New Testament procedures which, like all legal technicalities, exist to prevent miscarriages of justice. Whether excommunication is ignored, involves cult-like control, or tries to cut corners, biblical principles of justice and fairness are abandoned.

It is possible to have 'biblical blind spots' – we are not aware of what Scripture teaches on a particular subject. Our great need as Christians is to diligently read, carefully search, and humbly obey the Bible. Moses said to the children of Israel, 'Surely I have taught you statutes and judgments, just as the LORD my God commanded me, that you should act according to them in the land which you go to possess. Therefore be careful to observe them; for *this is your wisdom* and your understanding in the sight of the peoples who will hear all these statutes' (Deut. 4:5-6).

Biblical Basis

Christ quoted Deuteronomy 8:3 in Matthew 4:4: 'man shall not live by bread alone but by every word that proceeds from the mouth of God'. In Deuteronomy 32:46-47, Moses said, 'Set your hearts on all the words which I testify among you today, which you shall command your children to be careful to observe – all the words of this law. For it is not a futile thing for you, because it is your life, and by this word you shall prolong your days in the land which you cross over the Jordan to possess'. God said to Joshua, 'Only be strong and very courageous, that you may observe to do according to all the law which Moses My servant commanded you; do not turn from it to the right hand or to the left, that you may prosper wherever you go. This Book of the Law shall not depart from your mouth, but you shall meditate in it day and night, that you may observe to do according to all that is written in it. For then you will make your way prosperous, and then you will have good success' (Josh. 1:7-8). David said to Solomon, 'Only may the LORD give you wisdom and understanding, and give you charge concerning Israel, that you may keep the law of the LORD your God. Then you will prosper, if you take care to fulfill the statutes and judgments with which the LORD charged Moses concerning Israel. Be strong and of good courage; do not fear nor be dismayed' (1 Chron. 22:12-13). James 1:21-25 says, 'Therefore lay aside all filthiness and overflow of wickedness, and receive with meekness the implanted word, which is able to save your souls. But be doers of the word, and not hearers only, deceiving yourselves. For if anyone is a hearer of the word and not a doer, he is like a man observing his natural face in a mirror; for he observes himself, goes away, and immediately forgets what kind of man he was. But he who looks into the perfect law of liberty and continues in it, and is not a forgetful hearer but a doer of the work, this one will be blessed in what he does'.

CHAPTER 7

But the Bible is Dry, Boring and Difficult to Understand!

When I was twelve years old, I was given a book which, apart from the Bible, has probably been more of an encouragement to me in my Christian life than any other. It was the biography of George Müller[1]. As a twelve-year-old, however, I thought the book was a bit boring. The first chapter about Müller's godless youth as a petty thief, playboy and prison inmate, was interesting. The second chapter was good, too, about his conversion after attending a meeting at the home of a Christian where Müller was impressed by the reverence and sincerity of the prayers. But I put the book down after this; I thought that I had reached the end of any interesting parts. I didn't think there would be much more to the rest of the story. It was not until I was in my mid-teens that I picked up the book again, and read the rest of the story.

After his conversion in Germany in 1825, George Müller came to England and, in 1832, moved to Bristol where, with Henry Craik, he commenced a ministry which resulted in many people being converted. However, this was also the year of a terrible cholera outbreak which left many children orphans. In 1836 (one year before Charles Dickens published *Oliver Twist*), Müller opened his first orphan-house. He did so not only to help the needy, but also to demonstrate that God could be trusted to provide. He wrote, 'Now, if I, a poor man, simply by prayer and faith, obtained, *without asking any individual* the means for establishing and carrying on an Orphan-House: there would be something which with the Lord's blessing, might be instrumental in

---

[1] Roger Steer, *George Müller: Delighted in God*, London: Hodder and Stoughton, 1975

strengthening the faith of the children of God, besides being a testimony to the consciences of the unconverted of the reality of the things of God' (emphasis in original). Müller eventually built five huge Orphan Houses on Ashley Down, housing two thousand orphans. Over a period of sixty years, he cared for tens of thousands of orphans – without begging, borrowing or stealing the money to do so. Instead, he simply looked to God in childlike faith and prayer for the support of these children.

It was not only the story of George Müller's faith that left an impression on me. Some of his writings also had a great effect upon me, particularly Müller's description of how, as a young Christian, he started to study the Bible. In his autobiography he wrote:

'I fell into the snare into which so many young believers fall – the reading of religious books in preference to the Scriptures. I could no longer read French and German novels as I had formerly done to feed my carnal mind; but still I did not put in the place of those books the best of all books. I read tracts, missionary papers, sermons, and biographies of godly persons. The last kind of books I found more profitable than the others, and had they been well selected, or had I not read too much of them, or had any of them served to endear the Scriptures to me, they might have done me much good. I had never been in the habit of reading the Holy Scriptures'.

'Now the scriptural way of reasoning would have been: God Himself has condescended to become an author, and I am ignorant about that precious Book, which His Holy Spirit has caused to be written by His servants, and it contains that which I ought to know to lead me to true happiness; therefore I ought to read this precious Book most earnestly, most prayerfully, and with much meditation; and in this I ought to continue all the days of my life . . .'

'But instead of acting thus, for the first four years of my divine life, I preferred the works of uninspired men to the oracles of the living God. In consequence I remained a baby, both in knowledge and in grace'.

'All true knowledge must be derived by the Spirit from the Word. And as I neglected the Word, I was for nearly four years so ignorant that I did not clearly know even the fundamental points of our holy faith. And this lack of knowledge most sadly kept me back from walking steadily in the ways of God. . . .'

'When it pleased the Lord in August 1829 to bring me really to the Scriptures, my life and walk became very different. And though even since that I have very much fallen short of what I might and ought to be, I have been enabled to live much nearer to Him than before. . . .'

'When we read the Scriptures, it is of the greatest importance to meditate on what we read. . . . Learned commentaries I have found to store the head with many notions, and often also with the truth of God; but when the Spirit teaches, through the instrumentality of prayer and meditation, the heart is affected. The former kind of knowledge generally puffs up, and is often renounced when another commentary gives a different opinion, and often also is found to be good for nothing when it is put into practice. The latter kind of knowledge generally humbles, gives joy, leads us nearer to God, and thus having entered into the heart and become our own, is also generally carried out. . . .'

'The Holy Spirit alone can teach us about our state by nature, show us the need of the Saviour, enable us to believe in Christ, explain to us the Scriptures, and help us in our preaching. It was my beginning to understand this latter point in particular, which had a great effect on me; for the Lord enabled me to put it to the test of experience, by laying aside commentaries, and almost every other book, and simply reading the Word of God and studying it'.

'The result of this was that the first evening I shut myself into my room to give myself to prayer and meditation over the Scriptures, I learned more in a few hours that I had done during a period of several months previously. But the particular difference was that I received real strength for my soul in doing so'[2].

...

As we saw in an earlier chapter, because the Bible is the inspired Word of God, it is living and speaks to us powerfully (Heb. 4:12). However, there are some people who object that, instead of being living and powerful, the Bible seems dry, boring, and difficult to understand.

Christian Smith, an American sociologist and convert to Catholicism, argues in his 2011 book *The Bible Made Impossible*[3] that evangelicalism is awash with what he calls Pervasive Interpretive

---

[2] George Müller, *A Narrative of Some of the Lord's Dealings with George Müller*, Vol. 1, London: J. Nisbet, 1869, entries from 1827-29

[3] Christian Smith, *The Bible Made Impossible: Why Biblicism is Not a Truly Evangelical Reading of Scripture*, Grand Rapids, MI: Brazos Press, 2011

Pluralism. Instead of looking at the Bible and being able to agree on what it teaches, evangelicals have divergent interpretations on virtually every subject, with books like Four Views on the Atonement or Five Views on Church Government (or Baptism or Women's Ministry). He writes, 'If Scripture is as authoritative and clear on essentials as biblicists say it is, then why can't the Christian church . . . get it together and stay together, theologically and ecclesiologically?' (p175). Smith denies that we can open up the Bible and expect it to be clear and understandable.

In practical terms, the claim that the Bible is unclear, confusing or impossible to understand undermines the claim that it is really the Word of God. Millard Erickson asks, 'Of what value is it for us to have an infallible, inerrant revelation from God, if we do not have an inerrant understanding of it?'[4] The effect of a Bible that is difficult, or impossible, to understand is to discourage people from reading it, but reading is exactly what we should do if the Bible really is the Word of God.

Is the 'Clarity of Scripture' true?

The clarity of Scripture was a doctrine formulated at the time of the Reformation as a reaction to the abuses of the medieval Roman Catholic Church, specifically the refusal of the Roman Catholic Church to allow ordinary people to read the Bible for themselves in their own language. Because certain official Roman Catholic doctrines contradicted the plain teaching of Scripture (e.g. selling forgiveness of sins for money), the Reformers taught not only that Scripture is our final authority (as opposed to Church tradition), but alongside this they also taught that Scripture's meaning is plain and clear for all believers. The Reformation resulted in the Bible being translated into many languages for the ordinary person to read, starting with Luther's German translation of the New Testament in 1522.

The clarity of Scripture means that we do not need to be especially intelligent people to understand the Bible, nor do we need an authoritative Church to tell us what the Bible means, nor do we need an accredited theological education, nor do we need a special class of interpreters of Scripture (like priests or professors). Instead, all people in every culture may understand Scripture[5].

---

[4] Millard J. Erickson, *Christian Theology*, Grand Rapids, MI: Baker Academic, 1998, p272

[5] Another term for the Clarity of Scripture is the Perspicuity of Scripture, an expression whose obscurity is somewhat self-defeating.

But the Bible is Dry, Boring and Difficult to Understand!

Arguments For the Clarity of Scripture

Throughout the Bible, we are encouraged to read the Scriptures, implying that we can understand them. In the Old Testament, fathers and mothers were told to teach the Bible to children (Deut. 4:9, 6:6-7, 11:18-21), which implies that children could understand it, and that ordinary parents could explain it. Psalm 1:2 promises us of the blessedness of the person whose 'delight is in the law of the LORD, and in His law he meditates day and night'. In the Gospels, Christ reproached the Jews with words like 'Have you never read in the Scriptures?' (Matt. 21:42), implying that everyone should read the Bible. In the book of Acts, the Bereans in Acts 17:11 were commended as 'more noble' than others who rejected the Gospel, because they 'searched the Scriptures daily to find out whether these things were so'. The epistles were written to congregations of ordinary Christians, to whom Paul instructed these letters to be read aloud. 2 Tim. 3:15 speaks about the 'Holy Scriptures, which are able to make you wise for salvation through faith which is in Christ Jesus'. Similarly, in the last book of the Bible, Revelation, we are assured of a blessing if we read it (Rev. 1:3).

It is undeniable, then, that the Bible encourages all people to read it and promises to bless us if we do so. Much of the Bible is composed of easy-to-read material – stories like Moses, Joseph, Joshua, David, Daniel, Jesus and the book of Acts. A friend of mine once said, 'God is not so stupid to have communicated in such a way that only the intelligent can understand'.

Arguments Against the Clarity of Scripture

The problem with the doctrine of the clarity of Scripture is that there are many things in Scripture that are difficult, and there are some things that are very difficult to understand. Peter could write about Paul's letters, 'in which are some things hard to understand' (2 Pet. 3:16), while Paul himself could write in 1 Corinthians 8:3, 'if anyone thinks that he knows anything, he knows nothing yet as he ought to know'. The disciples failed to understand what the Lord was talking about on many occasions (Matt. 16:11, Mark 4:13, Luke 9:45, etc.).

When I was a boy, I remember my Mum reading to us children from Paul's letter to the Philippians. I was quite familiar with the stories from the gospels and the Old Testament, and thought I knew the Bible very well, but when I heard the book of Philippians, my reaction was, 'Why did God put *that* in the Bible?' I could not understand what it was saying, and was genuinely puzzled why God had put something so confusing in His Word. The book of Philippians was not at all clear to me. Nor is it just children who find parts of the Bible unclear. The book of Revelation contains many things that are difficult to understand; what does the number 666 refer to (Rev. 13:16), or what are the seven heads on the scarlet beast (Rev. 17:3)? Many people have suggested different ideas, but nobody knows for certain which is correct.

There are things in the Bible that human intellect cannot fathom – the Trinity, or the fact that God is without beginning, or how to balance God's sovereignty and human freedom. The Bible does not try to explain these mysteries. There are also things that we cannot know – like the day or hour of Christ's return. Even the parts of the Bible that make for relatively straightforward reading (like the 44% of the Bible that is narrative), while not presenting many difficulties in understanding, nevertheless prompt questions, in that we are often not sure of why a particular event is recorded in the Bible or what it is meant to teach us.

Roman Catholic Objections

The Roman Catholic Church rejected the idea of ordinary people reading the Bible, and pointed to the variety of different beliefs held by Protestant sects as proof that Scripture is not clear. The English poet Dryden (who later became a Catholic) wrote:

> *The book thus put in every vulgar hand,*
> *Which each presumed he best could understand,*
> *The common rule was made the common prey*
> *And at the mercy of the rabble lay.*
> (Religio Laici, or A Layman's Faith, 1682)

One day in a second-hand bookstore, I read through the preface to the Jerusalem Bible, a modern Roman Catholic translation, which observed that the modern availability of the Bible has not diminished disagreement over what it means. The Roman Catholic priest John O'Brien, in *The Faith of Millions*, writes, 'the Bible is not a clear and intelligible guide to all. There are many passages in the Bible which are difficult and obscure, not only to the ordinary person, but to the highly trained scholar as well. St. Peter himself tells us that in the epistles of St. Paul there are "certain things hard to be understood, which the unlearned and the unstable wrest, as they do also the other Scriptures, to their own destruction". . . . The simple fact is that the Bible, like all dead letters, calls for a living interpreter. . . . So the Catholic Church is the living, authoritative interpreter of the Bible'[6].

O'Brien is correct that there are difficult parts in the Bible, but he is wrong to call the Bible a 'dead letter', for it is the living Word of God, and he is even more wrong to call the Roman Catholic Church the living interpreter, for this is the Holy Spirit's role, as Christ taught in John 16:13, 'when He, the Spirit of truth has come, He will guide you into all truth'.

Catholics often quote 2 Peter 1:20 to prove that the Bible was not intended to be interpreted by individual Christians privately: 'no prophecy of Scripture is of any private interpretation'. However, ironically, the Roman Catholic interpretation of this verse is almost certainly wrong; the context shows that the verse is not talking about how people interpret Scripture, but rather the origin of Scripture as inspired by God.

Reformation Statements

Even some of the standard statements affirming the clarity of Scripture acknowledge that the Bible is difficult and insert many qualifications. Thus, the Westminster Confession of Faith says, 'All things in Scripture are not alike plain in themselves, nor alike clear unto all; yet those things which are necessary to be known, believed, and observed for salvation, are so clearly propounded, and opened in some place of Scripture or other, that not only the learned, but the unlearned, in a due use of the ordinary means, may attain unto a sufficient understanding of them' (WCF 1.7). Notice the qualifications:

(a) not everything in Scripture is clear in itself,
(b) nor is everything clear to all people, but
(c) only those things relating to salvation are clear, so that
(d) we may come to a sufficient (not perfect) understanding of them,
(e) if we make use of the ordinary means.

That seems like a lot of fine print to have to add to something that is supposed to be clear. The WCF does not state that everything in the Bible is clear; the qualifications tend to contradict the claim.

The Illumination of Scripture

Instead of speaking of the Clarity of Scripture, I think it is better to use a

---

[6] John O'Brien, *The Faith of Millions: The Credentials of the Catholic Religion*, Huntingdon, Indiana: Our Sunday Visitor, Inc., 1974, p135-138

more qualified and balanced term by speaking of the illumination of Scripture. The illumination of Scripture means that the Bible enlightens us. Rather than claiming that everything in the Bible is crystal clear or that we understand everything in it, we need to acknowledge that there are many things in the Bible that are difficult to understand, and that we are dependent upon God's illumination of Scripture for understanding. This was the great truth that George Müller taught me and encouraged me to put into practice.

> **Definition**: *The illumination of Scripture means that it is possible for us to understand God's Word through the teaching of the Holy Spirit, our meditation upon it, obedient observance of what it says, and interaction with other saints in the church.*

This truth was learned by Martin Luther in his great 'tower discovery' in 1514. Luther had been troubled by the expression, 'the righteousness of God' in Romans 1:17, which he thought referred to the way God must punish the wicked. He wrote about his discovery as follows: 'The concept of "God's righteousness" was repulsive to me, as I was accustomed to interpret it according to [the sense] in which God proves Himself righteous in that He punishes the sinner as an unrighteous person . . . until after days and nights of wrestling with the problem, God finally took pity on me, so that I was able to comprehend . . . "the righteousness of God" through which the righteous are saved by God's grace, namely, through faith; that the "righteousness of God" which is revealed through the Gospel was to be understood in a . . . sense in which God through mercy justifies man by faith, as it is written "the just shall live by faith". Now I felt exactly as though I had been born again, and I believed that I had entered Paradise through widely opened doors'[7].

Luther elsewhere wrote, 'If God does not open and explain Holy Writ, none else can understand it; it will remain a closed book, enveloped in darkness'[8]. 'Therefore the first duty is to begin with a prayer of such a nature that God in His great mercy may grant you the true understanding of His words'[9]. 'The Holy Spirit teaches man better than all books; He teaches him to understand the Scriptures better than he

---

[7] Martin Luther, *Werke*, Weimer Auflage, LIV, pp185, 187
[8] Martin Luther, *Works*, ed. J. Pelikan, XIII, p17
[9] Martin Luther, *Werke*, Weimer Auflage, XIII, p57

can understand from the teaching of any other'[10].

> **Biblical Basis**
>
> The Bible repeatedly assures us that we are dependent upon God the Holy Spirit for understanding of His Word. Thus, in the OT, we read the Psalmist praying, 'Open my eyes that I may see wondrous things from Your law' (Psalm 119:18). Later in the same psalm we read, 'Teach me, O LORD, the way of Your statutes, and I shall keep it to the end. Give me understanding, and I shall keep Your law; indeed, I shall observe it with my whole heart' (Psalm 119:33-34), and again, 'I have not departed from Your judgments, for You Yourself have taught me' (Psalm 119:102).
>
> When we come to the NT, Christ teaches us that any understanding of spiritual truth is dependent upon God's revelation: 'At that time Jesus answered and said, "I thank You, Father, Lord of heaven and earth, that You have hidden these things from the wise and prudent and have revealed them to babes. Even so, Father, for so it seemed good in Your sight. All things have been delivered to Me by My Father, and no one knows the Son except the Father. Nor does anyone know the Father except the Son, and the one to whom the Son wills to reveal Him"' (Matt. 11:25-27). Similarly, in John 6:45, Christ says, 'It is written in the prophets, 'And they shall all be taught by God'. Therefore everyone who has heard and learned from the Father comes to Me'.
>
> In 1 Corinthians 2:14, we learn that 'the natural man does not receive the things of the Spirit of God, for they are foolishness to him; nor can he know them, because they are spiritually discerned'. Similarly, verses 6-9 teach that unspiritual people and the wise of this world cannot receive the truths of God's Word: 'However, we speak wisdom among those who are mature, yet not the wisdom of this age, nor of the rulers of this age, who are coming to nothing. But we speak the wisdom of God in a mystery, the hidden wisdom which God ordained before the ages for our glory, which none of the rulers of this age knew; for had they known, they would not have crucified the Lord of glory. But as it is written: "Eye has not seen, nor ear heard, nor have entered into the heart of man the things which God has prepared for those who love Him"'. But verse 10 tells us that the Spirit of God is our teacher: 'But God has revealed them to us through His Spirit. For the Spirit searches all things, yes, the deep things of God' (1 Cor. 2:10).

---

[10] Martin Luther, *Works*, ed. J. N. Lenker, XII, pp16, 17

> 2 Timothy 2:7 says, 'Consider what I say, and may the Lord give you understanding in all things'. Similarly, 1 John 2:27 says about the Holy Spirit, 'But the anointing which you have received from Him abides in you, and you do not need that anyone teach you; but as the same anointing teaches you concerning all things, and is true, and is not a lie, and just as it has taught you, you will abide in Him' (see also 1 John 2:20). Thus, the Holy Spirit is our teacher, and without spiritual illumination, it is impossible to receive scriptural truth.

Qualifications and Explanations

The Bible promises us that God's Spirit will teach us and guide us into all truth. However, the Bible also adds some qualifications that we need to take note of.

1. There is a *moral element* to understanding Scripture. We must be willing to obey Scripture to properly understand it. In John 7:17, Jesus said, 'If anyone wills to do His will, he shall know concerning the doctrine, whether it is from God, or whether I speak on My own authority'. Psalm 111:10 says something which at first seems strange: 'The fear of the LORD is the beginning of wisdom; a good understanding have all those who do His commandments'. Whereas we sometimes postpone obedience until we have understanding, this verse says that 'all those who do His commandments' will have 'good understanding'. John Robinson sent off the Pilgrim Fathers to America in 1620 with the words, 'I am verily persuaded the Lord hath more truth and light yet to break forth from His holy word'. However, if we do not act on the light that God has given us, why should God give us more?

2. There is an *intellectual element* to understanding Scripture. We must meditate on God's Word, studying it patiently and carefully, prayerfully and regularly. Cursory reading is not enough. Joshua 1:8 says, 'This Book of the Law shall not depart from your mouth, but you shall meditate in it day and night, that you may observe to do according to all that is written in it. For then you will make your way prosperous, and then you will have good success'. Psalm 1:2 likewise says about the 'blessed man' that 'his delight is in the law of the LORD, and in His law he meditates day and night'. C. H. Spurgeon said, 'Some passages of Scripture lie clear before us – blessed shallows in which the lambs may wade; but there

> *Open my eyes that I may see wondrous things from Your law*
> Psalm 119:18

are deeps in which our mind might rather drown herself than swim with pleasure, if she came there without caution. There are texts of Scripture which are made and constructed on purpose to make us think. By this means, among others, our heavenly Father would educate us for heaven – by making us think our way into divine mysteries. Hence He puts the word in a somewhat involved form to compel us to meditate upon it before we reach the sweetness of it'[11].

3. There is a *progressive element* to understanding Scripture. There is milk for spiritual babes, as well as meat for the spiritually mature (1 Cor. 3:2). Augustine wrote: 'The Bible was composed in such a way that as beginners mature, its meaning grows with them'. We will not understand everything in the Bible all at once, let alone the hardest things first, but rather only gradually as we grow.

4. There is a *transformational element* to understanding Scripture. The purpose of reading the Bible is not to make us walking encyclopedias of Bible knowledge (although neither should knowledge of God's Word be despised). Instead, the Holy Spirit's purpose is primarily to transform us into the likeness of Christ. 2 Corinthians 3:18 says that 'we all, with unveiled face, beholding as in a mirror the glory of the Lord, are being transformed into the same image from glory to glory, just as by the Spirit of the Lord'. Romans 8:29 says, 'For whom He foreknew, He also predestined to be conformed to the image of His Son, that He might be the firstborn among many brethren'. Romans 12:2 says, 'do not be conformed to this world, but be transformed by the renewing of your mind, that you may prove what is that good and acceptable and perfect will of God'.

5. There is a *communal element* to understanding Scripture. God has placed us in the Church so that we 'all come to the unity of the faith . . . [by] . . . speaking the truth in love' (Ephesians 4:13-15). As 'iron sharpens iron' (Proverbs 27:17), so too Christians can help each other grow in our understanding of God's truth. By contrast, 'A man who isolates himself seeks his own desire; he rages against all wise judgment' (Proverbs 18:1). The illumination of Scripture does not mean that the Christian has no need of teachers in the Church. Instead, we need each other to grow in understanding. The communal aspect of illumination means that we need a good measure of humility when we find that other people have a different

---

[11] from a sermon, *How to Read the Bible*

idea to us about some passage of Scripture. We need to be prepared to listen to them and try to learn from their understanding.
6. There is an *element of faith* in following Christ, which involves trusting Him even though we do not know everything. The Bible does not tell us everything about God or salvation or the Christian life, nor was it intended to. Reading the Bible will not lead to us knowing everything. Instead, we 'walk by faith' (2 Cor. 5:7), and this faith involves trusting God about those things which we do not know or cannot understand.
7. There is a *need for humility* in approaching Scripture and in our interactions with other Christians about what Scripture means. The Bible does not promise us that Christians will always agree on everything, and there are issues over which Christians will have different opinions. It is quite possible that (a) we might be wrong about some idea we have, (b) even if we are right, we can still learn from other Christians who hold a different idea, or (c) we might be able to help them grow in understanding. In all three cases, we are wisest to adopt a humble attitude that is prepared to listen to other Christians.

Why do People Differ in their Understanding of Scripture?

There are many reasons why different people understand the Bible to mean different things. One major problem is that many people do not study the Bible very much. Another problem is that some people are not truly born again, and so are unable to understand Scripture, because 'the natural man does not receive the things of the Spirit of God, for they are foolishness to him, nor can he know them, because they are spiritually discerned' (1 Cor. 2:14). Yet again, others misunderstand the Bible because they have poor principles of interpretation (we will look at this subject in the next chapter). Differing interpretations of Scripture often also result from the biases, prejudices and presuppositions that we bring to the reading of the text. In other words, we misunderstand Scripture because human sin has warped our ability to understand divine truths. God's truth is often the very opposite of the way sinful human beings think, as God says: 'For My thoughts are not your thoughts, nor are your ways My ways, says the LORD. For as the heavens are higher than the earth, so are My ways higher than your ways, and My thoughts than your thoughts' (Isa. 55:8-9). We sometimes refuse to hear what Scripture is teaching because we tenaciously hold onto denominational or cultural traditions or because our authority source is something other than

Scripture (emotion, human reasoning).

Conclusion

The claim that the Bible is impossible to understand is not true. There is a false humility abroad that tells us that we are unable to be sure of anything we have learned from the Bible. Spurgeon mockingly wrote: 'You are not to be dogmatical in theology, brethren, it is wicked; but for scientific men it is the correct thing. You are never to assert anything very strongly; but scientists may boldly assert what they cannot prove, and may demand a faith far more credulous than any we possess'[12].

---

[12] C. H. Spurgeon, *Sword and Trowel*, 1877, p197

CHAPTER 8

That's Just Your Interpretation!

I once worked with a Roman Catholic who carefully avoided discussing anything to do with religion. Occasionally he might talk about a philosophical question, and once he asked me to pray for him, but he was very wary of talking about the Bible. I don't think he read the Bible very much. One day conversation turned to a subject that was related to the Bible, and I offered an opinion. His reply was dismissive: 'That's just your interpretation'.

On another occasion, as a schoolboy, I remember having a conversation with a school friend on a bus. We started discussing something related to religion, but as soon as I mentioned the Bible, his reply was equally contemptuous: 'You can make the Bible say black is white'. I think he was quoting a line he heard from a radio talk-show host. Actually, I have found a few ways to say that black is white without using the Bible (for example, I have met a few Mr. Blacks in my time who were all white), but I have not yet found a way to make the Bible say that black is white.

Nevertheless, we understand where these criticisms are coming from. People look at all the different Christian denominations, and assume they must all be teaching very different things, and they wonder how Christianity could be the true religion when so many people hold different opinions on the same subject. Or they get the impression that Christians are able to twist the Bible to make it say what they want it to. In their eyes, the numerous interpretations of the Bible tend to discredit Christianity altogether.

In the same way, however, that alternative political views jostle for attention, without leading us to conclude that all politics is thereby false, so the fact that people hold different interpretations on the Bible only shows that we need to think carefully about it. In a strange way, the many different interpretations of the Bible show that the Bible really is the Word of God, for the intensity of the spiritual war fought over the Bible goes beyond the normal levels of philosophical discussion.

This chapter is, in one way, a continuation of the subject we looked at in the last chapter. However, while in the last chapter we focused on the divine side of understanding Scripture – the Holy Spirit's illumination – here we are going to look at the same subject from the human standpoint, and think about how we actually go about correctly interpreting Scripture.

The Interpretation of Scripture

Not only are we dependent upon the Holy Spirit to illuminate Scripture, but we must also meditate upon the Bible. The Holy Spirit teaches us from Scripture as we think upon what it says; He will not teach us from Scripture if we never open a Bible and read it. We thus need to read the Bible intelligently as well as spiritually, using our mind to think about what the Bible is saying. In what follows, we will give a very brief and simple introduction to the practical steps we need to take to correctly interpret Scripture, observing four (or five) important principles that will help us to arrive at the right meaning of God's Word.

1. Text

Text refers to the actual wording of Scripture. The first principle of interpretation is simple: What does Scripture say? We must carefully observe what is right in front of us. This might seem obvious, but it is amazing how many times people break this rule, by reading things into the Bible that are not there, by not reading the Bible carefully, or by misunderstanding the meaning of words.

When I was a young Christian I sometimes heard 2 Timothy 2:15 quoted to encourage people to study the Bible. 2 Timothy 2:15 says, 'Study to shew thyself approved unto God, a workman that needeth not to be ashamed, rightly dividing the word of truth' (KJV). Later, however, I discovered that the Greek word translated 'study' in the KJV here does not mean 'study' in the way we use the word 'study' today. Instead, the Greek word *spoudazo* used here means to be 'diligent, eager, or zealous'. This is why most other translations read something like 'be diligent' (NKJ, NASB) or 'do your best' (NIV, ESV). So, this verse is saying that we should be diligent (*spoudazo*) and accurate ('rightly dividing') in our handling of Scripture ('the word of truth'). The point of this example is that the encouragement to study the Bible that I received, while well-meaning, leaned heavily on a misunderstanding of the meaning of the word 'study' in this verse.

We need to be careful, therefore, that we are accurately understanding the words the Bible uses. How can we determine the meaning of words that the Bible uses? Here are a few steps to take:

1. Check a few English translations for differences
2. Look up the meaning of the word in a Greek or Hebrew (not just an English!) dictionary, like *Vine's Expository Dictionary*.
3. Look up a concordance to see how a word is used in other verses
4. Determine the best meaning in context
5. If still stuck, look up some commentaries

Nowadays, we have many resources at our fingertips on the internet, or even on our phones. Some good websites for checking out the meanings of Bible words are www.biblehub.com or e-sword.net.

Here is a second example: Psalm 34:15 says, 'The eyes of the LORD are on the righteous and His ears are open to their cry'. Mormons believe that God was once a human being, who has now been exalted to Godhood, and that He has a body of flesh, including eyes and ears. They point to verses like Psalm 34:15 as proof that the Bible teaches that God has a physical body. However, if this were so, what do we make of verses like Psalm 91:4 which says, 'He shall cover you with His feathers, and under His wings you shall take refuge'? This verse mentions God's 'feathers' and 'wings', but it is obviously using a figure of speech – God is not a bird. Elsewhere in the Bible, we are told that 'God is not a man' (Num. 23:19), that 'God is a Spirit' (John 4:24). References to God's ears and eyes are figures of speech, just like God's feathers and wings.

While some people read figures of speech in the Bible literally, some people do the opposite – they spiritualize things in the Bible. Augustine suggested that Noah's Ark was meant to teach us about Christ: it was made of wood, just like Christ's cross, the door in its side represented Christ's side pierced by a spear, and the dimensions in length, breadth and height represent and foretell the dimensions of Christ's body. Augustine was less sure about what the three levels of the Ark represented: the three levels of Noah's Ark represented the three graces (faith, hope and charity) or the three harvests of the gospel, thirty-fold, sixty-fold and an hundred-fold. Or, for the most interesting interpretation, Augustine suggested that the ground floor represented marriage, the middle level represented chaste widowhood and the uppermost story represented celibacy (obviously the ideal state!). The idea that the three levels of the Ark were meant to teach us about different marital statuses is plainly ridiculous, as are Augustine's other alternative spiritualizing suggestions. What do the three levels of Noah's ark teach us today? That Noah's Ark was so large that it had three levels!

Richard Hooker, the Anglican theologian (1554-1600), wrote, 'I hold it for a most infallible rule in exposition of sacred Scripture that where a literal construction will stand, the farthest from the letter is commonly the worst. There is nothing more dangerous than this licentious and deluding art which changeth the meaning of words as alchemy doth or would do the substance of metals, making of anything what it listeth [i.e. wishes] and bringeth in the end all truth to nothing'[1].

2. Context

The second rule of interpretation is context. Context refers to what has been written before and after a verse or passage. This rule is important because the context will clarify and explain what is being said in a particular text. The Bible is not a string of pearls, a series of disconnected sayings. Observing the context will help prevent us taking a text in a way that was not originally intended by the author of Scripture. It will guard us against imposing our own personal, denominational or doctrinal biases upon a text. This is what heretics do, abusing Scripture by picking out and emphasizing one verse while ignoring what other passages teach. The danger of ignoring context has been summed up in the little saying: 'a text taken out of its context leaves us with a con'. It is possible, for example, to prove from the Bible that there is no God, if we rip the phrase 'there is no God' out of its context in Psalm 14:1. Muslims take John 14:16, 'I will pray the Father, and He will give you another comforter' to refer to Muhammed. However, the rest of the verse says 'that He may abide with you forever'. This verse cannot refer to Muhammed, but to the Holy Spirit, who is elsewhere in the context referred to as the Spirit of truth (John 14:17).

A second reason for the importance of context is that Scripture is its own interpreter. The Westminster Confession of Faith says, 'The infallible rule of interpretation of Scripture is the Scripture itself: and therefore, when there is a question about the true and full sense of any Scripture (which is not manifold, but one), it must be searched and

---

[1] Richard Hooker, *Laws of Ecclesiastical Polity*, V. lix. 2

known by other places that speak more clearly' (WCF 1:9). The fact that Scripture is its own interpreter means that we need to be regular and systematic in our reading of the Bible – reading through the entire Bible, book by book, not just reading isolated verses, or our favourite passages, or opening the Bible at random.

Context is also important because it will help us to be properly balanced in our understanding of Bible truths. Most heresies result from people refusing to accept the antitheses or paradoxes of Scripture, 'truths in tension', like the deity and humanity of Christ, the love of God and the wrath of God, or the fact that we are saved by faith not works, yet true faith is seen by its works. While Scripture balances these truths against each other, heretics try to resolve the difficulties by affirming certain verses in the Bible while ignoring other statements.

3. Genre

Although this principle of interpretation could be classified as another type of context (literary context), it is helpful to consider genre as a separate principle. Genre refers to the different types of literature we find in the Bible, which include narrative, discourse, poetry, proverbs, parables, letters, and apocalyptic literature. We have already seen, in an earlier chapter, that a historical narrative and a sermon are two different ways of communicating, and how they may emphasise different things even when looking at the same event.

Each of these different genres has different conventions that we need to be mindful of. For example, as we saw with God's eyes and ears in Psalm 34, poetry uses figures of speech, while proverbs are general principles (not iron laws or absolute promises). Thus, while 'evil pursues sinners, but to the righteous, good shall be repaid' (Prov. 13:21) or 'When a man's ways please the LORD, He makes even his enemies to be at peace with him' (Prov. 16:7) are true in a general way, they might not be true at any given moment. Most Christians are aware that Romans (a letter) is different to Revelation (apocalyptic literature), and that apocalyptic literature teaches by means of symbols. Thus, Daniel 7:8 says that 'in this horn, were eyes like the eyes of a man, and a mouth speaking pompous words'. A 'horn' symbolizes power, and a 'mouth speaking pompous words' symbolizes boastfulness. We do not take this verse to mean an animal's horn can see or speak; it speaks of the rise of a proud and powerful king.

4. Author's Intention

Probably the most important question we can ask when reading the Bible is, "what is the point of this passage?" or "why was this originally written?" Trying to discern the author's intention is an important principle because the book we are reading is God's Word; we want to hear what God is saying.

Instead of seeking to understand the author's original intention, we often come to the Bible with our own personal concerns and questions. Someone has said, 'By imposing our questions on a passage we may miss the questions it intended to raise'[2]. We need to make sure we do not just jump straight to the question of what a passage is saying *to me* without first of all asking what the author meant originally. If all we are interested in is practical application and 'what this means to me', then we reduce the Bible to a self-help manual or a feel-good fortune cookie.

Think about some well-known passages in 1 Corinthians. Why does Paul speak about spiritual gifts in chapter 12, or about love in chapter 13? We often hear chapter 13 read at weddings, or turn to chapter 12 when we want to discover our spiritual gifts, but why were these passages originally written? The church at Corinth had all sorts of divisions: by race, class, leadership, doctrinal opinions, and spiritual gifts. Paul's famous poem on love in chapter 13 is sandwiched between two chapters about spiritual gifts, and the point is that love has to be the motivation for using our spiritual gifts; they are to be used to help others, not for self-promotion. In chapter 12, Paul urges unity among the believers despite the fact they all have different gifts; some felt that because they didn't have certain gifts they weren't part of the body, but Paul teaches that we are all necessary. Both of these passages teach Christian unity, and while there are doubtless other points that Paul was trying to make and other lessons to be learned, it is crucially important that we learn this lesson before asking what else these passages teach.

There are many small Bible study groups where the study leader will ask what a verse means to one person, who will give an answer, and then the study leader will ask the same question of another person, who will give a completely different answer, and then the study leader will affirm both of these almost contradictory answers. The result is that small group Bible studies can produce a 'pooling of ignorance'. The point of Bible reading is not 'what this means to me', but 'what this means'. My opinion

---

[2] John Goldingay, "Expounding the New Testament", in *New Testament Interpretation*, ed. I. H. Marshall, Carlisle: Paternoster Press, 1992 reprint, p353

about, or reaction to, the Bible is not as important as what the author was trying to get across.

J. C. Ryle gave some good examples of preachers ignoring this principle in his little booklet called *Simplicity in Preaching*. He spoke of a man preaching on Isaiah 40:20, 'He that is so impoverished that he hath no oblation chooseth a tree that will not rot' (KJV). The preacher said: 'Here is a man by nature impoverished and undone. He has nothing to offer, in order to make satisfaction for his soul. And what ought he to do? He ought to choose a tree which cannot rot, even the cross of our Lord Jesus Christ'. However, if we look at the context, we would see that the passage is talking about someone chopping down a tree to make an idol. Isaiah's original intention was to warn against idolatry, not to point people to the cross of Christ. Ryle gave another example: 'On another occasion, being anxious to preach on the doctrine of indwelling sin, he chose his text out of the history of Joseph and his brethren, and gave out the words, "The old man of whom ye spoke, is he yet alive?" (Gen. 43:7)'. The lesson is obvious: before we try to apply a verse or passage of the Bible to ourselves we must first understand, and be faithful to, what the author intended to say to his original audience.

5. Application

While it is important that we don't jump straight to 'what is this passage saying to me', it is also important when we read the Bible that we do not simply leave it as dry, academic analysis of a text written thousands of years ago. The Bible is the living Word of God that speaks to us today. We need to hear and obey it. We need to ask what the Bible is saying to us today.

We must not think that the Bible is like a horoscope – each verse I randomly pick out gives a personalized prediction of my future happiness. Instead, to apply the Bible to ourselves, we must first of all make sure that have taken the preceding steps: reading the text carefully, allowing the context to clarify its meaning, and understanding the original author's intention. Having done all this, we want to see what lesson applies to our own lives. Is there a command to obey, or correction that I need to hear, or a good example to follow? Sometimes we struggle with the difficulties of life, and our responsibility is simply to trust what the Bible teaches, that 'all things work together for good to those who love God' (Rom. 8:28). In other chapters, even though we do not understand, our responsibility is simply to submit to what Scripture teaches (e.g. God's sovereignty in election in Romans 9).

Some parts of the Bible do not directly apply to us today due to the progressive revelation of Scripture – the fact that some truths and commands only applied at certain stages of history. Thus, we no longer offer animal sacrifices because they have been fulfilled in the work of Christ. We are no longer under certain dietary prohibitions because we are no longer under the Old Testament law. Nor is the preaching of the gospel restricted to Jews only (Matt. 10:5), for the Lord told His disciples to go into all nations and preach the gospel (Matt. 28:18-19).

Abuses of Interpretation

In addition to principles for correctly interpreting Scripture, we also need to beware of the interpretational tools and tricks that some people employ for twisting and abusing Scripture. We must stand up for the plain meaning of Scripture unless there are very good reasons not to, and we must resist attempts to argue that the Bible's hard truths are outdated. In the mid-1800s, Søren Kierkegaard, the Danish philosopher wrote: 'The matter is quite simple. The Bible is very easy to understand. But we Christians are a bunch of scheming swindlers. We pretend to be unable to understand it because we know very well that the minute we understand, we are obliged to act accordingly. Take any words in the New Testament and forget everything except pledging yourself to act accordingly. My God, you will say, if I do that my whole life will be ruined. How would I ever get on in the world? Herein lies the real place of Christian scholarship. Christian scholarship is the Church's prodigious invention to defend itself against the Bible, to ensure that we can continue to be good Christians without the Bible coming too close. Oh, priceless scholarship, what would we do without you? Dreadful it is to fall into the hands of the living God. Yes it is even dreadful to be alone with the New Testament'[3].

The problem is still with us; D. A. Carson, writing under the subheading of 'The Diminishing Authority of the Scriptures in the Churches', speaks of our 'exegetical and philosophical sophistication', the way we 'can by exegetical ingenuity get the Scriptures to say just about whatever we want – and this we thunder to the age as if it were a prophetic word, when it is little more than the message of the age bounced off Holy Scripture'[4]. The following are ten ways to abuse

---

[3] Søren Kierkegaard, *Provocations: Spiritual Writings of Søren Kierkegaard*, ed. Charles E. Moore, Farmington, PA: Plough, 2002, p201

[4] D. A. Carson, "Recent Developments in the Doctrine of Scripture", in

Scripture. Most involve clever-sounding half-truths that undermine the authority of the Bible in some area, or ignore its more radical and offensive parts. The result is not biblical Christianity, but a diluted, more comfortable and convenient Christianity of our own devising.

The 'Controlling Factor'

Some people try to play off one part of the Bible against another, arguing that one passage of Scripture controls (i.e. over-rides) what any other passage says. This is probably the most common way that people twist the Bible to suit themselves. It happens frequently in debates over controversial subjects like Arminianism versus Calvinism, or where two truths are balanced in Scripture, like Christ's deity and humanity.

Here are two examples from the debate over Christ's death. The British Baptist minister Steve Chalke argues against the idea of Penal Substitution (the idea that Christ bore the penalty for our sins on the cross); in fact, Chalke calls Penal Substitution 'cosmic child abuse'. He dismisses the entire sacrificial system in the Law of Moses as 'pagan' on the basis that the later prophets criticised Israel for offering sacrifices in the temple while hypocritically committing social evil in the streets: 'Yahweh's apparent appetite for continuous appeasement through blood sacrifice, present within some Pentateuchal texts, is to be understood in the light of the later prophetic writings as a reflection of the worship practices of the pagan cults of the nations that surrounded the people of Israel'[5]. The American New Testament scholar Scot McKnight also argues against Penal Substitution in his book *Jesus and his Death*. He suggests that it is doubtful that Jesus' words in Mark 10:45 about 'giving his life as a ransom for many' were really spoken by Jesus at all (he suggests Mark inserted his own ideas here)[6]. Using other 'genuine' words of Jesus in the Gospels, McKnight dismisses any 'notions of penal substitution and satisfaction' from the rest of the New Testament. However, we cannot just get rid of parts of the Bible we don't like. This is how to abuse Scripture, not properly interpret it.

Collected Writings on Scripture, Wheaton, IL: Crossway, 2013, pp107-8

[5] Steve Chalke, "The Redemption of the Cross", in *The Atonement Debate*, eds. Derek Tidball, David Hilborn and Justin Thacker, Grand Rapids, MI: Zondervan, 2008, p38

[6] Scot McKnight, *Jesus and His Death*, Waco: TX, Baylor University Press, 2005, p356

'Descriptive not Prescriptive'

A common slogan used today is that the New Testament is descriptive, not prescriptive. That is, the New Testament tells us the way things were done in apostolic times, but this does not mean that we have to do things the same way. There is some truth in this slogan: the book of Acts describes the foundational stage of the church. Paul was converted through a vision of Christ on the road to Damascus, but this is not meant to teach that all conversions have to happen the same way, nor do we need to cast lots to appoint new apostles (Acts 1). We do not have to meet every day (Acts 2), or have seven deacons in every church (Acts 6), although some new Christians are so keen they do meet every day, and some churches need seven deacons. However, while some things in Acts happened in many different ways (e.g. conversion), or were transitional, or foundational events never to be repeated, there are also many things in the book of Acts which are written to guide how we live as Christians. For example, we are to preach the gospel and to follow the early Christians' example in Acts 2:42 ('they continued steadfastly in the apostles' doctrine, and fellowship, in the breaking of bread, and in prayers'). Generally speaking, apostolic practice is apostolic precedent, because the apostles were given by Christ to be our authoritative guides in how to follow Him. The use of the 'descriptive not prescriptive' slogan is no longer limited to things in the book of Acts. For example, one of the most prescriptive passages in the New Testament is 1 Corinthians 14:26-40 where we have fifteen imperatives (commands) about the participatory nature of church gatherings – that is, the way church involves a variety of people using their spiritual gifts. But despite the apostolic commands (see particularly 1 Cor. 14:37), some even dismiss this passage as 'descriptive not prescriptive'[7]. Simplistic slogans used in this way subtly undermine the authority of Scripture.

"The New Testament does not provide a Unitary or Normative Pattern"

B. H. Streeter in his 1929 book, *The Primitive Church*, argued that there is no unitary picture of church organisation in the New Testament; some New Testament churches were charismatic (i.e. Spirit-prompted gifts were used) while others were presbyterian (i.e. elder-led). The obvious reply to this argument is, why cannot these churches have had both

---

[7] Basil Howlett, in the British Christian newspaper *Evangelicals Now*, April 2009, reviewing a book called *Biblical Church, A Challenge to Unscriptural Traditions and Practice*

features: the Spirit-led use of gifts under the shepherd-care of elders? In other words, these two features are not contradictory, but complementary. Once it has been argued that the Bible does not provide a clear picture of church life, we are left free to run affairs however we like. This is Millard Erickson's position in *Christian Theology*, where he argues that 'there is no prescriptive exposition of what the government of the church is to be like', and so 'we have little choice' but to 'build on . . . descriptive and narrative passages'. But here 'we find a second problem: there is no unitary pattern'. There is so much variation that we cannot discover an authoritative pattern. Lastly, 'even if it were clear that there is one exclusive pattern of organization in the New Testament, that pattern would not necessarily be normative for us today. It might merely be the pattern which was, not the pattern which must be'[8].

Modern evangelical scholars instinctively argue that the Bible is clear, sufficient and authoritative for establishing doctrines like salvation or the person of Christ, or practices like discipleship. The Bible is our go-to book, and it has the last word on such subjects. But it is a curious thing that when the subject turns to church, many turn around and argue that the Bible is neither authoritative nor adequate, and we must instead resort to pragmatism. Erickson works very hard elsewhere to synthesize a variety of sometimes seemingly paradoxical truths the Bible teaches about other areas of theology until he is able to present a coherent Christian doctrine, but with church government, he surrenders at the first sign of diversity, arguing the Bible is confused and presents no sure word from God. He argues that we cannot follow the Bible here because it is contradictory, but then admits he might not follow it even if it were clear. This suggests that it is not the Bible that is confused after all; perhaps the problem is rather an unwillingness to face up to and follow what it teaches. If the Bible is God's Word, given for our good, then it is indeed normative for us today, that is, authoritative over our lives. We should seek to obey it, not make sophisticated attempts at undermining its authority.

"Principles, not Patterns"
Once it is denied that there is any New Testament unity or definitive pattern, the claim is then made that we should follow 'principles'. While it is true that Scripture teaches us 'principles', there is a danger in

---

[8] Millard J. Erickson, *Christian Theology*, 2nd Ed., Grand Rapids, MI: Baker, 1998, pp 1094-5

elevating principles (which can sometimes be humanly-devised and contain flaws or half-truths) over the text of Scripture itself. A further problem arises if we cherry-pick certain principles which suit ourselves, while ignoring others that don't. We become the ones sitting in judgment on the Word of God, rather than the Word of God ruling us. This applies in all sorts of situations. For example, if we elevate the principle of 'love' to override what the Bible says about marriage, then homosexuality is alright as long as it is loving. But we do not have the right to pick and choose which 'principles' we want and which Bible passages to obey, ignoring those we don't like.

The Occasional (or Situational) Document Fallacy

Some scholars argue that because we only have fifty percent of the conversation preserved for us in New Testament letters (i.e. we only have Paul's words, not the questions that prompted them), we must reconstruct the situation behind the letter. Certain authors proceed to do this in highly imaginative ways that push a particular agenda. Thus, those who believe that women should be allowed to teach or lead in church argue there must have been some special circumstance that caused Paul to forbid women to teach or to be in authority in the church at Ephesus (1 Tim. 2:11-12). They suggest pagan high-priestesses occupying prominent social positions were influencing Christian women to teach in domineering ways, and that Paul was not forbidding women preaching *per se*, but just doing so in such a way that lords it over men[9]. It is argued that because Paul's words were occasioned by this 'special situation', they do not apply today, and women can indeed teach in church. However, this reconstruction reads things into the text to make it say the opposite of its plain meaning. Or, such commentators will dispose of problematic passages with words like 'We don't know what caused Paul to write this – there must have been some special circumstances that we know nothing about'. While it is true that the New Testament letters were 'situational documents', this is only half-right. They are also the timeless truth of God's Word, and were not just written for an ancient audience, but are authoritative over us still today.

---

[9] Linda Belleville, "Teaching and Usurping Authority: 1 Timothy 2:11-15", in *Discovering Biblical Equality*, eds. R. W. Pierce, R. M. Groothuis, Downers Grove, IL: IVP, 2005, pp207-223

Hermeneutical Consistency

Hermeneutical consistency is one of the most important principles in interpreting Scripture. 'Hermeneutics' means the art of interpretation, and hermeneutical consistency means to interpret the Bible consistently. For example, one of the favourite subjects of Jehovah's Witnesses is the 144,000 people mentioned in Revelation 7:1-8, who they believe were the first generation members of their cult. However, Revelation 7 says that the 144,000 are 'children of Israel' (Rev. 7:4), and then goes on to list the tribes they came from (verses 5-8). Hermeneutical consistency means the next time a Jehovah's Witness tells you about the 144,000, you can ask if they know which tribes their 144,000 members belonged to.

While we are on the subject of Israel in the Bible, here is J. C. Ryle on the inconsistency involved in another method of interpretation: 'We have got into a vicious habit of taking all the [Old Testament] promises spiritually, and all the denunciations and threats literally. The denunciations against Babylon and Nineveh, and Edom, and Tyre, and Egypt, and the rebellious Jews, we have been content to take literally and hand over to our neighbours. The blessings and promises of glory to Zion, Jerusalem, Jacob, and Israel, we have taken spiritually, and comfortably applied them to ourselves and the Church of Christ. Now I believe this to have been an unfair system of interpreting Scripture. I hold that the first and primary sense of every Old Testament promise as well as threat is the literal one, and that Jacob means Jacob, Jerusalem means Jerusalem, Zion means Zion and Israel means Israel, as much as Egypt means Egypt, and Babylon means Babylon. The primary sense, I believe, we have sadly lost sight of'[10].

For a modern example of this inconsistency, consider the following approach to reading Zechariah 12, replacing Israel with the church: 'In [Zechariah] chapter 12, we see the world opposing God's people. But God helps us to stand firm and ultimately He will give us victory . . . Zechariah 12 is being fulfilled today in the work of the church, as Christians proclaim the gospel of Jesus Christ to a hostile world, and in the church's experience of persecution'[11]. We are advised: 'Read the following quotes from Zechariah 12, where 'church' replaces 'Judah' or 'Jerusalem''. Thus, we should read verse 2 as, 'I am going to make the church a cup that sends all the surrounding nations reeling', or verse 8 as

---

[10] J. C. Ryle, *Prophecy*, Fearn: Christian Focus Publications, 1991, p24
[11] Tim Chester, *Zechariah: God's Big Plan for Struggling Christians*, The Good Book Company, 2005, pp40-41, 62

'On that day the Lord will shield those of the church, so that the feeblest among them will be like David'. So far, so good. But look what happens if we read verse 7 this way: 'The LORD will save the tents of *the church* first, so that the glory of *the church* and the glory of the inhabitants of *the church* shall not become greater than that of *the church*'. No wonder there is no attempt to offer commentary on this verse – it makes no sense.

Apocalyptic Abuse

We have already seen the value of understanding Bible 'genres' for interpretation. However, it is also possible to abuse 'genre' to undermine the Bible. Some scholars argue that certain passages of the Bible are 'apocalyptic' in order to advance a creative re-interpretation. For example, 1 Thessalonians 4:16-17 tells us how, at Christ's coming, 'we who are alive and remain shall be caught up together with them in the clouds to meet the Lord in the air. And thus we shall always be with the Lord'. Some try to treat this passage as 'clearly apocalyptic language' (despite 1 Thessalonians being an epistle, not apocalyptic literature) and argue that the 'clouds' are symbolic: 'cloud riding is a symbol of authority in apocalyptic literature'[12]. We are told that the verses are not meant to convey that we will actually be transported into the sky once we understand the symbolism involved: 'Paul's point is that when Christ's judgment falls on the earth believers will not be dangerously underneath it; instead they will be with the Judge on the "cloud". "In the air" just means at a safe distance from the judgment falling upon the world. There is no Rapture of the Church in Paul's teaching. The idea is a Christian myth'[13]. If it is the case, however, that 'clouds' in the Bible are just symbols used in apocalyptic literature, what shall we make of the cloud at Christ's ascension? Was the ascension a myth too?

In the same chapter of the book ("The rapture, Israel and other Christian myths"), the authors argue that Zechariah 14:3-4 do not teach that Christ will literally return and stand on the Mount of Olives, even though the verses themselves say, 'Then the LORD will go forth and fight against those nations, as He fights in the day of battle. And in that day His feet will stand on the Mount of Olives'. The authors state: 'It is said that Jesus the Judge will return to Jerusalem itself because Zechariah 14:4 prophesies, "On that day his feet will stand on the Mount of Olives,

---

[12] John Dickson and Greg Clarke, *666 and All That*, Sydney: Aquila Press, 2007, p42

[13] Ibid., p42

east of Jerusalem". *An apocalyptic scene is* interpreted as a preview of the historical event instead of *an imaginative way of saying* "he'll come home"'[14]. Even if we concede that Zechariah 14 is 'apocalyptic' literature (which is doubtful), why should we dismiss the idea that this passage teaches a literal return of Christ to the Mount of Olives? Pulling out the 'apocalyptic genre' trick allows us to dismiss anything in the Bible as simply 'an imaginative way' of speaking. Calvin in his commentary on Zechariah spiritualizes the entire passage to teach that God will deliver His Church (not Israel) from its persecutors, and that words that talk of God standing on the Mount of Olives are simply 'figurative expressions' picturing God as a military general supervising the victory of his Church. Despite the fact that the New Testament teaches that Christ is literally going to return, Calvin is reluctant to read this passage as relating to Christ because that would entail a return to a literal earthly Jerusalem.

'Out of Bounds' Bible Passages
Some who are happy to read the word 'Israel' to mean Israel in the Bible fall into a different error, and argue that the Lord's teachings in the Sermon on Mount (Matthew 5-7) and other chapters in Matthew do not apply to us today, because they are 'Jewish' and 'pure law', whereas we are under grace. Some would even argue that because the book of Acts represents a 'Jewish' transitional phase in the early church, only the prison epistles (Ephesians, Philippians, Colossians, etc.) apply to the Church today. However, all of the teachings in the NT epistles are developments of the Lord's teachings in the gospels (e.g. teachings on revenge or worry or forgiveness or prayer in the epistles come straight from the Lord's teachings in the gospels). If the disciple of Christ is not to follow Christ's own teachings, in what sense are we his followers? What is being done, again, is to rip pages out of the Bible. The opposite of this fault is to fail to understand (like the Seventh Day Adventists) the progressive nature of revelation, and the fact that we are no longer under law, thus continuing to observe Old Testament Jewish ceremonial, dietary and holiness rituals (like Sabbath-keeping).

The 'Big Picture'
While it is a good thing for us to understand the Bible's 'big picture' and get an overview of the Bible's entire storyline, it is also possible to promote one theme as the only way to understand the Bible. This

---

[14] Ibid, p45, emphasis added

'master-theme' is not only used to summarize the Bible, but can also be imposed as a straight-jacket upon every story or book. Common examples of such master-themes are 'the kingdom' or 'covenant' or 'blood sacrifice'. These themes are indeed biblical and it is helpful to trace the way they run through Scripture, but a problem arises when attempts are made to force every passage in the Bible into the one controlling theme. Rob Plummer gives a good example of the problem when he describes his four-year-old daughter's reaction to the story of Joshua and the battle of Jericho in *The Big Picture Story Bible*: "Where is the lady? Why did they leave out the lady?"[15] There was no mention of Rahab because the story of Jericho was made out to be all about the 'kingdom'. Trying to say that stories like Noah's Flood or the book of Ruth are about 'the kingdom'[16], or the Parable of the Good Samaritan is about 'covenant'[17] show the unconvincing lengths some will go. Another theme, perhaps the best of all, is 'Christ in all the Scriptures' (Luke 24:44, John 5:46). But it is not true that every chapter in the Bible is about Christ: Exodus 8 is about a plague of frogs, Isaiah 15 is about God's judgment upon Moab, and Psalm 119 is about God's Word. It is true that all roads lead to Christ in the Bible, but some take a roundabout route to get there. The truth is that there are many interwoven themes that we can trace through Scripture: sin, faith (read Hebrews 11), God's love, righteousness, the kingdom, judgment, Christ's sacrifice, etc. The problem with the 'big picture' approach is best explained using the oft-told story about a Sunday school child who, when asked what is grey, furry and lives in a tree, replied, "It sounds like a squirrel, but I know the answer to every question is 'Jesus'". Spending ten minutes in every sermon retelling the story of the Bible's 'big picture', or tracing a path to Christ from every chapter in David's life (by talking about the 'kingdom' theme) makes preaching repetitive and wearisome. The problem with the 'big picture' approach is that it can be a form of reductionism that shrinks everything down to one idea, robs us of the Bible's variety and multifaceted splendour, and is used to ignore or downplay important

---

[15] Robert L. Plummer, *40 Questions about Interpreting the Bible*, Grand Rapids, MI: Kregel, 2010, p153-4

[16] Graeme Goldsworthy, *Preaching the Whole Bible as Christian Scripture: the Application of Biblical Theology to Expository Preaching*, Leicester: IVP, 2000, p143-6

[17] Kim Huat Tan, "Community, Kingdom and Cross: Jesus' View of Covenant" in *The God of Covenant: Biblical, Theological and Contemporary Perspectives*, eds. Jamie A. Grant, Alistair I. Wilson, Leicester: Apollos, 2005, p129-39

themes which people do not like.

Postmodernism

Postmodernism 'denies and problematizes the existence of absolute truth and the ability of humans to know truth or to have objective historical knowledge'[18]. Just as different people see different things in a piece of modern art (or nothing at all!), so for postmodernists, there is no absolute truth or ultimate authority – there are only subjective opinions and individual perspectives. A postmodern attitude towards Scripture plays the Devil's advocate, delights in pointing out difficulties and problems, and probes for weaknesses in biblical positions. The best-selling and influential book, *How to Read the Bible for All Its Worth*, although not mentioning the term, is tinged with the cynicism typical of postmodernism. Early on, the authors attempt to show that even the apparently easy to interpret epistles are instead brimming with contradictions, difficulties and problems[19]. Thus, how can Paul's opinion (1 Cor. 7:25) be taken as God's Word, or how can we excommunicate someone nowadays (1 Cor. 5) if they can just walk down the street and go to another church, or what is the point of 1 Corinthians 12-14 if charismatic gifts are no longer valid, or how do Christians reconcile abstaining from alcohol with Paul telling Timothy to 'use a little wine for your stomach's sake' (1 Tim. 5:23), or how can men having their hair cut short be called 'natural' (1 Cor. 11:14)? The authors do not stop to answer these questions, most of which are not particularly difficult, but instead rush on, raising problem after problem, and poking fun at the inconsistencies of modern evangelical beliefs. By a process of 'deconstruction', postmodernism seeks to show that a 'text . . . contains irreconcilable and contradictory meanings', that 'its apparently solid ground is no rock but thin air' (J. H. Miller)[20]. Instead of approaching the Bible humbly, 'trembling at God's Word' (Isa. 66:2), our postmodern age prides itself on its lack of certainty and finds excuses to postpone obedience. Dogmatism is despised, indifference is counted sophisticated, and the result is Christians who 'stand for nothing and fall for anything'. In the words of the poet, 'The best lack all conviction, while the worst are full of passionate intensity'. Another way postmodernism manifests

---

[18] W. Randolph Tate, "Post-Modern Criticism", in *Interpreting the Bible, a Handbook of Terms and Methods*, Grand Rapids, MI: Baker, 2006

[19] Gordon D. Fee and Douglas Stuart, *How to Read the Bible for All Its Worth*, Grand Rapids, MI: Zondervan, 1993, pp45-77

[20] Wikipedia article on Postmodernism

itself is the attempt to avoid unpalatable truths by saying things like "We just don't know what this verse means". To say, "I don't know what this means" would be humble, but "We *just* don't know what this means" is an arrogant way to try to shut down conversation. Liberal theologians say the same about the resurrection: "Something happened, but we'll never know". Of course, there are passages which are difficult to interpret, but Scripture does not encourage us to be careless Christians or apathetic about understanding God's Word. We are to be people of conviction and action: 'let every man be fully convinced in his own mind' (Rom. 14:15).

Conclusion

Correctly understanding God's Word is not always easy. Neither is it as hard as some people today try to make it out to be. Thankfully, God has given us His Holy Spirit to be our Teacher and Guide. As we meditate upon His Word, He opens it up and illuminates its truth for us. If we obey the Bible, God promises to bless us.

CHAPTER 9

Didn't a Fourth Century Council decide which Books went into the Bible?

'The Bible did not arrive by fax from heaven . . . The Bible is the product of man, my dear. Not of God. The Bible did not magically fall from the clouds. Man created it as a historical record of tumultuous times, and it has evolved through countless translations, additions, and revisions. History has never had a definitive version of the book'[1].

'More than eighty gospels were considered for the New Testament, and yet only a relative few were chosen for inclusion – Matthew, Mark, Luke and John among them . . . The fundamental irony of Christianity! The Bible as we know it today was collated by the pagan Roman Emperor Constantine the Great'[2].

'From this sprang the most profound moment in Christian history . . . Constantine commissioned and financed a new Bible, which omitted those gospels that spoke of Christ's human traits and embellished those gospels that made him godlike. The other gospels were outlawed, gathered up, and burned'[3].

These are three quotes from *The Da Vinci Code*, the 2003 novel by Dan Brown which has (as of 2016) sold 80 million copies worldwide. Starting with the murder of curator Jacques Sauniere in the Louvre in Paris, it follows Robert Langdon, a Harvard 'symbologist', and Sophie Neveu, a

---

[1] Dan Brown, *The DaVinci Code*, Doubleday, 2003, p231
[2] ibid, p231
[3] ibid, p234

Didn't a Fourth Century Council Decide which Books went into the Bible?

French cryptologist, as they try to solve a number of clues while being chased by the police. These clues lead them to four amazing secrets hidden from the world for centuries:

1. Jesus married Mary Magdalene and had a child, who was the real Holy Grail, the sacred vessel, because it carried the bloodline of Christ. After Jesus' death, Mary and the child escaped to France.
2. The Roman Catholic Church covered up this history by destroying all the early gospels that told this story and instead promoted the idea that Jesus was divine.
3. The Kings of France were descended from the child of Jesus and Mary.
4. A secret society of historical figures such as Leonardo Da Vinci and Sir Isaac Newton faithfully passed on the true story of Jesus, waiting for the perfect moment to reveal it to the world.

While the last two 'secrets' might seem laughable to modern ears, most non-Christians today are willing to accept that the first two are perfectly possible, and that the entire edifice of Christianity is built upon ancient myths and the machinations of the Church.

Central to *The Da Vinci Code* is the claim that the Bible was 'forged' in the fourth century. Under the malevolent male chauvinist apostles and their successors, the Church tried to suppress the true story of Jesus by holding a council in the fourth Century in which they decided which books would be allowed in the Bible. Those that they approved made it into the Bible and those they disliked were burned. As one of the characters in the book puts it: 'Behold the greatest cover-up in human history'[4].

Now, of course, *The Da Vinci Code* is just a novel; no scholars take its historical claims seriously – despite the proclamation on the inside cover, 'FACT: . . . all descriptions of artwork, architecture, documents and secret rituals in this novel are accurate'. However, it is not simply works of fiction like *The Da Vinci Code* that promote the idea that there were actually many early gospels, only four of which were eventually included in the Bible.

The Jesus Seminar, a group of radical biblical scholars founded in 1985, used various coloured beads to vote on the authenticity of Jesus' sayings. They published their findings in *The Five Gospels* in 1993, based not only upon the four biblical gospels, but also upon the Gospel of

---

[4] ibid, p249

Thomas (discovered in 1945), a collection of 114 sayings attributed to Jesus, which they considered to provide equally reliable information about the life of Christ.

In 2006, making headlines around the world, the National Geographic Society held a press conference announcing the publication of the long-lost Gospel of Judas. National Geographic claimed that this gospel, which tells the story of Jesus' death from the point of view of Judas Iscariot, implies that 'Christ's betrayer was his truest disciple', the opposite of what the biblical gospels teach.

Again, in a special issue timed to coincide with Easter 2016, National Geographic published *The Story of Jesus*, in which it suggests that the Gospel of Peter, three fragments of which have been found since the 1880s, is based on even earlier evidence than the gospels of Matthew, Mark, Luke and John: 'Some [scholars] believe the Passion material [the story of Christ's death] in Mark is drawn from an older document, now lost, yet which may have survived in another Christian text, the so-called Gospel of Peter discovered in Egypt in 1886 . . . there is evidence the text enjoyed wide popularity in the first and second centuries. Of the 30 Gospel manuscripts uncovered since the 1880's, there is only one version of Mark but fragments of three separate copies of the Gospel of Peter'.

...

For some Christians, these issues are confusing and troubling. What are all these 'gospels', and where do they come from? Is there any truth to the idea that the church decided which books made it into the Bible? How can Christians really believe the Bible is the Word of God if a fourth Century Church Council of fallible men decided which books made it in and which did not?

The Canon of Scripture

In this chapter we will look at the issue of the canon of Scripture, the question of how we can know which books truly belong in the Bible.

> **Definition:** *The term 'canon' means the list or collection of books inspired by God and accepted as part of the Bible.*

The Greek word *kanon* means a 'standard' or 'rule' (from a Hebrew word *qaneh* meaning a 'measuring cane or reed'). When we speak of the canon of Scripture, we mean the list or collection of books which 'measured up' to the status of inspired, sacred Scripture.

Canonicity is an important issue – if we cannot determine which books belong in the Bible we will not be sure whether to believe or obey their words. The 'canon' presents a number of problems:

- The Roman Catholic Church and the Greek Orthodox Church accept additional books in between the Old and New Testaments which Jews and Protestants reject (these books, written in the 400 years before Christ, are called the Apocrypha).
- Some sceptical scholars suggest that other gospels besides our four gospels are equally worthy of admission to the New Testament (e.g. the Gospel of Thomas), and accuse the early Church of suppressing certain books so that they were not accepted in the New Testament canon.
- The Roman Catholic Church argues that, because the Church decided which books were to be included in the Bible at various synods and councils (Laodicea, AD 363, Hippo, AD 393, Carthage, AD 397), the Church is the ultimate authority for our faith, not the Bible.

These issues present a challenge to Christian faith. Because the Bible does not contain within itself an inspired table of contents, and because there was some uncertainty over the canonical status of some books at certain times in church history, we need to explain why we can put our trust in the Bible that we hold today.

Why We Can Trust the Canon of Scripture

The issue of how to distinguish divinely inspired books from merely man-made compositions is not nearly as hard as some people make it out to be. If God has inspired Scripture there will be a distinct difference between books that belong in the canon, and those that do not.

Let me illustrate. I have some Scottish friends who, in addition to being naturally proud of their national identity, occasionally say impolite things about the English. One of their milder comments involves something about 'the cream always rising to the top'.

The way whole milk separates into milk and cream if left to stand for a day presents us with a useful illustration to explain the issue of canonicity. There are three differences between cream and milk: a chemical difference (cream has a higher fat content), a physical difference (cream floats to the top) and a qualitative, subjective difference (milk and cream do not taste the same). But all three of these differences stem from the first, chemical difference. We could say that all these differences result from the different make-up of cream from milk.

Similarly, we would expect a divinely-inspired book to distinguish itself from an uninspired one in three ways. Firstly, inspired Scripture would be intrinsically different from any other human book because of its divine origin (its different 'chemical make-up'). Secondly, it should produce a different reaction in readers (a qualitative difference, the 'taste-test'). Christians believe that this is not simply a subjective, human reaction, but one in which the Holy Spirit is involved, as F. F. Bruce has written: 'the historic Christian belief is that the Holy Spirit, who controlled the writing of the individual books, also controlled their selection and collection'[5]. Lastly, given enough time, just like milk and cream, a clear line of separation should become evident between a list of inspired and uninspired books. Just like with milk and cream, all these contrasts result from the intrinsic difference[6].

There is, of course, a fourth difference between cream and milk: the label on a carton of cream in a shop, telling customers what it is. This distinguishes a carton of cream from a bottle of milk, which has its own different label. But nobody in their right mind would say that it is the label on the carton that *makes* cream different from milk. The idea that the labelling of certain books as canonical by fallible men somehow determined that these books were inspired is not true. The canon was just the final packaging of the product, the label on the wrapping paper.

It was ultimately God Himself who, by inspiration, determined which books should form part of the Bible. This resulted in these books becoming instant classics, or as we would say, 'runaway best-sellers', separated from other books by a gulf of class, credibility and popularity. Bruce Metzger used the analogy of 'survival of the fittest'[7] to describe the way the divinely-inspired writings outlasted and out-sold (if we may use a free-market economics illustration) those which were not. Canonicity is

---

[5] F. F. Bruce, *The New Testament Documents: Are they Reliable?*, Downers Grove, IL: Inter Varsity Press, 1987 reprint, p21

[6] These three differences correspond to three definitions of the canon: (1) the books inspired by God, (2) the books recognized as authoritative Scripture by the early Christians, and (3) the formal list of books a consensus emerged around. See Michael J. Kruger, *The Question of Canon: Challenging the status quo in the New Testament debate*, Nottingham: Apollos, 2013, pp27-46

[7] quoted in Lee Strobel, *The Case for Christ: a Journalist's Personal Investigation of the Evidence for Jesus*, Grand Rapids, MI: Zondervan, 1998, p67

not based on church authority, therefore, but on divine inspiration. To claim that certain books were accepted as canonical because of fourth-century church councils is to confuse cause and effect: divine inspiration was the cause, acceptance into the canon was the effect.

God's people had a secondary role in this process: they recognized these books as the Word of God. But this, again, was through the work of God's Spirit bearing witness in their hearts. This is not to say that any one individual's private opinion on the canon somehow carries the authority of the Holy Spirit. The Holy Spirit's work was church-wide, in the hearts of all Christians over many generations, so that over a period of time and through a process of interaction with Scripture and with each other, the views of Christians converged on the canon.

The inspired books were ultimately self-authenticating. They demonstrated the 'ring of genuineness' of the Word of God. Bruce Metzger said, 'The canon was not the result of a series of contests involving church politics. The canon is rather the separation that came about because of the intuitive insight of Christian believers. They could hear the voice of the Good Shepherd in the gospel of John; they could hear it only in a muffled and distorted way in the Gospel of Thomas, mixed in with a lot of other things. When the pronouncement was made about the canon, it merely ratified what the general sensitivity of the church had already determined. You see, the canon is a list of authoritative books more than it is an authoritative list of books. These documents didn't derive their authority from being selected; each one was authoritative before anyone gathered them together'[8]. F. F. Bruce writes, 'One thing must be emphatically stated. The New Testament books did not become authoritative for the Church because they were formally included in a canonical list; on the contrary, the Church included them in her canon because she already regarded them as Divinely inspired, recognizing their innate worth and generally apostolic authority, direct or indirect'[9]. Paul Wegner says something about the Old Testament canon that applies equally to the New: 'The books did not receive their authority because

> *The canon is a list of authoritative books more than it is an authoritative list of books.*
>
> B. M. Metzger

---

[8] Strobel, *The Case for Christ*, p69
[9] F. F. Bruce, *The New Testament Documents: Are They Reliable?*, Downers Grove, IL: Inter Varsity Press, 1987 reprint, p27

they were placed into the canon; they were recognized . . . as having divine authority and were therefore included in the canon'[10].

Therefore, arguments over the canon cannot finally be resolved by quoting various early Christian writers, documents or church councils which offered lists of canonical books because none of these authorities were infallible. Instead, there are deeper spiritual reasons for why we can trust the canon of Scripture. The validity of the biblical canon rests finally upon three pillars: God's inspiration, Christ's authentication, and the Holy Spirit's illumination.

We have already discussed the ultimate reason for the canon, God's work in inspiration. Because certain books were inspired by God, there must be a list of canonical books. But how do we know which books belong in the biblical canon? The decisive evidence comes from Christ Himself who authenticated the books of the Bible.

The Old Testament Canon

The Old Testament canon is where most of the 'canon controversy' centres. While Jews and Protestants accept 39 books (although the Jews have a different way of arranging and counting these books), the Roman Catholic and Eastern Orthodox churches accept other books. Paradoxically, however, it is in the Old Testament where the evidence for the canon is strongest.

The reason we can be certain about the limits of the Old Testament canon is that Christ confirmed it by speaking about the biblical martyrs 'from the blood of Abel to the blood of Zechariah' (Matt. 23:35, Luke 11:51). Abel was the first martyr killed (in Genesis) while Zechariah was the last martyr of the Old Testament killed in 2 Chronicles 24:21 (the Hebrew Bible has the books in a different order from our modern Bibles, and finishes with 2 Chronicles). Christ thus confirmed the precise limits of the Jewish canon of Scripture. Commenting on this, F. F. Bruce has written, 'No body of literature ever had its credentials confirmed by a higher authority'[11].

> *No body of literature ever had its credentials confirmed by a higher authority*
>
> F. F. Bruce

Christ repeatedly affirmed that the Old Testament books were

---

[10] Paul D. Wegner, *The Journey from Texts to Translations: The Origin and Development of the Bible*, Baker Books, 1999, p99

[11] F. F. Bruce, *The Books and the Parchments*, London: Marshall Pickering, 1991, p96

inspired by God, and thus implicitly confirmed that they were part of the canon of Scripture. He referred to the three-fold division of the Hebrew canon, 'the Law of Moses, and the Prophets, and the Psalms' (Luke 24:44). Christ quoted directly from the books of Genesis, Exodus, Leviticus, Deuteronomy, Psalms, Isaiah, Daniel, Hosea, Joel, Micah, Zechariah, and Malachi, as well as making allusions to Numbers, Job, Proverbs, Jeremiah, Ezekiel, Amos, Jonah and Zephaniah. While Christ quoted copiously from the Old Testament, He never quoted from the Apocrypha.

There are five additional reasons why we can be confident that the Apocrypha should not form part of the Biblical canon:

1. The Jews have never recognised the Apocrypha as a legitimate part of the canon. Josephus, the first-century AD Jewish historian wrote: 'our [divinely-inspired] books, those which are justly accredited, are but two and twenty and contain the record of all time'[12]. Josephus here counted twenty-two Old Testament books by combining the 12 minor prophets as one book, 1 and 2 Samuel as one, 1 and 2 Kings as one, 1 and 2 Chronicles as one, Ruth as part of Judges and Lamentations as part of Jeremiah. Intertestamental Jewish literature stated that the Holy Spirit departed from Israel with the deaths of Haggai, Zechariah and Malachi and that prophecy had ceased.

2. The books of the Apocrypha make no claim to be divinely inspired; in fact, some of them disclaim it.

3. The Apocrypha teaches things that contradict the New Testament: salvation by works (Tobit 12:9), purgatory (2 Macc. 12:41-45), and prayers for the dead (Baruch 3:4). The Apocrypha also contains chronological, historical and geographical mistakes and contradictions[13]. Some of the apocryphal books misleadingly claim to be the writings of earlier Biblical characters (Solomon, Ezra, Jeremiah, etc.); such deception disqualifies them from being divinely-inspired Scripture.

4. Early Christian writers largely rejected the Apocrypha. Thus, Origen (185-254 AD), an early church scholar, Athanasias, bishop of Alexandria (c. 296-373 AD) and Jerome (c. 345-420 AD), the pre-eminent scholar of the Roman church and translator of the Latin Vulgate, all held to the Hebrew Old Testament canon of twenty-two

---

[12] Josephus, *Contra Apion*, 1:37-39
[13] See a list of mistakes in the Apocrypha in Wegner, *The Journey from Texts to Translations*, p123

books that correspond with our thirty-nine books. It was not until Augustine (354-430 A.D) that a major Christian writer accepted the Apocryphal books, and this has been attributed by some to the fact that Augustine was not familiar with Hebrew and the Jewish Bible.
5. Even the Roman Catholic Church did not officially accept the Apocrypha as part of the canon until the Council of Trent in 1546 AD, called in response to the Reformation. This adoption was seemingly based upon the Apocrypha's support for some Catholic teachings, as well as being a reaction to Martin Luther's rejection of the Apocrypha. The Eastern Orthodox churches did not officially include the Apocrypha in their canon until 1692.

In addition to the Apocryphal books, there are also a number of other Jewish religious writings falsely claiming to have been written by biblical characters (called Pseudepigrapha, i.e. false-writings). These books were never considered canonical by either Jews or Christians, although the New Testament makes a number of allusions to them. Thus, 2 Timothy 3:8 may allude to the Assumption of Moses (Jannes and Jambres resisting Moses), Jude 9 may allude to the Assumption of Moses (Michael the archangel contending with the devil over the body of Moses), and Jude 14-15 quotes 1 Enoch 1:9 about the Lord coming to execute judgment upon the ungodly.

If these books are not divinely-inspired, why does the New Testament refer to them? The fact that the New Testament alludes to these books is no more proof that they are divinely-inspired than Paul's occasional quotations from pagan philosophers (Acts 17:28, Titus 1:12). Jude's letter warns against ungodly false teachers who had crept into the church (Jude 4), and he gives two examples that show that even the Pseudepigrapha teach reverence for authority (Jude 9), and the judgment of God that will come upon the ungodly (Jude 14-15). It appears that Jude was using well-known false-writings against the new false teachers, not to validate these spurious documents but to condemn the lifestyle of the false teachers even out of the mouths of forged pseudo-Scriptures.

The New Testament Canon
The ultimate authority for the canon of the New Testament is again our Lord Jesus Christ. Christ's authority is stamped on the New Testament canon in five ways:

Didn't a Fourth Century Council Decide which Books went into the Bible?

1. ***Christ's Coming Anticipated the Books of the New Testament.*** Christ's coming not only involved the arrival of someone far greater than the prophets, but also fulfilled their inspired prophetic Scriptures (Heb. 1:1-2). Therefore His coming virtually demanded the production of more Scripture, for if the history of Israel and the writings of the prophets were inspired, how much more important is the history of the Messiah which shows how the prophecies were fulfilled? Christ's coming was the culmination of the divine purposes and it is only natural that more Scripture would be inspired in addition to the Old Testament canon. Because the New Testament is essentially Christological, the New Testament is also canonical.

2. ***Christ Pre-Authenticated the Books of the New Testament.*** Christ predicted and added His authority to the production of more New Testament books which would permanently record His life and teachings. When Christ left His disciples, He promised the coming of the Holy Spirit, the Author of Scripture (Matt. 22:43, 2 Tim. 3:16, 2 Peter 1:21, etc), and in so doing promised the inspiration of more books of Scripture, in three ways:
    a. By causing the disciples to remember historical details ('He will ... bring to your remembrance all things that I said to you', John 14:26; 'He will glorify me', John 16:14)
    b. By instructing them in doctrinal truths ('He will teach you all things, John 14:26; 'He will guide you into all truth', John 16:13),
    c. By revealing to them future events ('He will tell you things to come', John 16:13)

    These correspond to the three divisions of the New Testament books: historical (Gospels), doctrinal (Epistles), and prophetical (Revelation). All three bodies of writing require ability of a supernatural order: perfect recall, revelation, and prediction. They require the inspiration of the Holy Spirit.

3. ***Christ Appointed Apostles as His Official Representatives.*** Christ not only personally conferred His authority upon the apostles by word ('As the Father has sent me, I also have sent you', John 20:21, Matt. 10:14-15, John 13:20, etc.), but also confirmed this apostolic authority through the miracles which the apostles did in Christ's name, as seen in the book of Acts. As a result, the apostles spoke (and wrote) in Christ's name and with His authority. Thus, Paul

said, 'the things which I write to you are the commandments of the Lord', (1 Cor. 14:37), and 'we command you, brethren, in the name of our Lord Jesus Christ', (2 Thess. 3:6). Similarly, Peter speaks of the need to be 'mindful of . . . the commandment of the Lord and Saviour through your apostles' (2 Pet. 3:2, ESV). Furthermore, the apostles commanded that their letters should be read in the churches (Col. 4:16, 1 Thess. 5:27) and that if some did not obey their letters, they were to be shunned (2 Thess. 3:14).

The New Testament writings of the apostles are the writings of Christ's officially authorised representatives. All of the books in the New Testament were either (a) written by apostles (Matthew[14], John, Peter, and Paul), or (b) written by close associates of the apostles under their oversight and with their apostolic sanction[15] (Mark was Peter's helper, Luke was Paul's), or (c) written by the Lord's brothers James and Jude, who possessed an authority nearly equal to the apostles (1 Cor. 9:4, Gal. 1:19, 2:9), being not only witnesses of Christ's entire life, but also the custodians of Mary and Joseph's witness about Christ's birth and early life. This last point is important in view of some non-canonical 'infancy gospels' which tell fairy tales about Jesus as a child.

---

[14] Although Matthew's Gospel is anonymous, the undivided testimony of early church writers attributed it to Matthew. For example, Origen (AD 185-254) wrote, 'The first gospel was written by Matthew, who was once a tax-collector, but who was afterward an apostle of Jesus Christ' (*Ecclesiastica Historia* 6.14.5).

[15] The Epistle to the Hebrews is anonymous, but notice that it was (a) written before the fall of Jerusalem in AD 70 (see, for example, how it uses the Greek present tense to describe the temple worship in Heb. 9:6, 7, 9, 25, 10:1), (b) written for the purpose of convincing Jewish believers that the OT temple worship, and the Law itself, have been replaced (see 7:5-12, 10:1-9), suggesting this was still a live issue, and the Temple still functioned, (c) written by multiple authors (see the notable 'we' passages, particularly Heb. 5:11, 6:9-11, 13:18), although also written by one main author (see Heb. 13:19-23) who was well-known to the readers, an outstanding theologian, a companion of Timothy (Heb. 13:23), and possibly a prisoner for the gospel's sake (see 10:34, 13:3, 18-19). The author thus lived in apostolic times, belonged to the apostolic circle, and the letter's doctrine and purpose were thoroughly Pauline, i.e. apostolic. Even if Paul himself was not the lead writer (for the style differs from Paul's writings), yet being written by an apostolic co-worker means it was probably written or promoted by apostolic approval.

4. **Christ's Apostles Accredited Inspired Books as Canonical.** The New Testament writings show evidence of apostolic promotion of inspired books, a process of canonical accreditation by the apostles which was already underway in the apostles' own lifetime. There were also attempts to carefully protect the apostolic canon from forgeries. Thus:

- Peter accredited Paul's letters as inspired Scripture by classing them alongside 'the rest of the Scriptures': 'as also our beloved brother Paul, according to the wisdom given to him, has written to you, as also in all his epistles, speaking in them of these things, in which are some things hard to understand, which untaught and unstable people twist to their own destruction, as they do also the rest of the Scriptures' (2 Pet. 3:15-16). By placing Paul's letters alongside the other divinely-inspired Scriptures, Peter is stating Paul's letters are also canonical.

- Paul accredited the inspiration of Luke's Gospel in 1 Timothy 5:18 when he quoted Luke 10:7 alongside Deuteronomy 25:4, calling both 'Scripture', and thus confirming Luke's Gospel as canonical. The fact that Luke is part of a two-volume work suggests that the second volume, Acts, is likewise inspired 'Scripture' and therefore canonical. Acts validates the claim of the apostles to be Christ's official representatives by the record of their preaching and their miracles in Christ's name. It also mirrors the trajectory of the Old Testament canon, in which historical records (e.g. Samuel, Kings) trace the development of God's acts following on from the foundation laid in the Law, providing a link with the later writings of the Prophets.

- Early church tradition describes the second Gospel as Peter's memoirs written by Mark in Rome at the very end of Peter's life[16]. Peter is probably referring to Mark's (forthcoming) Gospel in 2 Peter 1:15, where he says, 'Moreover, I will be careful to ensure that you always have a reminder of these things after my

---

[16] Thus Papias (in approx. AD 125) wrote, 'Mark, in his capacity as Peter's interpreter, wrote down accurately as many things as he recalled from memory—though not in an ordered form—of the things either said or done by the Lord' while Irenaeus who lived in the 2nd century, wrote, 'Matthew composed his gospel among the Hebrews in their own language, while Peter and Paul proclaimed the gospel in Rome and founded the community. After their departure, Mark, the disciple and interpreter of Peter, handed on his preaching to us in written form' (*Against Heresies* 3.1).

decease'. Notice that (a) Peter says that the time of his death is near (2 Pet. 1:14 – 'I must shortly put off my tent'), (b) Peter uses the future tense to write about an impending document, rather than using the past or present tense to refer to the current letter, (c) the context (vs 16-18, Peter's eyewitness testimony of Christ on the Mount of Transfiguration) shows that the subject matter Peter desires to permanently record concerns his testimony to the person and work of Christ, and (d) the way that Peter calls Mark *'my son'* and says that Mark is with Peter in 'Babylon' (1 Pet. 5:13), likely a veiled reference to Rome.

- The close similarity between 2 Peter 2 and Jude argues either that Peter is accrediting the message of Jude as inspired, authoritative and canonical by including it within his letter (just as Peter confirms Paul's writings), or that Jude has borrowed the message from Peter, thus accrediting 2 Peter as inspired and canonical, or that both are delivering (or borrowing) the same oracle, thus both mutually confirming the apostolic authority of the passage. We do not know which letter came first, but whichever way, their writings show the process of canonical accreditation in action, urging that 'the faith' has 'once for all been delivered to the saints' (Jude 3) and warning against false teachers trying to distort the Christian message.
- The apostles seemed to be alive to the danger of forged letters, and conscious of the need to protect believers from pseudo-apostolic writings (2 Thess. 2:2). Thus, Paul is careful to sign his letters personally (1 Cor. 16:21, Gal. 6:11, Col. 4:18, Phm 19, 2 Thess. 3:17). This speaks of a growing concern to protect an emerging canon of authoritative apostolic writings. Believers copying Paul's letters would be unable to reproduce Paul's personal signature, and so further anti-forgery measures would presumably require Paul authorising collections of legitimate letters. This would involve Paul making personal copies of own his letters and sending these copies out.
- Notice in 2 Peter 3:15-16 that Peter speaks of Paul's letters as a collection ('in *all* his epistles'), and that they were accessible not only to Peter but also to many other people (even 'unstable and untaught people'). This speaks of them being gathered together into a standard collection and published even in Peter's lifetime, i.e. a process of canonisation.

In response to the argument that the apostles did not leave behind a defined list of canonical Scriptures, it is clear from the above references that, while we do not have an inspired list of canonical books, Scripture itself shows us a process whereby the apostles promoted and accredited inspired writings which were thereby considered canonical. Virtually all of the New Testament books were written before AD 70 and were thus written with apostolic authority or verified by apostolic testimony.

5. ***Christ Completed the New Testament Canon.*** At the close of the Book of Revelation, John records Christ Himself saying that anyone who adds to the book of Revelation will endure its plagues, and anyone taking away from it will have his part taken away from the Book of Life and God's promised blessings (Rev. 22:18-19). Although this only refers to the Book of Revelation, the 'do not add or take away' formula is also found numerous times in Deuteronomy where it acted as a finish marker for the series of books making up the Law of Moses. The repetition of this formula in Revelation suggests likewise that the series of books making up the New Testament canon was closed. Two additional facts suggest the conclusion of the New Testament canon: (a) the subject matter of Revelation, concluding all Scripture by dealing with the end of all things, and (b) John the writer of Revelation being the last apostle and living link with Christ.

Apocryphal 'Gospels', 'Acts' and 'Letters'

We have fragments of over 30 non-canonical gospels, such as the Gospel of Thomas, the Gospel of Mary, the Gospel of Peter, and the Gospel of Judas. There are also other 'Acts', 'Epistles' and 'Apocalypses' (Revelations) named after various apostles, but we will focus here upon the apocryphal gospels, which present a somewhat different picture of Jesus. Although liberal Bible scholars champion some of these apocryphal gospels, the problems with these documents are:

a. These documents pretend to come from the real apostles in the first century, but there is far more evidence that they date from the second to fourth centuries. They are therefore not based on reliable eye-witness or apostolic testimony.

b. They contain legendary embellishments; e.g., the Gospel of Peter has a walking, talking cross coming out of the tomb after the resurrected Jesus, who Himself emerges supported by two angels whose height reaches to heaven.

c. They contain bizarre sayings, e.g. in the Gospel of Thomas, Jesus says that women are not worthy of eternal life unless they turn into males, and when the disciples ask when Christ will be revealed to them, He says 'when you disrobe and you are not ashamed nor afraid'. The Gospel of Thomas also has Jesus saying 'Lift the stone and there you will find me, split the wood and I am there'.
d. They lack historical realism; e.g. the Gospel of Peter has the Jewish authorities confessing their guilt to Pilate for putting Jesus to death and admitting that He was a righteous man. This shows a lack of familiarity with first-century Jewish hostility toward Christ.
e. They contain 'secret teachings' only revealed to special disciples; for example, the Gospel of Judas paints Judas as Jesus' most enlightened and greatest disciple, while the Gospel of Thomas presents Thomas as the favoured disciple whom Jesus secretly taught, and the Gospel of Mary presents Mary Magdalene as the favoured disciple who was taught things that the other disciples were not. Instead of a conspiracy by the early Church to suppress these writings, the real conspiracy theorists are the authors of these apocryphal gospels.
f. They draw much of their material from the canonical gospels, showing their dependence upon them. In other words, they are not primary sources about Christ's life, but secondary.
g. Some of the sensational claims made about these gospels go beyond the evidence. Thus, the claim that Jesus married Mary Magdalene is partly based on the very fragmentary and damaged Gospel of Philip which reads, 'And the companion of the [Saviour] is Mary Magdalene. [But Christ loved] her more than [all] the disciples [and used to] kiss her [often] on her [. . .]'. This line is speculatively reconstructed to read 'he used to kiss her often on her mouth'. However, this is pure conjecture – the document might have originally read 'hand', 'cheek', 'forehead', or 'mouth'; we do not know what it said.

In summary, the apocryphal gospels are 'legendary adaptations and expansions' of the canonical gospels (Rudolf Bultmann). Professor Philip Jenkins, speaking simply as a historian, says 'Reviewing suggestions for a potentially revised New Testament canon, we are repeatedly struck by just how weak are the claims of most of the candidates. . . . Contrary to recent claims, the more access we have to ancient "alternative gospels", the more we must respect the choices made by the early church in forming its canon'[17].

In their own strange way, even these apocryphal 'gospels', 'acts', and 'epistles' indirectly point to the truth of a settled canon, because (a) they borrow the same names as the apostles (Judas, Thomas, Peter, etc.), (b) they use the same writing categories (gospels, acts, etc.), (c) they depend on many of the historical facts in the canonical gospels (e.g. Jesus' death and resurrection) and (d) they borrow some of Jesus' sayings from the canonical gospels. This dependence upon apostolic names (and hence authority), canonical literary forms, historical details and sayings of Christ confirms that the canonical gospels were already accepted. Thus, the Gospel of Truth (written about AD 140) contains so many references to the canonical New Testament writings 'as to warrant the conclusion that in Rome at this period a New Testament was in existence that corresponded very closely with what we have today. Furthermore, what is utilized, whether from the Gospels, the Acts, the letters of Paul, Hebrews or the Revelation, is regarded as authoritative' (E. F. Harrison)[18].

Thus, the Church has not discarded 'one single work which after generations . . . have found cause to look back upon with any regret'[19]. In fact, we can go one step further and say that neither have we any reason to regret the inclusion of any of the books in our New Testament canon.

What about Church Councils?

Dan Brown claims in *The Da Vinci Code* that Constantine decided which books went into the New Testament when he convened a church council in Nicea in 325 AD. He also claims that at this council the church decided in favour of the divinity of Jesus: 'until that moment in history, Jesus was viewed by his followers as a mortal prophet . . . Jesus' establishment as the 'Son of God' was officially proposed and voted on by the Council of Nicea . . . a relatively close vote at that'[20]. In actual fact, the council of Nicea had nothing to do with deciding the canon of Scripture. It was called to deal with the heresy of Arianism, which denied that the Son was of the 'same substance' as the Father. Only two of the over three hundred bishops failed to sign the Nicene Creed which

---

[17] Philip Jenkins, *Hidden Gospels: How the Search for Jesus Lost its Way*, New York: Oxford University Press, 2001, pp105-6
[18] E. F. Harrison, *Introduction to the New Testament*, Grand Rapids, MI: Eerdmans, 1971, pp101-2
[19] W. Sanday, *Inspiration*, London: Longmans, Green and Co., 1893, p27-8
[20] Dan Brown, *The Da Vinci Code*, p233

affirmed the Son's equality with the Father. Constantine had nothing to do with deciding the canon of Scripture, neither did the Council of Nicea, and the 'vote' on Christ's Deity was hardly 'close'. So much for Christianity being the Big Lie – Dan Brown's book is a better contender for that title.

What of claims that the canon of Scripture was decided by a church council – some say the council of Hippo in 393 AD, or the council of Carthage in 397 AD? There is no more truth to this claim than the idea that a fourth-century council decided upon the deity of Christ. As in the case of the deity of Christ, the belief in the divine inspiration of certain books pre-dated any fourth-century council, and went right back to the earliest era of Christianity. The church councils that made declarations about the canon were remote (North African), local affairs of limited authority. They did not create the canon; all they did was restate what was already a 'fact on the ground'. They did not dictate a 'top down' decision the canon, but rather affirmed the already-existing position of the churches. F. F. Bruce says, 'The first ecclesiastical councils to classify the canonical books were both held in North Africa – at Hippo Regius in 393 and at Carthage in 397 – but what those councils did was not to impose something new upon the Christian communities but to codify what was already the general practice of those communities'[21]. B. F. Westcott, commenting on the various councils, wrote that the canon was 'fixed by usage rather than by law'[22]. Donald Guthrie echoes this view by saying, 'The content of the canon was determined by general usage, not authoritarian pronouncement'[23].

What about the Roman Catholic Claim?

The Roman Catholic Church argues that it gave us the Bible by settling the matter of the canon. John O'Brien writes, 'Far from being hostile to the Bible, the Catholic Church is its true mother. She determined which are the books of religion from the many writings circulated as inspired in the early Christian ages and assembled them all within the covers of a single book . . . Where did we get our Bible? Who assembled its various parts? Who determined which books were inspired by God and which were not? Who vouches for it as the inspired and authoritative word of

---

[21] F. F. Bruce, *The New Testament Documents: Are they Reliable?* p27
[22] B. F. Westcott, *A General Survey of the History of the Canon of the New Testament*, London: Macmillan and Co., 1896, p449
[23] Donald Guthrie, "Canon of Scripture", *The New International Dictionary of the Christian Church*, Rev. Ed. J. D. Douglas, Grand Rapids, MI: Zondervan, 1974

God? The answer to all these queries is: the Catholic Church . . . It was the Catholic Church which gathered up all these books, placed them within the covers of a single volume, and thus gave to the world what is known today as the Bible'[24].

However, the logic is flawed and the claim is false. The Church did not write the Bible, for the Bible was inspired by God – so that God gave us the Bible, not the Church. Nor can the Catholic Church claim to have given us the Bible by virtue of the fact that the Church agreed on the canon. This is as misguided as a scientist who claims he has 'given' the world gravity. Even if the scientist were to have discovered gravity, he would not claim that he gave it to the world. But even the Roman Catholic claim to have discovered the canon of Scripture is false. It is like a boxing match after which a referee announces the winner to a crowd which has just witnessed the loser being knocked out, leaving him lying flat on the mat. The crowd does not need a referee to tell them he has 'discovered' the winner. The church which had been reading the canonical New Testament books for 200 years hardly needed to be told that they were inspired, for the Holy Spirit, by His illumination of God's Word, had already confirmed in the hearts of countless thousands of ordinary Christians which were the inspired books.

Conclusion

Craig Evans, an expert on the extra-canonical Gnostic gospels, reviewing Dan Brown's *The Da Vinci Code* claims writes, 'Most of these assertions are either false or grossly misleading, as all trained historians know. Constantine apparently did commission the production of 50 copies of Scripture (as Christian historian Eusebius reports), but he did not decide which Gospels to include and which to omit. Furthermore, the claim that the Dead Sea Scrolls preserve the truth regarding Jesus is ludicrous, for the scrolls mostly date from the first century BC and do not refer to Jesus or to anyone in His following. Many of the Gnostic books found in Egypt (at Nag Hammadi) do refer to Jesus and His disciples, but all of these books are later not earlier than the Gospels in the New Testament. The "true" story of Jesus is not preserved in these writings. Indeed, the Gospels of the New Testament present Jesus as truly human, while the Gnostic Gospels exalt Jesus' heavenly status and often deny the reality of His humanity. And, of course, there is not a shred of credible evidence

---

[24] John O'Brien, *The Faith of Millions: The Credentials of the Catholic Religion*, Huntingdon, Indiana: Our Sunday Visitor, Inc., 1974, p126-7

that Jesus had a wife and children'[25].

---

[25] Craig A. Evans, "How Scholars Fabricate Jesus", in *Contending with Christianity's Critics*, eds. Paul Copan and William Lane Craig, Nashville: TN, B&H Publishing, 2009, p126-7

CHAPTER 10

All we have are Translations of Translations of Copies of Copies

Bart Ehrman is a prominent New Testament scholar. He became a 'born-again, fundamentalist Christian' as a teenager, and went to Bible college, then to Princeton Theological Seminary where he gained his Ph.D., eventually becoming a Professor of Religious Studies. Somewhere along the way on this educational journey, he abandoned his faith, and became an 'agnostic atheist'[1].

Ehrman's professional area of expertise is New Testament textual criticism. Despite the negative connotations associated with the word 'criticism', textual criticism is not an attack on Scripture, but the study of the manuscripts of our Bible and the attempt to establish the actual text the original authors wrote[2]. There are not a great many people in the world who consider this technical subject very interesting or exciting. But in 2005, Ehrman published a surprising bestseller, *Misquoting Jesus: The Story Behind Who Changed the Bible and Why*. Ehrman became a short-lived media celebrity, and was elevated alongside other atheist heroes like Richard Dawkins. In his book, he argues that the Bible was hopelessly corrupted in the process of its copying. To quote from its blurb on amazon.com, he believes that 'many of our widely held beliefs concerning the divinity of Jesus, the Trinity, and the divine origins of the Bible itself are the results of both intentional and accidental alterations by scribes'.

Ehrman's study of New Testament textual criticism might not have been the reason for his journey into unbelief, but it certainly seems to

---

[1] According to his Wikipedia page
[2] Paul Maas, *Textual Criticism*. Trans. B. Flower, Oxford: Oxford University Press, 1958, p1

play a major role in his continuing life-mission of attacking the Bible. Ehrman argues that not only do we lack the original manuscripts of the New Testament, but the copies we possess are riddled with scribal mistakes and, even more seriously, deliberate alterations. We have no certain way of knowing what the original New Testament said, but if we did, Ehrman is sure that it would teach a very different message to what modern Christians believe.

This is the same criticism made by Kurt Eichenwald on 23 December 2014 in a remarkable *Newsweek* magazine article entitled, 'The Bible: so Misunderstood it's a Sin'. Under a sub-heading reading 'Playing Telephone with the Word of God', Eichenwald wrote, 'No television preacher has ever read the Bible. Neither has any evangelical politician. Neither has the pope. Neither have I. And neither have you. At best, we've all read a bad translation—a translation of translations of translations of hand-copied copies of copies of copies of copies, and on and on, hundreds of times'.

This criticism is becoming more and more common today: how can we believe that the Bible really is the Word of God if we don't know for certain what the Bible originally said because its wording was changed as it was copied by hand many times before printing was invented?

...

In this chapter, we are going to look at the issue of the Bible's text and why we can put our trust in it.

The Text of Scripture

Some Definitions: *The Text of Scripture means the wording of the Bible. We can reconstruct the original text of the autographs (that is, the words written by the apostles and prophets themselves), as inspired by God, from the wealth of early manuscript (that is, handwritten) copies we still possess today.*

Just as we argued in the previous chapter that if we cannot determine which books belong in the canon of Scripture we won't be sure whether to believe or obey their teachings, so too, the issue of the text is important, for if we do not know what the original wording of Scripture is, we won't be able to have confidence in it.

All we have are Translations of Translations of Copies of Copies

Four Attacks on the Text of Scripture

Bible sceptics make four attacks on the text of Scripture. The first problem is that we no longer possess the original 'autographs' of Bible books, written by the authors themselves. Ehrman writes, 'For me, though, this [i.e. the fact we do not possess the original manuscripts of the New Testament] was a compelling problem. It was the words of Scripture themselves that God had inspired. Surely we have to know what those words were if we want to know how he had communicated to us, since the very words were his words, and having some other words (those inadvertently or intentionally created by scribes) didn't help us much if we want to know *His* words'[3].

Secondly, the Bible was copied many times by scribes down through time, until the invention of the printing press in the 15th Century. The result is that all we now have are manuscripts many centuries removed from the originals. No two of these manuscript copies agree completely, and their many differences suggest that there are mistakes in virtually all copies. 1500 years was a lot of time for the accumulated mistakes of scribes to build up in the text of the Bible. Just like a message gets mixed up in the 'telephone game' as people whisper a sentence round a circle, so the original words of the Bible may have been lost in transmission. Ehrman writes that the manuscripts 'differ from one another in so many places that we don't even know how many differences there are' (p10). He even claims that 'there are more variations among our manuscripts than there are words in the New Testament' (p90).

Thirdly, in addition to accidental mistakes, some scribes deliberately changed the wording and corrupted the message of the Bible. Ehrman writes, 'The more I studied the manuscript tradition of the New Testament, the more I realized just how radically the text had been altered over the years at the hands of scribes, who were not only conserving Scripture but also changing it' (p207). In fact, Ehrman's most important scholarly book (upon which *Misquoting Jesus* was based) is titled, *The Orthodox Corruption of Scripture*. Ehrman argues that it was not heretics who tried to change the Bible, but early Christians who changed certain parts of the New Testament to make Jesus divine.

Fourthly, at a more popular level, some people argue that the Bible is an ancient book written in foreign languages, and some things have got lost in translation. At best, the many different modern Bible versions

---

[3] Bart Ehrman, *Misquoting Jesus: the Story Behind Who Changed the Bible and Why*, San Francisco: Harper, 2005, p5

lead to uncertainty over wording. Well-educated Bible scholars like Ehrman do not make this accusation, but ordinary people who are not familiar with the process of Bible translation sometimes hold to this idea. We will look at this charge in the next chapter.

To summarise, the case against the text of Scripture alleges:
1. We do not possess the original manuscripts of the Bible
2. There are many copying mistakes in the manuscripts.
3. Scribes have also made deliberate alterations to the Bible.
4. Translations have also changed the Bible's message.

They conclude that we cannot have any confidence in the Bible, for we have no way of being sure that we have its original wording.

Arguments against the Reliability of the NT Text	Answers
We do not possess the original manuscripts	Our manuscript copies preserve the original text accurately
There are many copying mistakes in our manuscripts	Most mistakes are spelling or other inconsequential blunders
Scribes deliberately altered the text	On the contrary, scribes were very faithful conservationists
Translations change the meaning	Accurate translations faithfully convey the text's meaning

Why We Can Trust the New Testament Text

Contrary to what the critics argue, we have a huge amount of evidence that confirms the text of our Bibles. There are three very good reasons for believing that the text of our New Testament is reliable:
1. We can trust the text of our New Testament because we have over 5,800 manuscript copies of the New Testament in Greek, in part or whole, dating from the second century onwards. In addition to this, the New Testament was very early translated into other languages, and we possess about 20,000 manuscript copies of parts of the New Testament in other languages like Latin, Syriac, Coptic and Armenian. On top of all this, we have over a million catalogued quotations from the New Testament in the writings of early church theologians, commentators, apologists and preachers.
2. We can have confidence in our New Testament because of how early some of this textual evidence is. The earliest Greek manuscript, the John Rylands papyrus (containing part of John 18), is dated to approximately AD 125-150, less than 50 years after the writing of

John's Gospel. We have about 65 papyrus manuscripts of parts of the New Testament dating from before AD 300. Sir Frederick Kenyon of the British Museum wrote, 'The interval then between the dates of original composition and the earliest extant evidence becomes so small as to be in fact negligible, and the last foundation for any doubt that the Scriptures have come down to us substantially as they were written has now been removed. Both the authenticity and the general integrity of the books of the New Testament may be regarded as finally established'[4].

3. We can trust our New Testament because of the high levels of agreement among these manuscript copies. Apart from spelling differences and accidental blunders, the manuscripts are all telling the same story in the same words.

New Testament textual criticism has an 'embarrassment of riches' when it comes to manuscript evidence for its text. Even Bart Ehrman agrees. *The Text of the New Testament*, the leading textbook on New Testament textual criticism co-authored by Ehrman and Bruce Metzger, reads, 'Besides textual evidence derived from New Testament Greek manuscripts and from early versions, the textual critic compares numerous scriptural quotations used in commentaries, sermons, and other treatises written by early church fathers. Indeed, so extensive are these citations that if all other sources for our knowledge of the text of the New Testament were destroyed, they would be sufficient alone for the reconstruction of practically the entire New Testament'[5].

The New Testament's manuscript evidence is far more reliable than any other works of literature from classical antiquity. In the table below[6], there is a comparison of the New Testament with four other ancient writings, two Roman, one Greek and one Jewish: Julius Caesar's *Gallic Wars*, the Roman historian Tacitus' *Annals*, Homer's *Iliad*, the writings of the Jewish historian Josephus. Three of these were written at the same period of time as the New Testament, and the other was the greatest work of Greek literature, thus providing a comparison, in terms of

---

[4] F. G. Kenyon, *The Bible and Archaeology*, New York: Harper and Row, 1940, p288

[5] Bruce M. Metzger and Bart D. Ehrman, *The Text of the New Testament: Its Transmission, Corruption, and Restoration*, 4th Edition, Oxford: Oxford University Press, 2005, p126

[6] Many books defending the reliability of the New Testament text use figures that are now decades out of date; this table's figures will one day be so too.

popularity, with the New Testament:

Book	Written	Earliest Copy	Time Difference	No. Of Copies
Julius Caesar's *Gallic War*	50BC	AD 900	950 years	256
Tacitus' *Annals*	AD 100	AD 850	750 years	33[7]
Homer's *Iliad*	800 BC	400 BC[8]	400 years	1,900+[9]
Josephus	AD 78 – 100	AD 350[10]	250 years	134
The New Testament	AD 50-100	AD 125-150[11]	25-50 years	5,800+

Or, for another comparison, we may consider the text of Shakespeare's plays. Nineteen of the plays were printed multiple times before his death (the 'quartos'); however, these publications were not authorised, approved, or proofread by Shakespeare. They were pirated versions, either stolen by printers, or printed from actors' memories, and full of mistakes. Twenty-one of Shakespeare's plays remained in manuscript form at his death in 1616, but none of these manuscripts have survived, so that today we possess none of the original autographs of Shakespeare's plays. In 1623, thirty-six plays were printed (in 'folio') by two of Shakespeare's theatrical friends. They accused the previously published plays of being 'diverse stolen and surreptitious copies, maimed and deformed by the frauds of injurious imposters that expos'd them'. Shakespeare never gave his stamp of approval to any of the plays published in his name – either before his death or (obviously) after. The result is textual confusion: there are many parts of Shakespeare's plays

---

[7] Books 1-6 of Tacitus' *Annals* survive in only one copy.

[8] The earliest complete copy of Homer's *Iliad* comes from the 10th C. AD

[9] Graeme D. Bird, *Pointing at the Past: From Formula to Performance in Homeric Poetics*, Hellenic Studies Series 43. Washington, DC: Center for Hellenic Studies, 2010, http://nrs.harvard.edu/urn-3:hul.ebook:CHS_Bird.The _ Witness_of_Ptolemaic_Papyri.2010. accessed 5/5/2016

[10] The earliest copy of Josephus is a fragmentary papyrus from the 4th C. AD, the other copies come from the 11th C.

[11] The earliest complete copy of the New Testament is Codex Sinaiticus, which comes from the 4th Century AD.

All we have are Translations of Translations of Copies of Copies

which contain textual corruptions, and several plays which present problems so grave that editors are forced to emend the text (i.e. make wild guesses at what it originally said). Some of the plays exist in two quite different editions, like Hamlet and King Lear. Thus, the 1603 quarto version of Hamlet's famous soliloquy reads,

> "To be or not to be. Aye, there's the point
> To die to sleep, is that all? Aye all'.

The (far more well-known) folio version instead reads,

> 'To be, or not to be: that is the question
> Whether 'tis nobler in the mind to suffer
> The slings and arrows of outrageous fortune,
> Or to take arms against a sea of troubles,
> And by opposing end them? To die: to sleep . . .'

There is no such thing as a standard edition of Shakespeare's plays, and some plays exist in two quite different versions. By comparison with the corruption of Shakespeare's plays, the New Testament text has been transmitted to us in excellent condition: there are no parts of the New Testament text that are so corrupt that we have to make desperate guesses as to what the author originally wrote.

What About all those Textual Variants?
Ehrman claims that there are more textual variants[12] than there are words in the New Testament itself. He is right: there are about 400,000 textual variants (*Misquoting Jesus*, p89, but this is an estimate and the number could even be higher, maybe 500,000), while there are only about 140,000 words in the entire Greek New Testament.

This sounds an incredibly high number of alternative readings, but statistics can be misleading. When we realise there are about 2.5 million pages of New Testament manuscripts[13] (this is the estimate of Professor

---

[12] A textual variant is defined as any alternative wording found in the manuscripts. To clarify, if one word is spelled in five different ways in 2000 manuscripts, this is counted as five textual variants – not as 2000 variants.
[13] For the 2.5 million pages figure, see the interview with Daniel Wallace at www.evangelicaltextualcriticism.blogspot.com/2006/03/interview-with-dan-wallace.html. If we have over 5,800 NT manuscripts, and the average manuscript has 450 pages, then we have about 2,500,000 pages (for the 450

Daniel Wallace, who is involved in digitally preserving manuscripts at the Center for the Study of New Testament Manuscripts), the 500,000 textual variants amount to 1 variant per 5 manuscript pages. Thus, even if there are 500,000 variants, we are looking at very high standards of accuracy in copying.

Not only was the New Testament copied with impressive fidelity; in addition, the overwhelming majority of textual variants are entirely inconsequential. The vast majority of variant readings are cases of spelling differences, followed (in decreasing order) by obvious nonsensical blunders, the addition or omission of words like 'and' or 'the', or untranslatable variants including different grammatical ways of saying the same thing or changes in word order. The argument that the vast number of textual variants in our manuscripts undermines the reliability of the New Testament text is false. Ehrman knows all this, but he uses these big numbers to impress atheists, frighten believers, and sell books. His statistics are technically true, but by not putting the figures in context, his argument is morally deceptive and misleading.

What about the 'Textual Chaos' in the Earliest Period?
Other sceptical scholars attack the New Testament text on the grounds that copyists showed much more freedom with the text during the first few centuries than in later periods. William Petersen writes, 'Between the acts, words and life of Jesus and their text stands nearly 150 years of textual chaos'[14]. Indeed, one prominent textual scholar, David Parker, entitled a book, *'The Living Text of the Gospels'*, arguing that scribes felt free to change the text during the first few centuries. These scholars argue that we cannot hope to find the original text of the New Testament. It is lost in the 'turbid textual morass of the second century' (Harry Gamble).

To see the truth of the matter, however, we can look at how E. C. Colwell illustrated the difference between the early and later periods of copying as he compared two of our earliest manuscripts (P66 from about AD 200 and P75 from the third century) with two later manuscripts: 'from the [early] period, compare 34 verses (Jn 9:1-34) of P66 and P75. They are basically the same genetic strain, yet they differ from each other

---

page/manuscript figure, see https://blogs.thegospelcoalition.org/justintaylor/2012/03/21/an-interview-with-daniel-b-wallace-on-the-new-testament-manuscripts/). Pages accessed on 14/4/2016.

[14] William Petersen, "The Genesis of the Gospels", in *New Testament Textual Criticism and Exegesis*, ed. A. Denaux, Leuven: Leuven UP, 2002, p63

39 times in this short block of text – more than one to a verse. From the [later] period, take two manuscripts: the Isaac gospels and 2322. . . . In 31 verses of Mark 11 they never differ'[15].

Even if we examine the 39 differences between Colwell's two early manuscripts, 10 are trivial spelling differences or obvious blunders, 16 are additions or omissions of single words like 'and', 'that', 'the', 'therefore' and 'but', six are cases of grammatical changes which mean the same thing, and two are substitutions of words (and/therefore, for/but). None of these 39 differences affect the meaning of the text in any real way. It is true that there are some early manuscripts which have a 'free' text – that is, a text given to paraphrases. However, these manuscripts do not teach anything different to the others; the difference is merely stylistic. These 'free' texts relate to the 'strict' text in the way that the NIV does to the ESV. Moreover, these manuscripts are a minority; thus, among the 65 early manuscripts (before AD 300), 14 are classified as having a 'free' text (22%), while 51 have a 'normal' or 'strict' text (78%). In summary, we may agree that the standards of copying in the early manuscripts are not as high as in later periods, but even so, the vast majority of changes are entirely trivial, and the integrity of the NT text is not endangered by them.

Has the New Testament been Corrupted by Scribes?

Ehrman's main argument is that scribes deliberately changed the wording of the New Testament text to tamper with its message. However, Ehrman's entire case relies upon seven variants. This is not the tip of the iceberg – this is all he offers: seven examples of possible scribal changes. Seven examples are a drop in the ocean of 400,000 textual variants. If only 0.00175% of textual variants involve deliberate scribal corruption, then we have little to worry about. The claim that scribes have corrupted the New Testament is an inverted iceberg; it is an insupportable argument based on insufficient evidence.

Further, when we look at his examples, Ehrman's case becomes even weaker. Most of his seven examples are based on variant readings found in very few or very late manuscripts. For example, in 1 John 5:7-8, there are five manuscripts which add in the words, 'there are three that bear witness in heaven: the Father, the Word and the Holy Spirit, and these three are one'. Ehrman argues that this shows scribes trying to insert a

---

[15] E. C. Colwell, "Hort Redivivus", *Studies in Methodology in Textual Criticism of the New Testament*, Leiden: Brill, 1969, p168

reference to the Trinity into the New Testament. But this is a well-known case of scribal corruption found in very few, very late Greek manuscripts (the earliest is from the 14th C.). The passage is marked in most Bibles as not part of the genuine text of the New Testament, and the evidence for Jesus' Deity (and hence the Trinity) is found throughout the New Testament in numerous places, and does not depend on this verse.

For one other example, in Mark 1:41, instead of showing compassion for a leper, one solitary manuscript says that Jesus became angry. Ehrman suggests that scribes were uncomfortable with the image of an angry Jesus and changed the text to read He felt compassion. However, the 'angry' reading is found in one bilingual (Greek-Latin) manuscript, and in Latin the two words 'compassion' and 'anger' are very similar (*miseratus* and *iratus*). This suggests that it is more likely that a simple mistake occurred in this one manuscript tradition than that the scribes of all the other manuscripts changed the text to 'compassion'. In any case, the reading 'angry' does not change the meaning of Mark's gospel, for Mark presents other occasions where Jesus was angry: in Mark 3:5 (with the Pharisees), in 10:14 (with his disciples) and in 11:15 (the cleansing of the Temple). If scribes were intent on removing evidence of an angry Jesus, why were these readings not changed too?

As even one atheist blogger put it, reviewing Ehrman's book: 'if these verses are the strongest evidence for Ehrman's argument, his argument falls flat on its face'[16]. None of Ehrman's examples make any real change to our understanding of who Jesus was, nor the message of Christianity. This is because the doctrines of the Christian faith are repeated in numerous passages not suspect of textual corruption. Ehrman's examples typically consist of readings found in (a) very small numbers of (b) very late, or (c) quirky manuscripts – he uses these dubious and eccentric manuscripts to accuse the overwhelming majority of very faithful scribes of malpractice.

But We Do Not Have the Original Manuscripts!

Ehrman argues that we cannot really know what the original New Testament said because we do not possess the original copies, the autographs. However, there is no reason to doubt that the original text has been faithfully transmitted to us in our manuscript copies. As D. A.

---

[16] Luke Muehlhauser, *Misquoting Jesus by Bart Ehrman (Review)*, Feb. 5, 2009, http://commonsenseatheism.com/?p=27

Black has written, 'The sheer number of witnesses to the text of the New Testament makes it virtually certain that the original text has been preserved somewhere among the extant [i.e. existing] witnesses'[17]. F. F. Bruce wrote, 'Fortunately, if the great number of manuscripts increases the number of scribal errors, it increases proportionately the means of correcting such errors, so that the margin of doubt left in the process of recovering the exact original wording is not so large as might be feared; it is in truth remarkably small. The variant readings about which any doubt remains among textual critics of the New Testament affect no material question of historic fact or of Christian faith and practice'[18].

> *The sheer number of witnesses to the text of the New Testament makes it virtually certain that the original text has been preserved somewhere among the extant witnesses*
>
> David Alan Black

In fact, the irony here is that in Ehrman's seven examples of scribal corruption, he claims that he knows exactly what the original 'uncorrupted' reading is – he can work it out by looking at the manuscripts. How is it logically consistent for Ehrman to say that we do not have the original wording of the New Testament and then claim, time and again, to be able to tell exactly what it is? In reality, Ehrman believes that the discipline of textual criticism is able to reliably identify the original reading every single time. Even if we would not want to trust Ehrman's judgment in determining the original wording, it is reassuring that we not only possess all the possible alternative readings in the manuscripts that could lay claim to being the original text, but we also possess the tools to work out which readings are original and which are errors. Thus:

1. We are able to look at the manuscript evidence for different readings and assess which reading has better manuscript support.
2. We know the sorts of mistakes that scribes tended to make, and so may eliminate readings arising from scribal errors.
3. We can look at which reading makes more sense in its context. Here we not only rely on our 'common sense', but we have the Holy Spirit's help to illuminate Scripture for us.

---

[17] D. A. Black, *New Testament Textual Criticism: a Concise Guide*, Grand Rapids, MI: Baker, 1994, p24
[18] F. F. Bruce, *The New Testament Documents: Are They Reliable?* Downers Grove, IL: Inter Varsity Press, 1987 reprint, pp19-20

The Old Testament Text

How do we know that we have the Old Testament as it was originally written? There are three reasons we can have great confidence in our Old Testament text. Firstly, because of the care which Jewish scribes took in copying out the Scriptures. F. F. Bruce writes that the Jewish scribes 'treated [the sacred text] with the greatest imaginable reverence, and devised a complicated system of safeguards against scribal slips. They counted, for example, the number of times each letter of the alphabet occurs in each book'[19]. We can have great confidence in the copying practices of the Hebrew scribes.

Secondly, we can trust our Hebrew Old Testament because it was translated into other languages. After the exile in Babylon most Jews spoke Aramaic, and so the Hebrew Old Testament was translated into Aramaic paraphrases, or Targums, which eventually took the form of commentaries on the Old Testament. The Samaritan Pentateuch is a version of the first five books of the Hebrew Bible written in the Samaritan alphabet. The Old Testament was translated into Greek in the third and second centuries before Christ – this translation is called the Septuagint (based on a tradition that the translation was done by seventy scholars; 'Septuagint' comes from the Latin word for seventy and the Roman numerals LXX are sometimes used to refer to it). The Septuagint is the version of the Old Testament that was mainly used by the New Testament authors (in their Scripture quotations) and was widely used by early Christian believers. As a result, a number of other translations into Greek were made by non-Christian Jews: Aquila produced a very literal translation in AD 128, Theodotion revised the Septuagint about the same time, and Symmachus made an elegant paraphrase about the end of the second century AD. At the end of the fourth century, Jerome translated the entire Bible into Latin – this is called the Vulgate. We may compare the readings of these Aramaic, Samaritan, Greek and Latin versions of the Old Testament against the Hebrew copies to help determine the correct reading.

Thirdly, we can trust our Old Testament because of the Dead Sea scrolls. These were discovered in 1948 by a Bedouin shepherd boy who threw a stone into a cave near Qumran on the shores of the Dead Sea and heard the sound of something smashing. Investigating, he found pottery jars containing ancient scrolls. These scrolls had been hidden in

---

[19] F. F. Bruce, *The Books and the Parchments*, London: Pickering and Inglis, rev. ed. 1953, p115

All we have are Translations of Translations of Copies of Copies

caves by a community of Jews because of the advancing Roman army in AD 68. Some of the scrolls, however, dated from the second century BC, over one thousand years older than the previous oldest copy of the Hebrew Old Testament. The Dead Sea scrolls contained copies of every book of the Old Testament except for Esther. When the wording of the Dead Sea scrolls was compared with the Hebrew manuscripts from one thousand years later, the results were very reassuring. Gleason Archer writes, 'Even though the two copies of Isaiah discovered in Qumran Cave 1 near the Dead Sea in 1947 were a thousand years earlier than the oldest dated manuscript previously known (AD 980), they proved to be word for word identical with our standard Hebrew Bible in more than 95% of the text. The five percent of variation consisted chiefly of obvious slips of the pen and variations in spelling. Even those Dead Sea fragments of Deuteronomy and Samuel which point to a different manuscript family from that which underlies our received Hebrew text do not indicate any differences in doctrine or teaching. They do not affect the message of revelation in the slightest'[20].

Thus, the care taken by Jewish scribes, the other language versions we may compare the Hebrew Bible against, and the Dead Sea scrolls, all give us great confidence in the integrity of our Old Testament.

Conclusion
The claim that we cannot trust our Bible because it was copied by hand for centuries is baseless. It preys upon the obscurity of the subject; most ordinary Christians are not familiar with the wealth of manuscript evidence our Bibles are based upon, or the high copying standards of scribes of biblical manuscripts. We will look at the common accusation that something has got lost in translation in the next chapter.

---

[20] Gleason Archer, *A Survey of the Old Testament*, Chicago: Moody Press, 1964, p25

CHAPTER 11

What Bible Version should I read?

When I was growing up, there was an old man in our church who sometimes preached. He was a little eccentric and one Sunday in my mid-teens he digressed in his preaching to criticise modern Bible versions at length. After the meeting, as I walked by, I overheard the animated conversation of two ladies and, from what I picked up, they were a little upset by the old preacher's critical comments about a Bible version they were fond of using. I still remember feeling uncomfortable, both about the old preacher with a 'bee in his bonnet' over Bible versions, and also with the two ladies' criticism of the preacher in a semi-private conversation straight after the meeting.

Since my mid-teens, strangely enough, I have grown to appreciate the reasons why both the old preacher and the two ladies held the strong opinions about Bible versions they shared with the world that day. In this chapter I am going to explain why I think there is some wisdom in both positions they held. There are two sides to the issue of Bible versions, and we might entitle them, What the Old Preacher Got Right and What the Two Ladies Got Right.

The story of how I came to appreciate both sides of this debate is as follows. In my late teens, the old eccentric preacher died, and since his family did not want his books, they were given to my father. Around the same time, I started teaching myself New Testament Greek to help study the Bible better. When I came across the boxes of books that belonged to the old preacher, my respect for him increased. He had been a serious Bible student, and no mean Greek scholar. In fact, he had received a complimentary copy of the 1966 edition of the United Bible Society's Greek New Testament, (presumably) for help rendered to the secretary of the Editorial Committee, maybe in proof-reading. Amongst his books were numerous Greek New Testaments, marked up with his detailed textual notes, as well as many books about New Testament textual criticism. It was clear to me that here was someone for whom accuracy was very important, both in translating the Greek into English but also in translating from the Greek text that most closely represented the original text of the New Testament.

In my mid-twenties, I went to England where I was involved for three years in evangelistic ministry in inner-city London, primarily to children in deprived housing estates. There I started to learn another lesson: the need to relate the Bible's message to children in terms they can understand. I have seen first-hand the way that children and teenagers find it easier to read and comprehend some Bible versions than others. This was what prompted the concern of the two ladies in my church: both were heavily involved in children's ministry.

In my thirties, I went back to England, during which time I did five years of part-time research at Tyndale House, Cambridge in the area of New Testament textual criticism, an interest which had grown out of things I read in some of the old preacher's books. As a result of this research, I had a number of academic papers accepted for publication. It is strange to think how the life-work of the old preacher, dismissed as an eccentric crank, had borne some fruit in someone else's life.

Both the old preacher's concern for accuracy in Bible translation and the two ladies' concern for using language that reached and related to people, need to be balanced and married in any Bible version.

...

The subject of Bible versions is a controversial and sometimes heated one. Far be it from me to try to tell anyone which Bible version to use, for as the translators of the King James Version wrote, in their Epistle to the Reader, 'whosoever attempteth anything for the public (especially if it pertain to Religion, and to the opening and clearing of the word of God) the same setteth himself upon a stage to be gloated upon by every evil eye, yea, he casteth himself headlong upon pikes, to be gored by every sharp tongue. For he that medleth with men's Religion in any part, medleth with their custom, nay, with their freehold; and though they find no content in that which they have, yet they cannot abide to hear of altering'.

Instead of telling readers what version they ought to use I will instead attempt to set out some principles that allow readers to understand why Bibles differ at certain points. Certain Bible versions are better for certain purposes, but it is also true that some Bibles sometimes make poor choices. We need to know which Bibles are best in certain situations and why. There are two main reasons why our English Bibles differ from one another: the first is translation preferences (the issue the two ladies were exercised about), and the second is textual choices (the concern of the old preacher). In this chapter, we are going to look at translation preferences, and in the next chapter, we will look at textual choices.

The Translation of Scripture

One common misconception about the Bible held by non-Christians is that something has got lost in translation. They see the different Bible versions available in English and reason that there must be something unreliable about a book that has been translated so many different ways. There is indeed something disconcerting about the fact that we have over 900 different types of Bibles on the market in English, but the problem here is really the Bible publishing industry making money by marketing new editions: from the NKJV John Hagee Prophecy Study Bible to the NIV Study Bible for Women of Colour to the NLT Girls Life Application Study Bible with Glow in the Dark Dots.

The objection about different translations arises primarily in the English-speaking world where most people only speak one language. It is very different in many other countries where people are bi-lingual or tri-lingual as, for example, in most European countries, where schoolchildren learn two or more languages. In these cultures, everybody is aware of the fact that there are different ways that a sentence in one language can be translated into another without changing the essential message. The idea that we cannot trust the Bible because the original meaning has been lost in translation is simply not true.

The reality is that people saying that something has been lost in translation either know very little about language translation, or have never opened up a Bible and started reading it. There is very little that is lost in translation in our English Bibles, and even if we come across a difference between Bible translations, we can always consult the meaning of the words in the original languages of the Bible: Hebrew and Aramaic for the Old Testament and Greek for the New Testament.

Translation Differences

The first main reason why our Bibles differ is translation preferences.

What Bible Version should I Read?

There are six reasons translators use alternative ways of rendering the Bible out of the original languages into the 'receptor' language: translation approach, age of readers, antiquated language, advances in understanding, ambiguity in interpretation, and literary artistry.

Translation Approach: There is always more than one way of translating from one language into another. Some Bible versions try to be very literal, and employ a word-for-word translation technique, while other versions are more flexible, and try to capture the sense of a verse. The first approach is referred to by some linguists as 'formal equivalence', while the second is sometimes marketed as 'dynamic equivalence'. Others describe the two approaches as 'formal equivalence' versus 'functional equivalence'. In addition to this, there are some versions which take even more liberties; these paraphrases completely reword a verse in a fresh and punchy style. At the very opposite extreme, there are interlinears which are useful for study; they give a very literal translation but make no attempt to use readable English.

Interlinear	Word-for-Word	Thought-for-Thought	Paraphrase
Jay Green's Interlinear, Englishman's Greek NT	KJV, RV, NKJV, NASB, ESV	NIV, NLT, Good News Bible	Living Bible, The Message

Whereas we might say that we love someone with all our 'heart', in New Testament times the 'bowels' were spoken of as the seat of the affections. The bowels are not used as a figure of speech for love or compassion today. If a young man tried to ask a young lady to marry him by saying that he loved her with all his bowels, the result would probably be shock, and perhaps even swift rejection. The KJV translates 'bowels' word-for-word in some verses ('the bowels of the saints are refreshed by thee, brother', Phm 1:7; 'ye are straitened in your own bowels', 2 Cor. 6:12, etc.), whereas other modern Bible versions use the word 'heart' or 'affections' instead. These other versions try to convey the same idea in words we are familiar with, using a term that is less crude, and it would seem hard to fault them for doing so.

No English Bible version gives us a totally literal, word-for-word translation. For example, if we were to translate the first phrase of John 3:16 absolutely literally, it would read, 'So for loved the God the world'.

All versions try to translate the Bible into readable English. Thus, all English Bibles are found somewhere on a spectrum between more literal and less literal translations. For example, Matthew 10:10 in the KJV reads, 'Nor scrip for *your* journey, neither two coats, neither shoes, nor yet staves: for the workman is worthy of his meat'. The word 'your' in italics here is not present in the original Greek text, it has been added by the translators to make the English more readable. The NIV reads, 'no bag for the journey or extra shirt or sandals or a staff, for the worker is worth his keep'. This is somewhat literal, but it also uses a colloquial expression at the end of the verse: 'the worker is worth his keep'. *The Message*, a modern Bible paraphrase by Eugene Petersen, tries to give us a lively and inventive rewording of Christ's instructions: 'You don't need a lot of equipment. You are the equipment, and all you need to keep that going is three meals a day. Travel light'. Some paraphrases may help convey the meaning of the Bible in an interesting way, but if we believe that the very words of Scripture are inspired by God, we will want a more literal translation for our normal reading and study.

Age of Readers: A second way to compare different Bible translations is by the reading level they are aimed at. The readability of a Bible version not only depends upon the translation approach (less literal and more paraphrased versions are easier to read) but also on the vocabulary and sentence structure. Thus, the NIV is marketed as a Bible that an average 12-year-old is able to read. The New Living Translation and the Good News Bible employ even simpler English words and sentences, and are able to be read by the average ten-year-old. By comparison, the reading level of the ESV is about 14 years old, the NKJV is 16 years old, the NASB 17 years old and the KJV is 18 years old.

The idea of making a Bible version for children to read is hardly a new, strange or evil idea. William Tyndale famously told a Roman Catholic clergyman that if God spared him life, before many years he would cause a boy driving a plough to know more of Scripture than a clergyman who preferred what the pope taught to what God said. Most Christians agree with Tyndale's view that children should be able to read the Bible. The same is true for people whose first language is not English. It is a fact, and I have observed it myself, that non-Christian children and young people find it far easier to understand what they are reading when they are using the NIV or the Good News Bible than even the NKJV, let alone the KJV. To encourage children and teenagers to read from versions that they can follow and understand is, surely, a good idea. The result is that beginners understand the main lessons the Bible teaches and do not get bogged down with unfamiliar words. On the other side of the ledger, however, the reason that certain versions are easier to read is because they substitute simple and plain words for more precise and complex Biblical words. To speak bluntly, they dumb down the Bible's language. The problem with this is that if every word of the original text is inspired by God, it is important that we try to understand its richness in our reading and study of it. As Spurgeon put it, the Bible not only contains 'blessed shallows in which the lambs may wade' but also 'deeps in which our mind might rather drown herself than swim with pleasure'. The Bible does not always speak in words suited to ten-year-olds, but often deals with complex ideas using technical vocabulary and intricate arguments. Children's evangelism is important, but it is not the only reason that God gave us His Word.

Antiquated Language: A third reason for differences between Bible versions is that translations made in previous centuries will contain words that are no longer understood in the same way today. In Matthew 10:10, we read about the 'scrip' in the KJV, an obscure word for a 'bag' which is no longer used in spoken English. Not only do some Bibles contain obscure words we no longer use today, sometimes they use words whose meaning has changed over time. For example, in Matthew 10:10, the KJV also says that the 'worker is worthy of his meat', but the word 'meat' here does not mean 'animal flesh' as we use the word today, but is an archaic word which meant 'food' in a broad and general sense.

There are also words that mean something very different from what they did a few hundred years ago. For example, in Ephesians 2:3 (KJV) we read, 'Among whom also we all had our conversation (Greek: *anastrepho*) in times past in the lusts of our flesh', but the word 'conversation' no longer means what it did when the KJV was translated. Today it means to talk with someone but in past times conversation referred to a person's conduct or manner of life. Philippians 3:20 (KJV) says, 'our conversation is in heaven', and here the KJV uses 'conversation' to translate a quite different Greek word (*politeuma*) which means citizenship. In 1 Thessalonians 4:15, the KJV says that 'we which are alive and remain unto the coming of the Lord shall not prevent them which are asleep'. The word 'prevent' here means almost the exact opposite of what we understand it to say today: 'prevent' in olden times meant to precede or go before someone or something else. There are also words which meant simple things in more innocent times, but now sadly have negative connotations. In the KJV in James 2:3 we read about a man who comes into the church wearing 'gay clothing'. This expression could be taken to mean something quite different from when the KJV was translated.

C. S. Lewis wrote about the need for updating language in his introduction to J. B. Phillips' translation: 'The truth is that if we are to have translation at all we must have periodical re-translation. There is no such thing as translating a book into another language once and for all, for a language is a changing thing. If your son is to have clothes it is no good buying him a suit once and for all: he will grow out of it and have to be re-clothed'.

On the other hand, even though the NIV has been the best-selling version of the Bible for a few decades now, the KJV is still the most-read version of the Bible, at least in the USA. Thus, in the American Bible Society's *State of the Bible Report* (2013)[1], 38% of Bible readers said they read the KJV most often, 14% said NKJV, 11% said NIV and 3% said ESV. This shows that those who are serious about reading the Bible are not put off by slightly archaic language, and that having the Bible in easier English does not ensure that people actually read it.

Advances in Understanding: A fourth reason for differences in translation arises from the fact that our understanding of the original languages has advanced with time. For example, in 1 Samuel 13:21, the KJV reads, 'Yet they had a file for the mattocks'. However, virtually all modern versions translate the phrase as 'the charge was two-thirds of a shekel for the plowshares' (ESV). The reason for this difference is because archaeologists discovered the Hebrew word *piym* inscribed on weights, and realised it meant two-thirds of a shekel. In the days of the KJV translators, the meaning of this Hebrew word was unknown and they were forced to guess its significance, translating with the erroneous word 'file'. The Brown Driver Briggs Hebrew lexicon even said that the Hebrew text had been corrupted here. Now, however, the reading makes perfect sense: the Israelites were forced by their Philistine overlords to pay for the sharpening of iron implements.

Similarly, in the New Testament, light has been thrown on the meaning of words through the papyri discoveries over the last hundred years. These secular documents from Egypt show how Greek language

---

[1] American Bible Society, *State of the Bible Report 2013*, http://www.americanbible.org/uploads/content/State of the Bible Report 2013.pdf

was commonly used in the time of Christ. Thus, the expression in Philippians 4:18, 'I have all and abound' (KJV) is translated in some modern Bibles, 'I have received full payment and more' (ESV, see also NIV, RSV). The change from 'have' to 'received payment' results from the very common use of the Greek word *apecho* among the papyri in the sense of a receipt for monies received or taxes paid. These receipts commonly also used the word 'all' (just like here in Philippians 4:18 where Paul acknowledges, with a hint of humour, a monetary gift from the church) to mean 'fully paid'.

Ambiguity in Meaning: Another reason for differences in Bible versions is because of ambiguity of meaning. There is more than one way we could possibly understand a particular word or phrase in the original Greek or Hebrew. The act of translation sometimes requires interpretation: the translator has to choose whether to adopt one meaning, a second alternative, or perhaps try and find an ambiguous English word which means both.

Thus the Good News Bible's translation of Matthew 10:10 is, 'Do not carry a beggar's bag for the trip . . .'. By translating 'beggar's bag', the Good News Bible was arguing that the disciples were not to imitate travelling religious beggars who scrounged off others. However, the expression 'beggar's bag' is only one possible interpretation (other translators suggest it was a shepherd's bag or traveller's bag or a wallet). Because we are not certain of the exact type of bag, it is better to simply translate with the general word 'bag', and not to try to read too much interpretation into the word.

Another example of the danger of interpreting instead of translating is found in 1 Corinthians 7 where Paul writes about the Christian and marriage. He addresses different groups of people: husbands and wives, the unmarried and widows. But in verse 36, Paul gives instructions about a man and 'his virgin'. Some Bibles interpret this as referring to a man and the young lady he is engaged to marry (NIV, NRSV, ESV, NLT). Other Bibles interpret this as referring to a man and his daughter (RV, NASB). Darby interprets this to refer to the man's own virginity. Other Bibles (KJV, NKJV) simply translate the word 'virgin' as it is, leaving the matter undecided, and allow the reader to make up his or her own mind. The danger of interpreting this expression, one way or another, is that the translator might get it wrong and force a false interpretation upon readers instead of letting them come to a conclusion by exploring all the possible options. I personally believe it refers to the situation where the father is involved in the decision of whether his daughter can marry – the arranged marriage situation not only common in Paul's day but still prevalent in most parts of the world until the 20th century. However, if you hold a different interpretation of this verse, you would hardly be happy to have my opinion forced down your throat by a Bible version which, instead of letting you think about the options for yourself, only gives you one possible interpretation. The best option is to use the word 'virgin', retain some ambiguity, and let the readers decide for themselves (as the KJV and NKJV have done). It is not the job of the translators to interpret the Bible here – that is the responsibility of the readers.

The 1984 NIV often translated the word 'flesh' as 'sinful nature' instead of letting the reader work out that 'flesh' was being used in some passages in a metaphorical way to refer to our inability in our own strength to keep God's law due to our sinful nature. Paul used the word 'flesh' as a powerful and complex metaphor. The word 'flesh' is used to tie together a number of related ideas:

- Physical: flesh = muscle/body (e.g. 1 Cor. 15:39, 2 Cor. 4:11)
- Moral: flesh = our failing efforts at self-righteousness, our sinful weakness (e.g. 'when we were still without strength, Christ died for the ungodly, Rom. 5:6; 'weak through the flesh', Rom. 8:3,); thus, flesh = our sinful nature (Rom. 13:14, Gal. 5:13-24)
- Natural: flesh = our natural human abilities, human wisdom (e.g. Rom. 6:19, 1 Cor. 1:26, 2 Cor. 1:17),
- National: flesh = Jewish descent (e.g. Rom. 1:3, 4:1, 9:3, etc.),
- Religious: flesh = connected with circumcision (e.g. Rom. 2:28)

Paul used the 'flesh' metaphor to teach the truth that we are not saved by our own works, nationality or religious rites but need God's salvation. To uniformly interpret 'flesh' as 'sinful nature' robs Paul's message of some of its richness, and in some places, is in danger of missing the sense in which he used the word. The 2011 NIV wisely removed most of the references to 'sinful nature' and reverted to 'flesh'. The 2011 NIV has come in for criticism itself on one issue; it replaces masculine terms with 'gender-neutral' expressions. Thus, 'brothers' is translated as 'brothers and sisters', 'man' as 'mortals', 'father' as 'parent', 'son' as 'child', and 'leading men' as 'leaders' (Deut. 5:23). This was done to make the Bible more acceptable in our modern egalitarian culture, and in keeping with the view of certain editors of the NIV that men and women should both occupy positions of public leadership in the church. This is again allowing an interpretational agenda to override translation.

Literary Artistry: One last reason for different versions is that certain Bibles, whether by design or otherwise, have more literary quality than others. Thus while the KJV has been called 'the noblest monument of English prose', by contrast, one reviewer wrote about the RV (1885) that it 'cheerfully ruined many of the loveliest passages in English literature'. Similarly, the poet T. S. Eliot described the New English Bible (1970) as 'a symptom of the decay of the English language in the middle of the twentieth century'. Some Christians prefer the KJV, not just because it is the version they are familiar with, but also because of its literary beauty. There is no doubt that the KJV was translated at a high water-mark for the English language, the same period that gave us Shakespeare, Milton and the Book of Common Prayer.

However, literary artistry also has its downsides. J. N. Darby's *New Translation* lamented one of the principles of the KJV translators: 'There is one principle which the translators avow themselves, which is a very great and serious mistake. Where a word occurs in Greek several times in the same passage or even sentence, they render it, as far as they possibly can, by different words in English. In some cases the effect is very serious; in all the connection is lost. Thus in John 5 we have 'judgment' . . . 'condemnation' . . . 'damnation'. The word is the same in Greek, and everyone can see that 'not coming into judgment' is a very different thing from 'not coming into condemnation'. The whole force of the passage depends on this word, and its contrast with life. Here the sense is wholly changed'[2]. By striving for more literary effect, the original simplicity of the Bible's message can be lost.

Another problem is that the Bible in its original Hebrew and Greek was not written in beautiful language. The New Testament was not written in Greek of the literary quality of the classical authors like Homer, Plato or Aristotle. Instead, just as 'the common people' heard Christ gladly (Mark 12:37), so the New Testament was written in Koine (i.e. 'common') Greek, the language of the man in the street, used throughout the Roman world. It was not the language of the political, academic, or literary elites. As C. S. Lewis, himself a Professor of Medieval and Renaissance Literature, wrote in his introduction to J. B. Phillips' translation of the New Testament, 'It is possible that the reader . . . may ask himself why we need a new translation of any part of the Bible . . . "Do we not already possess," it may be said, "in the Authorized

---

[2] J. N. Darby, *The Holy Scriptures: a New Translation from the Original Languages*, Revised Preface to Second Edition, Kaduna, Nigeria: Word of Truth, 1987, pxix

Version the most beautiful rendering which any language can boast?"' Lewis replies that 'the New Testament in the original Greek is not a work of literary art: it is not written in a solemn, ecclesiastical language . . . In it we see Greek used by people who have no real feeling for Greek words because Greek words are not the words they spoke when they were children. It is a sort of "basic" Greek'. He even cautions, 'we must sometimes get away from the Authorized Version if for no other reason, simply because it is so beautiful and so solemn. Beauty exalts, but beauty also lulls. Early associations endear but they also confuse. Through that beautiful solemnity the transporting or horrifying realities of which the Book tells may come to us blunted and disarmed and we may only sigh with tranquil veneration when we ought to be burning with shame, or struck dumb with terror, or carried out of ourselves by ravishing hopes and adorations'.

The argument that we should prefer literary excellence over clumsy and wooden renderings is surely true, but we also need to careful of the danger of mere aesthetics, the triumph of art over substance, ornament over truth. Just as some modern Christian songs are popular more for their catchy tune than any depth in their words, and just as some church buildings are architecturally beautifully yet lack any gospel proclamation, so we must not confuse the outer literary clothing of a particular version with the inner content. The prominent atheist Richard Dawkins applauds the King James Bible[3], even though he says it is full of horrible myths, because it is 'one of the glories of English literature', showing that it is possible to appreciate the beauty of English language while rejecting the message of the Bible.

Summary: There is a story of a temperance advocate, protesting against the consumption of alcohol, walking down a street one night who came across a drunkard leaning against a lamp-post. Trying to reason with the drunkard, he said, "Don't you know that beer is bad?" The drunkard shook his head and said, "No, there is good beer and better beer, but there is no such thing as bad beer". Without wishing to endorse the opinion of the drunkard, or trying to imply that there is an exact parallel (for there are bad Bibles, like the doctrinally corrupt Jehovah's Witnesses *New World Translation)*, there is a sense in which the same applies to the

---

[3] Richard Dawkins, "Why I want all our children to read the King James Bible", https://www.theguardian.com/science/2012/may/19/richard-dawkins-king-james-bible

What Bible Version should I Read?

Bible: there are good Bibles and there are better Bibles. People have been converted and blessed reading many different versions. Reading any Bible is better than reading none at all, and the best translation is one that is read! However, before we say any more about which Bible versions are better, there is a second big issue we need to examine that has a major effect upon on the outcome.

CHAPTER 12

The Parable of the Four Fishing Boats

The second reason for differences between Bible versions relates to the underlying Hebrew or Greek text from which they are translated. This was the issue to which the old preacher in the last chapter devoted much of his study. In my teens I started noticing footnotes in Bibles mentioning alternative readings from various manuscripts. Then I stumbled across some books of the old preacher which I found to be quite interesting – eye-opening even – and I realised that the subject was quite important. The old preacher's notes and his choice of books showed that he was quite an independent thinker, and had concerns about the mainstream views on the matter. Over time, having read these books and done my own research, I came to appreciate his concerns.

The subject of the texts underlying our Bible versions contains a few technicalities that some people will struggle with. So, to help us understand the matter more easily, we are going to use a parable.

The Parable of the Second-Hand Fishing Boats
Imagine a fisherman who needs to buy a fishing boat and goes down to the harbour to look at what is on sale. The fisherman is told there are no new boats for sale, so he asks if there are any second-hand boats. He is taken down to a quiet corner of the harbour where he is shown four boats. The first is a small old brown boat that has been lovingly cared-for, but is covered in barnacles. The second boat looks very strange: it was once a fishing boat, but after being bought by city-folk, it was painted in multi-coloured flowers and remodelled so that instead of going fishing it could take passengers on river cruises. The third boat looks sleek and fast, and not very old, but it is damaged: its red paintwork is scratched and it even has holes in places, as if it has hit

The Parable of the Four Fishing Boats

some rocks. The fourth blue boat is much bigger than the others and looks to be in good condition – its woodwork is nicely polished. However, the fisherman has heard rumours about this boat – some say it has been rebuilt from other boats; it is literally two boats bolted together.

Which boat would you buy if you were the fisherman? All seem to have their drawbacks. You would probably want to investigate more before spending any money. These four boats represent four different texts of the Greek New Testament that modern Bibles are translated from (the once brand-new 'original' documents are no longer available). Which text should we use? Some underlying Greek New Testament texts are 2000 words (ten pages) longer than others, making the question of whether we should translate our Bibles from the shorter or longer versions of the Greek New Testament quite important. Most Christians are not aware that there is any issue, and choose a Bible largely based on its translation style. Some Christians have strong preferences for one of our 'fishing boats', despite being largely unfamiliar with the issues that determine which 'boat' is best. Yet others consider themselves educated about this isssue, but only repeat second-hand opinions based on long out-of-date scholarship. In what follows, we will hopefully get a clearer understanding of the matter. Before we explain the parable of the fishing boats (which only applies to the NT text), we need to briefly mention the less troubled matter of the OT text.

The Old Testament Text

In Isaiah 53:11, the KJV reads, 'He shall see of the travail of his soul, and shall be satisfied', whereas the NIV (1984) reads, 'After the suffering of his soul, he will see the light [*of life*] and be satisfied'. The NIV reading 'the light' is found in the Dead Sea scrolls and the Greek Septuagint, and suggests that the Servant will rise from the dead – he will see the light of life. Similarly, in Psalm 145:13b, many modern versions (ESV, NIV, RSV, NLT) add in some extra words not contained in the KJV: 'The LORD is faithful in all his words and kind in all his works'. These extra words are found in the Dead Sea scrolls, the Greek Septuagint and the Latin Vulgate. Psalm 145 is an acrostic psalm, in which the first letter of every verse spells out the Hebrew alphabet. However the Hebrew letter *nun* is missing, and the extra words in verse 13b start with the letter *nun*. In addition, the theme of this psalm concerns the attributes of God: The Lord is great (v3), the Lord is gracious (v8), and the Lord is righteous (v17). The missing words (v13b) continue this theme ('the Lord is faithful'), and the following words in v14 speak of God's faithfulness too:

'The Lord upholds all who fall', etc.. All this would indicate that these words were an original part of the psalm.

In the Old Testament, virtually all Bibles, ancient and modern, follow the standard Masoretic Hebrew text in their translation. Some modern versions will have the occasional reading from the Dead Sea scrolls, particularly if this reading has support from other ancient versions. Most modern Bibles will not use such readings in their main text; instead, they will note such readings from the Dead Sea scrolls or the Septuagint in the margins. This makes for a very standard text across all Bibles.

Glossary of Textual Terms	
originals	the original copies written by apostles and prophets
manuscripts	hand-written copies (singular: ms; plural: mss)
edition	a version of a text, prepared by a publisher
text	the words of a verse, book, manuscript or edition
papyri	early manuscripts written on papyrus
majuscules	parchment manuscripts written in capital letters
minuscules	later parchment mss in small running writing
codex	a manuscript in book, as opposed to scroll, format
Masoretic Text	the text of the majority of Hebrew OT manuscripts
Dead Sea Scrolls	very early Hebrew OT manuscripts
Septuagint (LXX)	the Greek translation of the OT
Vulgate	the Latin translation of the Bible
Textus Receptus	the Greek NT text underlying the KJV
Byzantine Text	the text of the majority (95%) of Greek NT manuscripts
UBS Text	the scholarly edition of the Greek text underlying the NT in most modern English Bibles

The New Testament Text

While the Old Testament text is very settled, due to the consensus that the standard Masoretic Text is very dependable, the situation is quite different in the New Testament. There are many variations between Bible versions based on different underlying Greek texts. In our parable of the four fishing boats, we have pictured the four main Greek NT texts, but before we head back to the boats and try to decide which one is best, we need to explain a little about what sort of differences our Greek texts contatin. Although these textual differences do not affect any fundamental doctrine (because doctrines never depend on one isolated verse), and most of them are of minor significance, nevertheless some have considerable consequences for our understanding of individual passages.

These textual differences primarily involve (a) the inclusion or omission of words, phrases, entire verses and whole passages, and (b) substitutions of alternative wordings in different verses. Here are a few examples of additions and omissions – the following phrases and verses are not found in Matthew's Gospel in some Bible versions, because some Greek manuscripts do not contain them:

- Matt. 5:44, *'Bless those who curse you, do good to those who hate you'*
- Matt. 6:13, *'Thine is the kingdom, the power and the glory'*
- Matt. 17:21, *'this kind does not go out except by prayer and fasting'*,
- Matt. 18:11, *'the Son of Man has come to save that which was lost'*
- Matt. 19:9, *'whoever marries her who is divorced commits adultery'*
- Matt. 23:14, *'Woe to you, scribes and Pharisees, hypocrites! For you devour widows' houses, and for a pretense make long prayers. Therefore you will receive greater condemnation'*

These examples from Matthew's Gospel involve major instances of addition or omission, and there are other cases of large-scale differences in other New Testament books. There are also many cases of textual differences that only involve one or two words.

To illustrate the big difference a small change makes, let's return to Christ's instructions for His disciples on their evangelistic journey. The KJV in Matthew 10:10 says that the disciples were not to take 'two . . . staves' (plural) on their journey, but some other Bibles say that the disciples were not to take a 'staff' (singular). This is not a matter of translation style or preference, but of different Greek manuscripts underlying the KJV and modern Bibles. In the KJV, the Gospels are all saying the same thing in different ways: only take one staff. But in other Bibles there seems to be a clear and obvious contradiction: were the disciples told to 'take nothing for the journey – no staff' (Matthew 10:10, NIV, ESV, NASB, and NLT, etc.)[1] or to 'take nothing for the journey except a staff' (Mark 6:8)? Some attempts have been made to reconcile these verses, but they seem half-hearted and far from convincing. If we

---

[1] We find the same textual variant in Luke 9:3 where the KJV says the disciples were not to take 'staves' (pl.) while the NIV, ESV, NASB, NLT, etc. read they were not to take a 'staff' (sg.).

believe that the Bible does not contradict itself and is without error, and that all Scripture is inspired and therefore important, then we need to understand what is going on in verses like this one where underlying textual differences make a significant impact on the meaning of the verse.

This is hardly the only case of a verse where an underlying textual difference radically changes the meaning; there are many other cases like this. Unfortunately, while some people want brief answers to such issues, to understand what is going on behind all these differences, big and small, and which readings are correct, we need to understand a little about the history of how our Bibles came to us. Let's go back to the fishing boats.

The Small Old Brown Boat with Barnacles: the Textus Receptus
The KJV was translated from what is called the Textus Receptus. The Textus Receptus (or Received Text) is the name given to the first printed Greek New Testament published in 1516[2]. The Textus Receptus (TR) was an instant bestseller, partly because it was the first published edition of the Greek New Testament and partly because of the reputation of its editor, Erasmus, as the foremost scholar of the day. It was quickly used by the Reformers like Luther and Tyndale for their German and English Bibles. Some people believe that, as the Greek text behind the KJV, it is the only trustworthy Greek text of the New Testament.

However, it was based on only a very small number of hastily assembled Greek manuscripts. These manuscripts were also late, dating from the 12th Century onwards. Erasmus published it in a race to beat another edition of the Greek New Testament; it was prepared in such a short time that Erasmus himself said that it was 'precipitated rather than edited'. Its first edition contained hundreds of typographical errors that were gradually cleared up over four more editions.

---

[2] More accurately, there are about fifteen or more slightly different editions of the TR. Erasmus produced five editions of his Greek New Testament (1516-1535, each different), the Paris printer Stephanus produced four editions (1546-1551), Theodore Beza published nine editions (although really only four distinct editions, 1565-1598), and the Elzevir brothers of Leiden also published a number of editions of the Greek New Testament (1624, 1633). It was the second of these Elzevir editions in 1633 (obviously produced after the KJV of 1611) that claimed that its text was the text 'received by all' - i.e. the Textus Receptus. All of these Greek New Testaments are generally similar (although with differences) and all are referred to as the Textus Receptus. The KJV was based on a mixture of these editions.

There are a number of problems with the TR. Firstly, it only used a very small number of Greek copies that Erasmus had on hand at the time. As a result, the TR has many irregular and eccentric readings that are only found in a very small minority of Greek copies. We have nearly 6000 Greek manuscripts – we should not be restricted to just six late ones. Secondly, because parts of the book of Revelation were missing in the few copies Erasmus used, he had to 'make up' some of the Book of Revelation by back-translating certain verses into Greek from the Latin Vulgate, meaning that in these places the TR lacks Greek manuscript support. For example, the TR reads 'book of life' in Revelation 22:19, but every single Greek manuscript we have reads 'tree of life'. Thirdly, the TR includes a number of whole verses which are found in very few Greek copies. These verses include Luke 17:36, Acts 8:37, Acts 9:5b-6a and Acts 15:34. How did they get into our Bibles? These verses were incorporated by Erasmus from the Roman Catholic Latin Bible. Lastly, perhaps the most famous problem with the TR is found in 1 John 5:7-8. Erasmus' first edition was criticised for not including the words about there being 'three who bear witness in Heaven: the Father, the Word and the Holy Spirit, and these three are one'. He included these words in his third edition after this criticism, but these words are only found in Latin manuscripts and a handful of very late (i.e. 16th and 17th century) Greek manuscripts. They have very little right or reason to be in our Bible.

Some would argue that the TR is the best text of the Greek New Testament because it is the text of the vast majority of the manuscripts. This claim is not quite true. The text of the vast majority of the manuscripts (called the Byzantine, or Majority, Text) differs from the TR in 1,838 places[3]. It would be more accurate to describe the TR as a distant cousin of the family of Byzantine manuscripts.

Yet others would make the claim that the KJV was translated from the TR in God's providence and by men of superior godliness and learning. But this is the same argument that Roman Catholics advance for the superiority of Jerome's Latin Vulgate. Thus, the Roman Catholic translators of the Douay-Rheims Bible (a 1610 translation into English from the Latin Vulgate) argued that 'the Hebrew and Greek Editions are foully corrupted by Jews and Heretics since the Latin was truly translated out of them'. They also claim that Jerome was used by 'God's particular

---

[3] Daniel Wallace, "The Majority Text Theory: History, Methods, and Critique", *The Text of the New Testament in Contemporary Research*, S&D46, ed. Bart D. Ehrman and Michael W. Holmes, Grand Rapids, MI: Eerdmans, 1995, p302, footnote 28.

providence in this great Doctor' to produce 'the true text and Edition of Holy Scriptures'. But since any Bible translator may claim divine help and providence, such an argument proves little.

Other defenders of the TR would claim that it is a better text than current Greek texts which were edited by people who (allegedly) did not believe in the deity of Christ, the inspiration of the Scriptures or other important doctrines like justification by faith. Unfortunately, this argument also backfires somewhat on the TR because Erasmus, the scholar who originally prepared the TR, was (1) a Roman Catholic priest (and the illegitimate son of a Roman Catholic priest) who never left the Catholic Church during the Reformation (though he did criticise it in his time), and (2) in it, with the printer who persuaded him to prepare the TR, for the fame and the money that could be earned by publishing the first printed Greek text of the New Testament. This was why the TR was such a hurried job and contained so many mistakes.

The TR is like the small old boat covered in barnacles in our parable because (a) it was based on a very small number of manuscripts, (b) it was based on very late manuscripts, and (c) it contains some extra verses, like barnacles, added to the New Testament. We have many more ancient copies of the Greek New Testament that need to be consulted and whose evidence must be heard. The only reason the TR has its defenders today is because it was the basis for the KJV and some of the other great versions of the New Testament (like Tyndale's and Luther's). As greatly as we may admire Tyndale, Luther and the KJV, this should not blind us to the faults of the TR.

The Big, the Fast and the Flowery: Three Alternative Texts

After Erasmus' day, many more Greek New Testament manuscripts came to light and were compared with the TR. Many of these manuscripts were far older than the manuscripts used by Erasmus for the TR. Scholars studying these manuscripts classified them into three main 'text-types':

1. ***The Big Blue Boat***: The Byzantine text-type is found in the majority (95%) of Greek manuscripts (hence it is also called the Majority Text); it dominated the period from the 4th to the 16th centuries, as seen in the writings of Greek church 'fathers' of this period. The most important manuscript of this type is the 5th century Codex Alexandrinus, which has a Byzantine text in the gospels. Despite looking big and beautiful, this boat has a question mark hanging over it: it is accused of having been remodelled – cobbled together from

two other boats – in the fourth century.
2. ***The Fast Red Boat***: A smaller number of early manuscripts are called Alexandrian because their text is similar to that found in the Coptic (Egyptian) versions of the New Testament and the early Church 'Fathers' from Alexandria. Their text is also (2000 words) shorter than the other two text-types. Most of the early papyrus manuscripts found in Egypt within the last one hundred years are Alexandrian, as well as some of the major manuscript finds of the 19th century like Codex Sinaiticus and Codex Vaticanus, both from the 4th century. Not only is this boat quicker (its text is shorter), it also appears to be a somewhat 'damaged' text, with readings that make less sense.
3. ***The Flowery Boat***: A very small number of manuscripts are called Western, because they share affinities with the early Latin versions of the New Testament. The most important Western manuscript is the very eccentric Codex Bezae (5th C.), which is especially fond of paraphrases, as well as omissions and additions large and small. Some of these eccentric 'Western' readings made their way, via the Latin Vulgate, into the Textus Receptus, and hence, the KJV. The Western text of Codex Bezae is most eccentric in Acts; its text has many embellishments and is about 8% longer than other manuscripts.

Very few scholars advocate translating our New Testament from the few, 'flowery', eccentric 'Western' manuscripts. Faced with the choice between the 'blue' Byzantine and 'red' Alexandrian manuscripts, the United Bible Societies (UBS) Greek New Testament[4], upon which most modern Bible versions are based, is heavily Alexandrian. There are four main reasons why most biblical scholars prefer the readings of the Alexandrian manuscripts instead of the Byzantine 'Majority Text':
1. The Alexandrian manuscripts are earlier than the Byzantine manuscripts, and therefore presumably closer to the original.
2. The Alexandrian text is shorter, and scholars prefer shorter readings, believing that scribes tended to add to the text down through the centuries, thus producing the longer Byzantine text-type.
3. Many scholars believe that the Byzantine majority of Greek manuscripts sprung from a 'recension', an official 'revised edition' of

---

[4] The Greek text of the United Bible Societies NT is identical with the *Nestle-Aland* Greek New Testament, the only difference being the Nestle-Aland GNT gives more variant readings in its critical apparatus.

the Greek New Testament composed in the fourth century.
4. Scholars argue that Alexandrian readings better explain the origin of the alternative Byzantine and Western readings. Thus, because it is believed that scribes tended to harmonise parallel gospel accounts, remove apparent difficulties and polish up the style of readings, the Alexandrian readings, which are more difficult, less polished and less harmonised, are preferred.

These reasons are worth exploring and evaluating, so that both their strengths and weaknesses are better understood. Like the fisherman looking at second-hand boats, we have four decisions to make.

Old Boats or New?
The argument that the Alexandrian manuscripts are earlier and therefore closer to the originals has great force. Just as we would ordinarily prefer to buy a newer boat than an old one, so textual scholars prefer early manuscripts to late. However, as anyone buying cars knows, age alone is no guarantee of quality; a newer car might have higher mileage and be in worse condition. One problem with the preference for earlier manuscripts is that in some works of ancient literature the earliest manuscripts we possess are the most eccentric. Just as the earliest editions of Shakespeare are not necessarily the most reliable, so too the early papyri of Homer's *Iliad* vary wildly from the standard text (possibly due to the fact that, like Shakespeare, the *Iliad* was oral performance literature). The Dead Sea scrolls are the earliest evidence we possess for the Hebrew Old Testament, but some scrolls also exhibit eccentricity: they show an 'astonishing range of textual variants . . . While some of the Qumran biblical manuscripts are nearly identical to the Masoretic, or traditional, Hebrew text of the Old Testament, some manuscripts of the books of Exodus and Samuel found in Cave Four exhibit dramatic differences in both language and content'[5]. Similarly, the early Latin versions of the New Testament are among the most unreliable witnesses to its text, with 'almost as many types of text as manuscripts'[6].

The sensational discoveries of the early NT papyri in the last century have great apologetic value, i.e. for defending the reliability of

---

[5] Brian M. Fagan and Charlotte Beck, "Dead Sea Scrolls" in *The Oxford Companion to Archaeology*, Oxford University Press, 1996

[6] This was what Jerome, who was commissioned to translate the Latin Vulgate by Pope Damasus in the late AD 300s, said about the earlier Latin translations of the New Testament.

the Bible, but most papyri are 200-300 years after the original manuscripts. Further, all the early papyri come from remote locations hundreds of miles up the Nile, preserved under desert sands. Whether they contain an idiosyncratic and isolated text, or how it compared with manuscripts in other Christian centres at the same period, is uncertain. We have little evidence that the Alexandrian text existed anywhere other than Egypt. If it was close to the original text, why do we find no early language versions being made from it, other than the Coptic (Egyptian) versions? This would appear to suggest that the Alexandrian text was not widespread, but a localised variant only found in Egypt. Bird, writing about the analogous case of the early Homeric papyri (found in the same Egyptian locations), mentions scholars 'falling on their knees before the papyri' and cautions that, 'our examination of the [early Homeric] papyri must bear in mind that our surviving amount of evidence is tiny, and cannot automatically be assumed to be a "representative sample." However, neither can its evidence be ignored'[7]. Age alone is no proof of the superiority of the Alexandrian text; age is less important than history, as anyone buying second-hand vehicles knows. Sadly, none of our manuscripts come with a record of their history, like a ship's logbook, verifying how well their text has descended from the originals. Age is important, then, but further supporting evidence is required.

A Boat Covered in Barnacles or a Boat Full of Holes?
Not only are the Alexandrian manuscripts earlier than other manuscripts, they are also shorter. Scholars have long believed that scribes tended to add to the NT text over time, thus producing the longer Byzantine text found in the majority of later manuscripts. The Byzantine text, they argued, is thus proved guilty of scribal corruption, and the brevity of the Alexandrian text provides extra evidence of its superiority.

Is this theory true? This was the research question that I spent a number of years studying at Cambridge: have copyists added to the text over time, or did scribes omit material? My interest in this question was sparked by a study on scribal habits by E. C. Colwell which I found in a book that had belonged to the old preacher. Colwell was an independent-minded and innovative textual scholar, who pioneered a method of testing scribal habits. Since Colwell, half a dozen academic studies examining the sorts of errors scribes made have shown that,

---

[7] Graeme D. Bird, *Pointing at the Past: From Formula to Performance in Homeric Poetics*, http://chs.harvard.edu/CHS/article/display/4853, accessed 5/5/2016

contrary to the received wisdom, scribes tended to omit rather than add to the New Testament[8]:

Study	Type	Additions	Omissions
Royse (1981)[9]	6 Major Papyri in Gospels	130 (28%)	337 (72%)
Robinson (1982)[10]	220 Manuscripts in Revelation	451 (40%)	678 (60%)
Head (1990, 2004)[11]	30 Minor Papryi in Gospels	10 (34%)	19 (66%)
Hernández (2006)[12]	3 Majuscule Manuscripts in Revelation	57 (40%)	87 (60%)
Wilson (2011)[13]	3000+ Manuscripts in 10% of the NT text	1088 (39%)	1712 (61%)

It should not be surprising that scribes tended to omit rather than add; after all, accidental omission is the easiest of all copying mistakes to make. The present author's study showed scribes of our earliest papyri omitting 75% of the time and adding 25%, meaning that scribes of our

---

[8] These studies are based on singular readings among the manuscripts, that is, readings only found in one lone manuscript, and therefore highly likely to be scribal errors. The table shows the numbers of singular additions and omissions.

[9] J. R. Royse, *Scribal Habits in Early Greek New Testament Papyri*, Th.D. Dissertation, Graduate Theological Union, Berkeley, California, 1981. Subsequently updated and published as *Scribal Habits in Early Greek New Testament Papyri*, Leiden: Brill, 2008

[10] M. A. Robinson, *Scribal Habits among Manuscripts of the Apocalypse*, Ph.D. Dissertation, Southwestern Baptist Theological Seminary, Ft. Worth, TX, 1982

[11] P. M. Head, "Observations on Early Papyri of the Synoptic Gospels, especially on the 'Scribal Habits'", *Bib 71* (1990), pp240-47, and "The Habits of New Testament Copyists: Singular Readings in the Early Fragmentary Papyri of John", *Bib 85* (2004), pp399-408

[12] J. Hernández, Jr., *Scribal Habits and Theological Influences in the Apocalypse: The Singular Readings of Sinaiticus, Alexandrinus, and Ephraemi* (WUNT 2.218), Tübingen: Mohr Siebeck, 2006

[13] Andrew W. Wilson, "Scribal Habits in Greek New Testament Manuscripts", *Filologia Neotestamentaria*, Vol. 44 (2011), pp95-126. See also Andrew W. Wilson, "Scribal Habits and the New Testament Text", *Digging for the Truth: Collected Essays regarding the Byzantine Text of the Greek New Testament; A Festschrift in Honor of Maurice A. Robinson*, eds. Mark Billington, Peter Streitenberber, Norden: FocusYourMission KG, 2014, pp21-39.

early Alexandrian manuscripts were some of the most prone to this error.

As a result of these studies, NT textual scholars are slowly acknowledging that the long-held view that scribes tended to add to the text is wrong. Royse, whose magisterial study has set the standard for all others, said: '(It is my) conviction that the preference for the shorter reading is fundamentally mistaken'[14]. One of the central supporting pillars of Alexandrian superiority is quietly collapsing.

How does this affect our Bible? Would we prefer to sail on a ship covered in barnacles or a ship full of holes? The answer is obvious. But ideally, we would prefer a ship with neither barnacles or holes. The evidence shows that a longer Greek text is preferable to a shorter. The current scholarly UBS Greek NT is about 2000 words (or 10 pages) shorter than the Byzantine text (UBS: 138,000 words; Byzantine: 140,000 words), largely because of the preference for 'shorter readings' (i.e. omissions in early Alexandrian manuscripts). Many of these omissions are single words like 'and' or 'the' which hardly change the message at all. However, the verses listed earlier from Matthew's Gospel, omitted in many modern Bibles, are representative of many other verses and phrases, most of which should be reinstated in our Bibles.

A Ship that has been Cobbled together from Two Other Boats?

A third reason many scholars prefer the shorter Alexandrian manuscripts is because it is believed that in the fourth century, the text of the majority of manuscripts (i.e. the Byzantine text) was cobbled together by combining readings from the earlier Alexandrian and Western texts. This revised NT text was then imposed by official authority upon the Greek-speaking churches. The term 'Lucianic Recension' refers to this recension (i.e. revision) of the NT text, carried out (perhaps) by Lucian of Antioch. On this theory, the numerical superiority of Byzantine manuscripts counts for little since they all sprung from one late 'doctored' version of the original text. As a result, the 'corrupt Byzantine text' (Metzger[15]) is considered virtually worthless for determining the wording of the original New Testament.

The main problem with this recension theory is that there is not the slightest documented evidence of such a thing ever happening; there is no historical evidence of anyone 'remodelling' the Greek NT to produce

---

[14] see http://evangelicaltextualcriticism.blogspot.com.au/2009/06/sbl-boston-book-review-of-james-royse.html, accessed 11/5/2016

[15] B. M. Metzger, *A Textual Commentary on the Greek New Testament*, 2nd Ed., Stuttgart: Deutsche Bibelgesellschaft, 1994, p10*

the Byzantine text, or of any authorities officially imposing a new text upon the churches. The contrast with the strong historical evidence for the official revision of the Latin Bible by Jerome is stark.

Among the books left behind by the old preacher I mentioned earlier, there were two books by Pickering and Sturz on the Byzantine text[16]. After reading these books I was fairly convinced that the evidence showed that the Byzantine text had not originated in a 'Lucianic Recension'. But what really confirmed this was the way that other scholars responded to these arguments. Gordon Fee and Daniel Wallace, two leading textual critics, replied that the Byzantine text was indeed late and corrupt, but ignored the question of whether the Lucianic Recension theory was true or mythical[17]. Instead of addressing the crucial issue upon which the history of the Byzantine text hinges (the Lucianic Recension theory), they attacked Pickering and Sturz's motivation, suggesting that they favoured the Byzantine text for theological reasons. This surprised me: why would leading textual critics refuse to grapple with the evidence for the Lucianic Recension? It reminded me of the old lawyer's adage: when the evidence is on your side argue the evidence, when the law is on your side argue the law, but when neither the law nor the evidence is on your side, attack the motives of your opponent.

Some of today's leading textual experts are openly abandoning the entire idea. Thus, Klaus Wachtel, one of the editors of the standard UBS Greek NT, says, 'Above all, these readings make it improbable that the Byzantine text could have had its beginning in a proper recension of the 4th century', and again, 'So also from the perspective of the development of the Byzantine text the traditional concept, namely, that the

---

[16] Wilbur N. Pickering, *The Identity of the New Testament Text*, Nashville, TN: Thomas Nelson, 1980 and Harry A. Sturz, *The Byzantine Text-Type and New Testament Textual Criticism*, Nashville, TN: Thomas Nelson, 1984

[17] Gordon Fee, "The Majority Text and the Original Text of the NT", in *Studies in the Theory and Method of New Testament Textual Criticism* (S&D 45), Grand Rapids, MI: Eerdmans, 1993, pp183-208; Daniel Wallace, "The Majority Text Theory: History, Methods and Critique", in *The Text of the New Testament in Contemporary Research: Essays on the Status Quaestionis* (S&D 46), Grand Rapids, MI: Eerdmans, 1995, pp297-320. Both seem to believe in a Lucianic Recension: for Daniel Wallace, see *Mark 1:2 and New Testament Textual Criticism* (2004) at https://bible.org/article/mark-12-and-new-testament-textual-criticism (accessed 11/5/16), while Gordon Fee (ibid., p188) argues that the influence of Chrysostom accounts for the numerical majority of Byzantine manuscripts, thus sidestepping the real issue: the origin of the text-type.

transmission history of the New Testament was determined by recensions, proves to be no longer viable'[18]. Earlier textual experts were scathing in their contempt for this idea. F. H. A. Scrivener referred to recension theories as a playground for 'pleasant speculations which may amuse the fancy but cannot inform sober judgement'[19]. S. P. Tregelles and Sir Frederick Kenyon were others who dismissed the idea as imaginary and implausible[20].

There is no good evidence, historical or otherwise, that the Greek New Testament was revised in the fourth century to produce the majority of 'corrupt' Greek manuscripts. The idea is just another conspiracy theory, right up there with Dan Brown's theory that Constantine chose which books went into the New Testament. The big, blue boat was not cobbled together from two other boats; its construction is solid and sound; we can be confident it is not going to fall apart on us.

Once the myth of the recensional origin of the Byzantine text-type is dispelled, the 95% majority of Greek manuscripts become more significant. If they did not originate in some revision, these manuscripts must have been copied from earlier manuscripts. If they were not created (*de novo*), or edited (in a recension), they must have been transmitted (the default for any text), descending ultimately from the originals. Their dominance of the Greek manuscript tradition from AD 400 to AD 1600 is significant. The fact that they also come from the Greek-speaking heartland of the post-apostolic church (from Antioch through Asia Minor to Greece), the area where two-thirds of the New Testament documents were originally sent, further serves to underline the respect they deserve.

A Boat with Polished or Damaged Woodwork?

The last difference between the Alexandrian and Byzantine texts is that the Byzantine is more polished and pleasing, both in sense and style, while the Alexandrian text is more rugged, terse, jagged and difficult. Scholars have tended to prefer Alexandrian readings precisely for this reason, claiming that scribes would have been more likely to polish up

---

[18] Klaus Wachtel, *Der Byzantinische Text der Katholischen Briefe* (ANTF 24), Berlin: de Gruyter, 1995, pp199, 201.

[19] F. H. A. Scrivener, *A Plain Introduction to the Criticism of the New Testament*, 4th Ed., London: George Bell and Sons, 1894, Vol. 2, p273

[20] For Tregelles, see his *Account of the Printed Text*, London: Samuel Bagster and Sons, 1854, p90; for Kenyon see his *Handbook to the Textual Criticism of the New Testament*, London: Macmillan and Co., 2nd ed., 1912, pp324-5

originally harder readings rather than create such difficulties. Thus, it is claimed, the early rugged and difficult Alexandrian NT text was 'improved' by scribes to produce the more sensible and smooth Byzantine text. However, there are three problems with this claim: one logical, one empirical, and one historical. Firstly, the theory that scribes improved the NT text is somewhat illogical. Not only does it imply that the original text was full of problems, but as John Dobson argues: 'Any error made in copying a sentence is likely to make it more difficult to understand'[21]. As one friend put it, 'Prefer the Dumber Reading' seems like a really dumb rule. If we were to take 'Prefer the More Difficult Reading' to its logical conclusion, we should adopt a New Testament full of strange readings.

Secondly, over recent decades, theoretical speculation about what scribes did has given place to empirical research into what they actually produced in our manuscripts. While there is indeed evidence of scribes improving and polishing up the text, there is far more evidence of scribes making the text more abrupt, terse, austere and difficult. These were not deliberate attempts by scribes to mangle the NT text, of course, but rather the accidents and blunders of normal copying. In the present author's study, there were 244 scribally-created harder readings to only 8 'improved' readings (less than 1% of all readings). Readers need not take my word for it either. In Royse's monumental study, there are so few cases of scribes creating 'improved' readings that the scholarly rule 'Prefer the Harder Reading' is not listed in the Index, and only mentioned once in the book (on p713)[22]. Head's studies showed no scribal 'improvements' at all.

Thirdly, historically, one final piece of evidence suggests that the more sensible and smooth Greek of the Byzantine text is preferable to the more abrupt, terse, jagged and difficult readings of the Alexandrian text. This is the fact that, as discoveries of secular documents have shown, first century Greek was more like the Byzantine text than the Alexandrian. Sturz wrote, 'The Byzantine text does tend to be simple, lucid, full, unpretentious, and plain in style. . . . However, it should be noted that [this] description . . . , with few changes, could also be taken as an acceptable description of the Hellenistic Greek of the First Century!'[23] The Alexandrian text, on the other hand, is characterised by the terse austerity of Classical Greek used centuries before Christ and

---

[21] John H. Dobson, *Learn New Testament Greek*, 3rd Ed., Grand Rapids, MI: Baker Academic, 2005, p316
[22] Royse, *Scribal Habits*, 2008, p713, footnote 30
[23] Sturz, *The Byzantine Text-type*, p108

preferred in Alexandria, the great centre of classical learning.

'Prefer the More Difficult Reading' is one of the main rules behind most of our modern English Bibles. Thus, many 'difficult readings' have been incorporated into our modern NT precisely because they make less sense, most of them from the Alexandrian manuscripts. Ordinary Christians might be surprised to hear that 'prefer the reading that makes less sense' is a rule of modern textual scholarship, but sadly, many modern textual scholars do not believe in the inspiration or inerrancy of Scripture, and so are happy to include readings in our NT which are clumsy, confused and even contradictory. We mentioned earlier the reading in Matthew 10:10 about the disciples' staff/staves, but there are other 'difficult' readings in our modern Bibles, e.g.:

- 'Asaph' and 'Amos' as ancestors of Christ (Matt. 1:7, 10, ESV), instead of 'Asa' and 'Amon' (i.e. two prophets instead of two kings).
- In Matthew 5:22 we read Christ warning that 'whosoever is angry with his brother *without a cause* shall be in danger of the judgment' (KJV), but many Bibles[24] leave out the words 'without a cause' (Gk. *eike*). This omission makes the verse seem a bit extreme, for Christ himself was angry (e.g. Mark 3:5), implying that there is a place for righteous anger (see Eph. 4:26).
- In Matt. 19:17 (NIV etc.), Christ says, 'Why do you *ask me about what is* good? There is One who is good', instead of 'Why do you *call me* good? There is One who is good' (cf. Mark 10:18, Luke 18:19)
- Christ being *angry* with the leper (NIV), instead of feeling compassion for the man who He healed (Mark 1:41)
- In Mark 5:1, 'they came to the region of the Gerasenes' (NIV, ESV, etc.), but did the swine run a marathon (50km) before drowning in the lake? A scribe here confused 'Gerasenes' with 'Gergesenes'.
- When Herod listened to John the Baptist, 'he was greatly *puzzled*, and heard him gladly' (NIV, etc.), instead of he 'did many things (i.e. obeyed John's teachings) and heard him gladly' (Mark 6:20)
- Mark 6:22 says 'his (i.e. Herod's) daughter Herodias' (NET, NLT, NRSV) danced (instead of the 'daughter of Herodias'), cf. Matt. 14:6
- Mark 7:31 says that departing 'from the region of Tyre he came *through Sidon* to the Sea of Galilee' (NIV, ESV, etc.) instead of 'from the region of Tyre and Sidon He came to the Sea of Galilee'. The journey to Sidon (in the wrong direction) would have added 50km to the trip for no good reason.

---

[24] RSV, NIV, NASB, NRSV, ESV, NLT, NET, etc.

- Anna being a widow *until* 84 years, instead of being a widow 'about' 84 years, Luke 2:36-37. Is it more likely that a woman of 'great age' who 'served God with fastings and prayers night and day' was a widow of about 105, or a romantic, recently remarried 85 year old?
- Luke 4:44 tells us Christ was preaching in the synagogues of *Judea* (NIV etc.) but the context and parallel passages say He was in Galilee
- Christ being the 'only begotten *God* in the bosom of the Father' (ESV etc.) instead of the only begotten *Son* in the bosom of the Father, John 1:18, cf. John 1:14, 3:16, 18, 1 John 4:9
- In John 7:8, Jesus says, 'I am *not* going up to this feast' (NIV etc.) instead of '*not yet*' going up; see context: Jesus did go up to the feast
- Paul and Barnabus returned *to* Jerusalem (after their trip to Jerusalem), instead of returning *from* Jerusalem, Acts 12:25 (cf. 13:1)
- 'if I give my body *to boast*', instead of 'to be burned', 1 Cor. 13:3 (ESV etc.); but it would seem hard to boast of being martyred

Not all modern Bibles print all of these 'difficult' readings, just as they are hesitant to completely remove passages like Mark 16:9-20 (the resurrection appearances), Luke 22:43-44 (the angel strengthening Christ in Gethsemane), Luke 23:34 (Christ's prayer of forgiveness on the cross) and John 7:52-8:11 (the woman taken in adultery) from our Bibles, all of which are missing in Alexandrian manuscripts. But this is due to a 'tradition of timidity' (Daniel Wallace) that most modern scholars are keen to reverse, printing the New Testament, 'warts and all'.

Some readers may find it hard to believe that the modern world of biblical scholarship could be wrong about something so important as the best Greek text of our New Testament. Surely we should accept the fruit of expert scholarship? However, just as secular academic scholarship has its 19th century 'junk science' (Marx, Darwin and Freud), so too modern biblical scholarship is still dominated by the speculative and unproven 19th century theories of unbelievers which persist as academic orthodoxy despite having little proof: the Documentary Hypothesis (Moses did not write the books of the Law – 'J', 'E', 'D', and 'P' did), the Deutero-Isaiah theory (the second half of Isaiah was written two centuries after the first by a different author), and NT pseudonymity theories (the Pastoral Epistles, etc., were not written by Paul but by a second century forger). Biblical scholarship is divided over these theories (but Bible sceptics and even some professing believers hold them). It should come as no great surprise that the same scholars hold a theory about the NT text itself that dismisses the vast majority of manuscripts as 'corrupt', cuts 2000 words from their text, and prefers readings which make less sense. We should not uncritically accept everything that biblical scholarship tells us, but rather examine whether the supporting reasons are valid. In the case of our NT text, increasingly it seems they are not.

The Big Blue Boat: the Byzantine 'Majority' Text

If we cannot wholeheartedly follow the Textus Receptus or the modern scholarly United Bible Societies text, should we follow the Byzantine text found in the majority of our Greek manuscripts? The Byzantine text is certainly superior to the TR (both in numbers of manuscripts and in their age). In many respects it also seems better than the modern UBS text (the Byzantine text has less evidence of scribal corruption, and presents a more sensible text than the Alexandrian manuscripts). However, there are some readings in the Byzantine text which just seem plain wrong, including:

- the Roman doxology (Rom. 16:25-27) is out of place in the Byzantine text, occurring at the end of Romans 14 where it awkwardly interrupts Paul's argument,
- James 2:18 has the meaningless reading, 'Show me your faith *by* your works, and I will show you my faith by my works' (instead of 'show me your faith *without* your works . . .').
- 1 Peter 1:8 reads 'whom not *knowing* you love' instead of 'whom having not *seen* you love'
- In John 5:4, the Byzantine text (and the TR) tells us about the angel coming down to stir the water, healing the first person to jump in, but angelic healing on a lottery-style basis seems more like a Jewish superstition than the inspired truth.
- In Matthew 28:9a, the Byzantine text (and the TR) include the words, 'as they went to tell his disciples', but this contradicts the other Gospel accounts about when Christ appeared to the women.

The problem most scholars have with the Byzantine text is that no manuscripts of this type have been found from before the fourth century. Neither do any early church 'fathers' quote exclusively from this text. These deficiencies could be excused on the grounds that we have in our possession only the smallest percentage of manuscripts known to have existed in these early centuries, and all our early evidence comes from remote locations in Egypt. Nor are there many church 'fathers' of note who lived and wrote in the 'Byzantine' area (Greece and Asia Minor) before the fourth century. Absence of proof for an early Byzantine text-type is not proof of absence.

However, we not only have over 5800 Greek New Testament manuscripts, we also have about 20,000 manuscripts in other early language versions: Latin, Syriac, Coptic, Gothic, Armenian, Georgian, and Ethiopian. In some places virtually all this evidence sides against the Byzantine Text (as in Matt. 28:9a above), so that the Byzantine reading is not really the 'majority' reading. We should prefer readings that have more early, widespread, geographical attestation among our witnesses, rather than readings only found in one area (whether Egypt or Byzantine lands).

The Byzantine text is the official NT of the Greek Orthodox church and a few scholars argue the Byzantine text is the original text of the NT. However, there was great persecution (including the destruction of biblical books) during the first few centuries. It is unlikely that the Byzantine manuscripts emerged from this difficult period of transmission completely unscathed. In addition, our earliest Byzantine witnesses (like Codex Alexandrinus and Chrysostom) have many differences from later forms of the same Byzantine text-family. We should be cautious about accepting the later Byzantine text as identical with the original NT text for the simple reason that we do not possess any Byzantine-text ancestors in the first few centuries. Another reason why we should not just simply assume that the Byzantine text is without any errors is because of the analogous case of the OT Majority text, the Masoretic Text, found in the majority of Hebrew manuscripts. The Masoretic Text is often not used when the Old Testament is quoted in the New; for example, in Hebrews 1:6 we read 'let all the angels of God worship him', but we search in vain for the source for this quote in the KJV because it is lacking in the Hebrew Masoretic Text, upon which the KJV was based. The verse is instead found in Deuteronomy 32:43 in the Dead Sea Scrolls and the Greek Septuagint. The inspired NT writers show us that the later Masoretic 'Majority' text we possess today is sometimes wrong, and instead give us readings now only found in other witnesses. Just because a reading has the majority of copies supporting it today does not mean it is the original. All that can be said about the Byzantine (Majority) text is that it has every right to a place at the top table when we sit down to work out the original NT. There are reasons to think it is very often correct, but like all the text-types, it also contains mistakes.

A Balanced Approach

Modern scholarship has swung from one extreme position (the TR) to another (an Alexandrian text), swapping an eccentric minority of late manuscripts for an eccentric minority of localised early ones. Instead of relying on a few late, eccentric manuscripts (the TR), or the modern 'critical' UBS text which dismisses 95% of the evidence as 'corrupt' on the basis of a scholarly conspiracy (the 'recension' theory), we should adopt a balanced approach based on the abundant evidence we possess for determining the wording of our Greek NT. Steering a middle course that tries to take account of all the evidence, a more balanced and sensible approach involves adopting readings that are able to marshall the broadest spectrum of supporting evidence. This means favouring readings whose evidence is more early, numerous, widespread, in line with proven scribal habits, consistent with the context, in keeping with the author's theology and style, and respectful of the divinely inspired origin and message of Scripture. This was the balanced policy of earlier textual scholars like Griesbach, Wordsworth and Scrivener, as well as modern scholars like Sturz. Professor David Alan Black also advocates this approach, calling it 'Reasoned Conservatism' in his book, *New Testament Textual Criticism, A Concise Guide*[25].

Which Bible to Use

Which Bible we should use depends on what we are trying to use it for. If we are trying to evangelise children or young people, we should use a Bible with age-appropriate English. Why confuse them with big words if our aim is to see these young people grasp the simple message of salvation? Let them understand the Bible's main truths before we try to teach them the finer points of the faith. On the other hand, older and supposedly more mature Christians need to be weaned off dumbed-down translations and paraphrases. Even though some less literal versions will use striking, insightful or powerful phrases, we should prefer a Bible that uses a more word-for-word translation approach, because the very words of Scripture are inspired by God. It is also preferable to use a Bible without archaic words that need to be re-translated into modern English. Ideally, if we are studying the Scriptures it is best to compare a number of different Bibles; such a policy will perhaps save us misconstruing the meaning of a word or missing the message of a verse. For those who are serious about studying the Bible, it is best to try to learn the original

---

[25] *New Testament Textual Criticism, A Concise Guide* (Baker Academic, 1994).

languages, even at a basic level, so that we are able to understand why different translations adopt different renderings.

As far as which Bibles are more textually dependable, regrettably, none of our English Bibles are perfect in terms of their underlying NT text. Most of our translations are based on the two extreme ends of the spectrum, the TR and the UBS Alexandrian text. Thankfully, while the Byzantine 'Majority' Text is not perfect, on balance it seems the best text, but on occasions we should prefer an alternative UBS reading, if it has early and widespread manuscript support. Just as the Dead Sea Scrolls sometimes give the original reading in the OT, allowing us to correct the Hebrew Masoretic Text, so the UBS text often provides readings that correct the NT Byzantine 'Majority' text. Some will suggest that God must have preserved His Word prefectly for us in one solitary text, but Psalm 119:89 asserts that 'Forever, O LORD, Your word is settled *in heaven*'. Thankfully, due to our abundant manuscript resources, the true reading of the NT is indeed preserved for us, either in the Byzantine 'Majority' text or in an alternative UBS reading.

Where do we look to find these alternative manuscript readings? Most modern versions (including the NIV, NRSV, NKJV and ESV) have helpful marginal notes in the OT, allowing us to see alternative readings from the Dead Sea scrolls, the Septuagint, and other early language versions. Sadly, in the NT most modern Bibles give too limited information in their marginal notes about textual variants, only saying that '*Some manuscripts read . . .*'. The best Bible to see what different texts read in the NT is NKJV, which shows what the alternative NU (ie. Nestle-Aland/UBS text) and M ('Majority'/ Byzantine) texts read at points of variation from the TR. This gives us something of the weight of evidence, and allows readers to think through the issues for themselves, looking to the Holy Spirit's help in understanding and interpreting Scripture[26].

If we were to rank Bibles by how well they handled the forty OT and NT textual variants we have mentioned in this chapter, the worst versions (in equal last place) would be the NRSV and the NLT, managing a score of 19 correct readings out of 40. The others (from worst to best) are ESV (21), NIV (21), NASB (22), RV (26), Darby (28), KJV (31) and NKJV (31), but of course, such results are shaped by

---

[26] For more accutate information necessary to make textual decisions, the critical apparatus of the *Nestle-Aland* Greek New Testament or the *Biblia Hebraica Stuttgartensia*, and a knowledge of Greek and Hebrew to read them, are required.

the number and selection of variant readings (as well as my textual judgments). If we had an accurate translation of a 'Majority Text' (Hebrew Masoretic for the Old Testament plus the New Testament Byzantine text), it would come equal first with the KJV and NKJV, but even so, it is only scoring 31 out of 40. Thus, while the Byzantine (Majority) Text and even the TR are better than the Alexandrian text underlying most modern versions, they are far from textually perfect.

In summary, it is impossible to understand the differences between Bible versions without a knowledge of some of the textual issues that have been explored in this chapter. Some might argue that a little knowledge is a dangerous thing, but a little education is preferable to the perpetuation of myths and misinformation. As Thomas Newberry said, in the Introduction to *The Englishman's Greek New Testament*[27] with its literal, interlinear translation and the alternative readings of various editors, 'It may be true that a little knowledge is a dangerous thing; yet let our object be not to stamp out the little, but to give the means to use it to profit, and, it may be, to increase it. A Christian needs the grace and help of God to read his English Testament profitably: the same grace and help will prevent his using in any other way the present work'.

---

[27] *The Englishman's Greek New Testament*, London: Samuel Bagster and Sons Ltd., 1877. Although anonymous, by all accounts it was the work of Newberry.

EPILOGUE

How to Read the Bible

A little boy noticed a big black book covered with dust lying on a shelf high up in a cupboard. He asked his mother what it was, and she replied, 'That's a Bible'. 'What's a Bible?' the little boy asked. 'That's God's book', said the mother in an embarrassed tone of voice. The little boy thought for a moment and then said, 'Well, if it is God's book, we should give it back to him, because nobody here is reading it'.

Here is one final way we can deny that the Bible really is God's Word – by not reading it. There are many Christians who read the newspaper or watch the television with an eagerness that they cannot find when it comes to opening the Bible. Spurgeon preached, 'Ah! You know more about your ledgers than what God has written; many of you will read a novel from beginning to end, and what have you got? A mouthful of froth when you have done. But you cannot read the Bible; that solid, lasting, substantial and satisfying food goes uneaten, locked up in the cupboard of neglect'.

Despite being the world's best-selling book, it seems that people read the Bible less today than ever. While 88% of households in the USA own a Bible, and Bible owners have an average of four Bibles per household, only 13% say that they read the Bible daily and only 34% say they read it at least once a week[1]. Surveys in the USA have found that only half of Americans know the name of one of the gospels, less than half can name the first book of the Bible, 60% cannot name half the ten commandments, only a third know who spoke the Sermon on the Mount (Billy Graham is a popular answer), 12% think Noah was married to Joan

---

[1] http://www.americanbible.org/uploads/content/State of the Bible Report 2013.pdf

of Arc, and three-quarters believe the Bible teaches that 'God helps those who help themselves'.

If the Bible is the Word of God, then putting a yellow smiley-face sticker on it is not enough. Nor is taking it to church. We should read it. However, reading the Bible is a routine that many Christians find difficult. In this chapter we are going to try to give some practical advice on how to make reading the Bible an integral part of our lives.

How to Read the Bible

How do we go about reading the Bible? I once read an article by a missionary doctor who said that we should read the Bible three ways. Firstly, we should read it telescopically, that is, reading the whole Bible to understand the entire story. Secondly, we should read the Bible microscopically, that is, studying it in detail. Thirdly, we should read the Bible stethoscopically, that is, reading the Bible and applying it personally, for our own spiritual health and blessing.

We Have to Make a Plan to Read the Bible.
As the old saying goes, to fail to plan is to plan to fail. If we don't have a plan for Bible reading, Bible reading will not happen very much. It is not enough to read the Bible occasionally – we need to have some plan for regular Bible reading.

You need to make a plan to read the Bible both regularly and systematically. Unless you make a plan to *regularly* read the Bible, your reading will be sporadic and fitful and before you know it, you will not have read it for a week or even a month. If you do not plan to *systematically* read the Bible, you will tend to keep on reading the same 'happy verses' and favourite chapters, and remain ignorant of vast areas of biblical territory. Do you believe that the whole Bible is inspired by God? Having a Bible reading plan will help you to get back on track if you miss a day or two, and give you a target to try and achieve. Remember: a verse a day will *not* keep the Devil away.

My personal suggestion is that you should try to read the entire Bible through every year. It only takes two Old Testament chapters and one New Testament chapter per day to read the whole Bible through in one year. Or, if that sounds too much, read the Bible over two or three years. The important thing is to read the Bible regularly and consistently – every day. Split the reading so you do some early in the morning and some in the evening. Draw up your own schedule for how you want to do it, or use one of the many Bible reading plans available (you'll find them in the back of Bibles or on the internet). If you are in the middle of the year, just start from the date you are at now, and finish off the rest of the year on the Bible-reading plan, then you can go back and start from the beginning of the Bible in the New Year. Get yourself a friend who agrees to do the Bible reading plan with you so that you can encourage and help each other through the year.

There really is no excuse for a Christian not to read the Bible. The average person in the Western world spends 3.5 hours watching TV or on the internet per day, so it's not as if you don't have the spare time. When my son first started playing the piano as a boy, he had to go for an interview with his piano teacher, who asked him if he really wanted to learn the piano. Then he was asked if he was prepared to practice for 5-10 minutes per day. That didn't sound like too much, so he agreed. It's the same with reading the Bible – it is a spiritual discipline that requires time, effort and self-denial.

We Need to Read the Bible On its Own

Some Christians think that listening to Christian sermons is a suitable substitute for reading the Bible. Others think that listening to Christian music, or reading a Christian biography or a Christian novel is as good as the Bible. Others like to use a devotional book in place of reading the Bible.

> *You shall find that reading the Word of God for yourselves, reading it rather than notes upon it, is the surest way of growing in grace*
>
> C. H. Spurgeon

Reading Christian books or even daily devotionals are no substitute for reading the Bible itself. Christian books have their place, and we can all learn from them. If we didn't believe that, we might as well not worry about listening to Bible teaching in church – we should all go home and read the Bible on our own. However, good Christian books are not as good as reading the Bible.

The most important reason for reading the Bible is that it cultivates a personal relationship with the Lord. Bible-reading notes may be helpful, but they are not as good as reading the Bible on its own. Reading the Bible should not be a conversation between you, the Lord and someone else. Two is company, but three's a crowd, and the third person wouldn't be such a problem, except in this case, when we use a devotional book, we are letting the third person do all the talking. If you are depending on some other author to tell you what the Bible says, instead of thinking upon God's Word and listening for God's voice in it, then you are swimming with floaties on, or riding a bike with the training wheels on. You need to take the plunge and start trusting the Lord to help you as you look into his Word for yourself. We need to hear God's voice directly, not second-hand, through an intermediary, like the priests in the middle-ages. We all have direct access to God.

Here is Spurgeon: 'Sermons and books are well enough, but . . . you shall find that reading the Word of God for yourselves, reading it rather than notes upon it, is the surest way of growing in grace. Drink of the unadulterated milk of the Word of God, and not of the skim milk, or the milk and water of man's word'.

We have to meditate on God's Word

No, this doesn't mean we have to sit down, cross our legs, close our eyes and hum. Meditating on the Bible means thinking carefully about what we have read.

Joshua 1:8 says, 'This Book of the Law shall not depart from your mouth, but you shall *meditate* in it day and night, that you may observe to do according to all that is written in it. For then you will make your way prosperous, and then you will have good success'. Psalm 1:1-3 also stresses the need for meditating upon God's Word: 'Blessed is the man who walks not in the counsel of the ungodly, nor stands in the path of sinners, nor sits in the seat of the scornful; but his delight is in the law of the LORD, and in His law he *meditates* day and night. He shall be like a tree planted by the rivers of water, that brings forth its fruit in its season, whose leaf also shall not wither; and whatever he does shall prosper'.

Every now and then I hear a Christian saying that they try to read the Bible but are unable to retain anything: "When I read the Bible I don't get anything out of it". Some people try to comfort these readers with the humorous illustration, 'I have got a brain like a sieve, but at least the water keeps the sieve clean'. However, we need to meditate on the Bible until we get something that sticks in our minds.

Spurgeon said, 'Much apparent Bible reading is not Bible reading at all. The verses pass under the eye, and the sentences glide over the mind, but there is no true reading. An old preacher used to say, the Word has mighty free course among many nowadays, for it goes in at one of their ears and out at the other; so it seems to be with some readers – they can read a very great deal, because they do not read anything'[2].

The solution to the problem of superficial or forgetful reading is to

---

[2] From the 1879 sermon, *How to Read the Bible*

meditate upon what we have read. That is, we need to turn the words over in our minds. Here are some ways we can do this:
- We can focus on one part of our reading that seemed to speak to us, whether challenging or comforting our hearts
- We can try to summarise what we have just read, that is, try to identify the main idea in a passage
- We can try to paraphrase what we have just read, that is, put the verses in our own words
- We can try and divide up a passage that we have read into its paragraphs and summarise these paragraphs
- We can try and ask questions of what we have just read. Rudyard Kipling put it in a rhyme: 'I have six honest serving men, they taught me all I knew; their names are What and Why and How, and When and Where and Who'.
- Occasionally we might notice puzzling features in the Bible passage we have read. We can turn these over in our mind, and pray for understanding. Remember: the bumps are what we climb on.
- Sometimes, one verse of Scripture will prompt us to think of another verse elsewhere. Other passages of Scripture will help explain the truths of the verses before us.

Meditation is important because when we wrestle with the words of Scripture, we build up our spiritual strength, and as we think about the Bible, we increase in spiritual intelligence. No doubt, at the beginning, our attempts to meditate upon the Bible will be difficult, and all we will be able to handle is milk. But the more we persist in meditating on the Bible, the more we will be able to chew on the meat of God's Word.

We have to remember that our own intellect cannot fathom the Scriptures. We must, in true humility of soul wait upon God, that He, by His Spirit, would be pleased to instruct us
George Müller

When should we meditate on the Bible? The best time is in the morning when our mind is clear and before we are distracted by the affairs of life. Have you ever tried talking to someone while they are watching the TV? In the same way that they don't give you their full attention, God does not get our full attention when we allow our minds to be filled with the distractions of the world around us.

We need Divine Illumination

George Müller wrote, 'We have to remember that our own intellect cannot fathom the Scriptures. We must, in true humility of soul wait upon God, that He, by His Spirit, would be pleased to instruct us. We must also seek to couple with this, meditation upon the Word of God. It is not enough that we go through it in a cursory way, just to satisfy our conscience. In a greater or lesser degree, we should seek to dwell upon what we read'.

Psalm 119:18 is a prayer: 'Open my eyes, that I may see wondrous things from Your law'. This verse teaches us that God Himself must reveal truths to us if we are going to understand spiritual reality. Of course, we cannot very well ask for the Holy Spirit to 'open my eyes that I may see wondrous things from Your law' if we have not even got our Bible open in front of us. There is a divine-human partnership in the understanding of Scripture, so that God reveals things to us when we, for our part, meditate upon His Word. Other verses that teach this same truth of illumination include Psalm 119:102 ('You Yourself have taught me'), John 6:45, and 1 Corinthians 2:10.

Spurgeon says, 'Beloved, I would next remind you that for this end we shall be compelled to pray. It is a grand thing to be driven to think, it is a grander thing to be driven to pray through having been made to think. . . . Do you wish to begin to be true readers? Will you henceforth labour to understand? Then you must get to your knees. You must cry to God for direction. Who understands a book best? The author of it. If I want to ascertain the real meaning of a rather twisted sentence, and the author lives near me, and I can call upon him, I shall ring at his door and say, "Would you kindly tell me what you mean by that sentence? I have no doubt whatever that it is very clear, but I am such a simpleton, that I cannot make it out. I have not the knowledge and grasp of the subject which you possess, and therefore your allusions and descriptions are beyond my range of knowledge. It is quite within your range, and commonplace to you, but it is very difficult to me. Would you kindly explain your meaning to me?" A good man would be glad to be thus treated, and would think it no trouble to unravel his meaning to a candid enquirer. Thus I should be sure to get the correct meaning, for I should be going to the fountain head when I consulted the author himself. So, beloved, the Holy Spirit is with us, and when we take his book and begin to read, and want to know what it means, we must ask the Holy Spirit to reveal the meaning. He will not work a miracle, but He will elevate our minds, and He will suggest to us thoughts which will lead us on by their natural relation, the one to the other, till at last we come to the pith and marrow of his divine instruction. Seek then very earnestly the guidance of the Holy Spirit, for if the very soul of reading be the understanding of what we read, then we must in prayer call upon the Holy Ghost to unlock the secret mysteries of the inspired word'.

Bible reading is no mere intellectual exercise – it is a *spiritual* discipline. That is, it involves interaction and communication with a holy and all-knowing God. Unconfessed sin will hinder blessing when we try to read the Bible. Similarly, we need to put right any relationship breakdowns at a horizontal, human level that grieve God's Spirit. We need to realise we are dependent upon God for light and understanding, and seek Him patiently and confidently for it. The wonderful fact is that we can go directly to the author of Scripture and ask Him what He meant by its words.

Looking to God in prayer for understanding of His Word means that Bible reading becomes a two-way conversation between a person and God. Some of the most precious times of fellowship with God upon earth will be found here.

Most importantly, Bible reading is all about knowing God Himself – not filling our heads with facts or information. Bible reading is not primarily an intellectual journey, but ultimately a walk with God. God wants to reveal Himself to us through His Word. We might not yet be ready to understand everything there is to know about the Book of Revelation; God may think that there are other things we need to learn beforehand. But, ultimately, the purpose of our Christian lives is to know God, and only God can reveal Himself to us. We need to pray that God, 'the God of our Lord Jesus Christ, the Father of glory, may give [us] the spirit of wisdom and revelation in the knowledge of Him' (Eph. 1:17).

We need to Obey God's Word

The aim of reading the Bible is not to become a walking encyclopaedia. The goal of Bible reading is to do what God says, firstly through coming to know Christ as our Saviour. After we have become Christians, the purpose of reading the Bible is for us to grow in our new life and become more like Christ. That means that we have to start doing what God tells us to do in His Word. James 1:22 says, 'Be doers of the Word, not hearers only', and the Lord Himself said, 'If you know these things, blessed are you if you do them' (John 13:17).

On the other hand, and it might seem paradoxical, but to understand God's Word, we must first obey it. This is what Psalm

111:10 says: 'A good understanding have all those who do His commandments'. Mark 4:24-25 say the same thing: 'to you who hear, more will be given'. Why should God give us more light if we do not obey the light He has given us already?

If there is a sense in which obeying the Bible is an essential element involved in understanding it, this means that reading the Bible is an exercise of faith. We must step out in obedient faith, putting what we read into practice, even if we do not fully understand what it means. A willingness to obey what the Bible teaches is therefore completely essential for understanding the Bible.

Conclusion

There is a story about an English preacher named E. W. Rogers who was approached by two young men asking him how to study the Bible. Mr. Rogers answered, "Read it!" The subject of how to study the Bible is beyond the scope of this chapter, but Mr. Rogers' answer covers both that question and the message of this chapter: we need to read the Word of God. Another English preacher, G. H. Lang, gave some advice for how to preach: 'the way to do it is to do it'. The same answer applies to Bible reading: the way to read the Bible is to read the Bible!

General Index

Aesop's Fables 37
Albright, William 10
Alexandrian text-type . 183, 184, 185, 187, 189, 191, 192, 193, 195, 197
Amish 90
Anglican Thirty-Nine Articles 81, 93
Apocrypha 135, 139, 140
Aquila 162
Archer, Gleason 163
Assumption of Moses 140
Athanasias 139
Augustine   7, 36, 71, 111, 116, 140
Authority of Scripture.... 3, 13-17, 26, 33, 34-47, 81, 84, 85, 89, 93, 94, 104, 112, 123
Barth, Karl 26
Belgic Confession, 1561 74
Belleville, Linda 125
Bible
  authority ...... See Authority of Scripture
  Christ's testimony 12-16
  clarity See Clarity of Scripture
  errors 18-20, 48-71
  historical accuracy 9
  human authors 11-12
  illumination . See Illumination of Scripture
  inspiration.. See Inspiration of Scripture
  interpretation .... See Interpretation of Scripture
  living power 16
  necessity 99-100
  permanence 5
  popularity 6
  progressive nature of revelation 121, 128
  prophecy 8, 9
  scientific accuracy 10
  unity 7
Biblia Hebraica Stuttgartensia 196
Bird, Graeme D 156, 185
Black, D A 161, 195
Book of Common Prayer 173
Book of Enoch 140
Brooks, Ron 13-14
Brown, Dan . 132, 147-149, 189
Bruce, F F ...7, 32, 23, 88, 136, 137, 138, 148, 161, 162
Brunner, Emil 26
Bultmann, Rudolf 38, 146
Bunyan, John 21-22
Byzantine recension 184, 187, 188, 189
Byzantine, or Majority, Text 181-189, 193-197
Calvin, John 128
Canon of Scripture........ 134-152
Carson, D A 121
Chalke, Steve 122
Charismatic Christianity.... 40, 46, 78, 80, 81, 94, 123, 130
Chester, Tim 126
Chicago Statement on Biblical Inerrancy 29, 69
Clarity of Scripture 104-107
Clarke, Greg 127
Codex Alexandrinus 182, 194
Codex Bezae 183
Codex Sinaiticus 156, 183
Codex Vaticanus 183
Colwell, E C 158, 159, 185
Constantine . 132, 147, 149, 189

Council of Nicea 147
Council of Trent 140
Cowper, William 11
Da Vinci Code, The 132, 133, 147, 149
Darby's *New Translation* 171, 173, 196
Dawkins, Richard 151, 174
Dead Sea Scrolls 149, 162, 163, 177, 178, 184, 194, 196
Deere, Jack 78
Demarest, Bruce 39
Dickens, Charles 6, 101
Dickson, John 127
Douay-Rheims Bible 181
Dryden, John 106
Eddy, Mary Baker 76
Edwards, David 48
Ehrman, Bart 151-161, 181
Eichenwald, Kurt 152
Eliot, T S 173
English Standard Version 69, 115, 159, 167, 168, 170, 171, 177, 179, 191, 196
Englishman's Greek New Testament 167, 197
Erasmus 180-182
Erickson, Millard 104, 124
Eusebius 149
Evans, Craig 149
Fee, G D 130, 188
Frost, Henry 78
Gamble, Harry 158
Geisler, Norman 13-14
Goldingay, John 62, 119
Goldsworthy, Graeme 129
Good News Bible ... 167, 168, 171
Gospel of Judas 134, 145, 146
Gospel of Mary 145, 146
Gospel of Peter 134, 145, 146
Gospel of Philip 146
Gospel of Thomas 134, 135, 137, 145, 146
Graham, Billy 18-20
Griesbach, J J 195
Griffith-Thomas, W H 7, 81
Grudem, Wayne .. 17, 81, 84, 85
Guthrie, Donald 148
Ham, Mordecai 18
Harrison, E F 147
Head, P M 186, 190
Henry, Matthew 68
Hernández Jnr., J 186
Homer . 155, 156, 173, 184, 185
Hooker, Richard 117
Hoste, W E 14, 15, 24
House, H. Wayne 30
Howlett, Basil 123
Illumination of Scripture 26, 84, 107-112, 115, 138, 149, 203
Inerrancy 56, 68-70, 191
    abbreviation 59
    approximations 52
    copying mistakes 55
    discrepancies 63
    figurative language 51
    free quotations 54
    hyperbole 52
    language of appearance 51
    reported speech 53
    reporting of falsehoods 50
    selective use of material 58
    translation 54
Inspiration of Scripture. 2-5, 15, 20-33
Interpretation of Scripture 37, 107, 114-131, 167, 171, 172
Irenaeus 143
Jefferson, Thomas 39

Jehovah's Witnesses 39, 76, 126, 174
Jenkins, Philip 146, 147
Jerome . 139, 162, 181, 184, 188
Josephus 139, 155, 156
Julius Caesar 155, 156
Keller, Tim 13
Kenyon, Sir Frederick 10, 155, 189
Kierkegaard, Søren 121
Kim Huat Tan 129
King James Version 28, 30-31, 42, 66, 69, 115, 120, 167-174, 177-183, 191, 194, 196, 197
Knox, John 41, 91
Koran 12, 27, 77
Kruger, Michael J 136
Kuyper, Abraham 16, 32-33
Lang, G H 205
Latin Vulgate 31, 140, 162, 177, 181, 184
Lewis, C S 170, 173, 174
Liberal theology .. 23, 38, 48, 94, 131, 145
Lightfoot, J B 82
Lincoln, Abraham 6
Living Bible, The 167
Luther, M 34, 35, 39, 45, 46, 104, 108, 109, 140, 180, 182
Maas, Paul 151
MacArthur, John Jr 78, 79
Mackintosh, C H 28, 42, 43, 74, 75
Masoretic Text ... 178, 184, 194, 196, 197
McKnight, Scot 122
Message, The 167, 168
Messy Church 93

Metzger, B M 136, 137, 155, 187
Miller, J H 130
Miller, J. Graham 23
Milton, John 173
Morgan, Robert 2
Mormons 12, 72, 73, 76, 116
Müller, George 101-108, 203
Mykytiuk, Lawrence 9
National Geographic 134
Neo-orthodoxy 26
Nestle-Aland Greek NT 183, 196
New American Standard Bible 115, 167, 168, 171, 179, 191, 196
New International Version 21, 115, 159, 166, 167, 168, 170, 171, 172, 177, 179, 191, 196
New King James Version 166-168, 170, 171, 172, 196, 197
New Living Translation 21, 166, 167, 171, 177, 179, 191, 196
New Revised Standard Version 196
New World Translation 174
Newberry, Thomas 197
Newman, John Henry 81
Normative Principle ... 92, 93, 94
O'Brien, John 106, 107, 148, 149
Origen 139, 142
Packer, J I 23, 28, 69
Papias 143
Parker, David 158
Petersen, Eugene 168
Petersen, William 158
Pharisees . 15, 38, 43, 44, 51, 77, 92, 160, 179
Phillips, J B 170, 173
Picard, Rosalind 1, 16

Pink, A W 12
Piper, John 74, 85
Plummer, Rob 129
Prefer the Harder Reading ....
    190, 192
Prefer the Shorter Reading ....
    185, 187
Queen Elizabeth II 6
Ramm, Bernard 6
Regulative Principle ... 91, 92, 94
Revised Version 167, 171, 173,
    196
Reymond, Robert 92
Riplinger, Gail 30
Robertson, A T 28
Robinson, John 110
Robinson, M A 186
Rogers, E W 28, 205
Roman Catholic Church 5, 31,
    37, 38, 77, 104, 106, 107,
    133, 135, 140, 148
Royse, J R 186, 187, 190
Russell, Charles Taze 76, 77
Ryle, J C 24-25, 29, 43, 120, 126
Ryrie, Charles 29
Sadducees 39
Samaritan Pentateuch 162
Sanday, W 147
Scrivener, F H A 189, 195
Septuagint .. 162, 177, 178, 194,
    196
Shakespeare .. 22, 156, 157, 173,
    184
Smith, Christian 103
Smith, Joseph 12, 72, 73
Smith, Wilbur 8
Spurgeon, C H 33, 110, 113,
    169, 198, 201, 203
St. John, Harold 55, 88
State of the Bible Report 170, 198

Stoner, Peter 8
Stott, John 12-13, 48
Streeter, B H 123
Stuart, Douglas 130
Sturz, Harry 188, 190, 195
Sufficiency of Scripture ... 42, 63,
    74-85
Symmachus 162
Tacitus 155, 156
Targums 162
Tate, W Randolph 130
Templeton, Charles 18-20
Text of Scripture .. 152-154, 176
Textus Receptus   180-182,
    193, 195- 197
Theodotion 162
Toronto Blessing 40
Tozer, A W 38, 46
Tregelles, S P 189
Tyndale, William .. 13, 168, 180,
    182
UBS Greek NT 183, 187, 188,
    193, 195, 196
Vine, W E 82, 83
Wachtel, Klaus 188, 189
Wagner, Peter 78
Wallace, Daniel .. 157, 158, 181,
    188, 192
Wallace, J. Warner 63, 64
Warfield, B B 3, 27, 32
Watson, J B 89
Watts, Isaac 86, 87
Wegner, Paul 137
Wesley, John 45, 46, 48
Westcott, B F 148
Western text-type 183, 184
Westminster Confession of
    Faith 17, 42, 74, 91, 107
Wilson, A W 186
Wordsworth, C 195

ABOUT THE AUTHOR

Andrew Wilson grew up in Sydney, Australia. In his mid-twenties, he spent three years in London, England, involved in Christian ministry, mostly doing children's evangelism in deprived housing estates. For over twenty years since, he has been involved in full-time Bible teaching and evangelism. Andrew returned to England for another five years in his thirties, and was engaged in ministry as well as doing part-time research at Tyndale House, Cambridge. As a result, he published a number of academic articles on scribal habits in New Testament Greek manuscripts. He is the author of two other books, *Matthew's Messiah, a Guide to Matthew's Gospel*, and *The Most Amazing Prophecy in the Bible: Daniel's Prophecy of the Seventy Sevens*. He lives in Brisbane with his wife Gillian and three children.

www.ingramcontent.com/pod-product-compliance
Lightning Source LLC
Chambersburg PA
CBHW050534300426
44113CB00012B/2101